Wildlife of Madeira and the Canary Islands

A Photographic Field Guide to Birds, Mammals, Reptiles, Amphibians, Dragonflies and Butterflies

John Bowler

PRINCETON
press.princeton.edu

Contents

Introduction

Types of Species Covered

The aim of this book is to enable anyone, visitor or resident, to identify all the birds, land mammals, marine mammals, reptiles, amphibians, dragonflies and butterflies that are likely to be encountered on these magical islands, as well as to give an introduction to the habitats in which these animals occur. The photographs and text highlight the key differences between all similar species occurring in the islands, so that given suitable views, the subject can be identified with confidence. Where there are major differences in appearance between sexes and/or age classes, these also have been illustrated when appropriate. The photographs were largely taken on the islands and therefore illustrate the local subspecies of wide-ranging species and the correct plumages of migratory birds that one is most likely to encounter.

Acknowledgements

A very large number of people have helped in the production of this book in a variety of ways, and thanks are due to them all, although any errors that may remain are entirely my own. Rob Still at Princeton WildGuides was instrumental in encouraging me to write this book following a wildlife-watching visit to Fuerteventura in 2004, when a guide of this nature would have been much appreciated. Rachel Still's skills with the layout of the images, together with those of Rob Still, have really brought this book to life, whilst much assistance in getting the book off the ground was given by Robert Kirk at Princeton University Press. Latterly, Andy Swash at WildGuides helped greatly with the book production, as did Ellen Foos at PUP, and Amy K. Hughes did a fantastic job of copy-editing. Alejandro de Vera Hernández of Museo de Ciencas Naturales de Tenerife pointed us to invaluable mapping data. Jaime A. de Urioste of the Fundación Neotrópico was incredibly helpful in sourcing photographs of reptiles in the Canaries, and in addition carefully reviewed all of the text on reptiles and amphibians, which greatly improved its accuracy. I am also greatly indebted to Martin Wiemers for checking through the text on butterflies and for updating their taxonomy. Matt Rowlings was extremely helpful in providing photographs of many of the butterflies from his excellent euroButterflies website, whilst Luís Dias at venturadomar.com provided all but three of the sea mammal images, as well as some Madeiran endemics. I would also like to thank Noemí Rodríguez for her detailed help with the Tenerife Speckled Lizard account and for helping to source photos of other Canarian endemics, as well as Teresa Farino of Iberian Wildlife for her help in tracking down photographs of some of the endemic butterflies. Particular thanks go to Marc Guyt and everyone at agami.nl for sourcing and providing images, particularly of, but not limited to, birds. Thanks also to Domingo Trujillo González for his help with sourcing photographs of bats from the Canaries and Yeray Monasterio León for his help with Canarian butterflies.

The photographic plates are a key feature of this book and I would like to thank all the photographers for allowing us to use their images. There are too many to list individually here, but all the photographic credits are listed on *pages 214–216*.

Thanks are also due to the many friendly and helpful people we met on our visits to all of the islands, which made our research trips all the more enjoyable and valuable. Lastly, I would like to thank my wife, Janet, for her uncomplaining support and help during countless hours of research for this book, both in the field and at home on the computer, and for her companionship throughout.

The geography and climate of Madeira and the Canary Isles

Geography

Madeira and the Canary Islands are two neighbouring archipelagos in the eastern Atlantic Ocean lying off the north-western coast of Africa, which together with the more remote Azores to the north and the Cape Verde islands to the south, form the island region known as Macaronesia. All of these islands are the tips of a series of undersea volcanoes, some of which are still active. As a result of their oceanic birth, the islands are home to a distinctive range of flora and fauna, including many endemic species, which have been able to evolve here in isolation. Madeira and the Canary Islands are the most readily accessible of the island groups and, fortuitously, are also among the most interesting from a wildlife perspective.

The location of the Atlantic islands

Madeira

The Madeira archipelago belongs to Portugal and lies just under 400 km to the north of the Canary Island of Tenerife and 520 km west of Morocco. The archipelago is dominated by the main island of Madeira, which is by far the largest island, with a surface area of 741 km² (see page 8 for detailed map). It holds 98% of the archipelago's human population, of which around 85% live in the warmer and drier south, including some 100,000 in the capital, Funchal. Madeira is a rugged mountainous island with a high central ridge rising to 1,862 m at the summit of Pico Ruvio. The mountain slopes drop steeply to the sea and then drop quickly, resulting in deepwater habitats close inshore. The island of Porto Santo lies 37 km north-east of Madeira. It

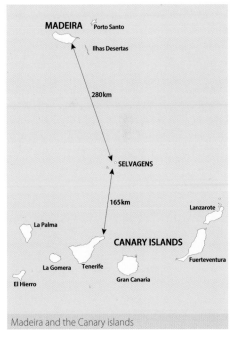

Madeira and the Canary islands

covers around 50 km² and has a population of some 5,500 residents, although numbers swell greatly during the summer months. It has a more gently sloping terrain than Madeira, with the highest point of just 517 m at Pico de Facho, in the more rugged north-eastern part of the island. The coastal plain in the island's south-west is home to a spectacular 9-km-long white-sand beach. There are many offshore islets, and these are home to large numbers of breeding seabirds. The Desertas Islands lie 16 km south-east of Madeira. This is a chain of three small, uninhabited islands (except for permanent wardens), with elevations rising to 442 m on Deserta Grande, 348 m on Bugio and 98 m on Ilhéu de Chão. The Desertas are very important for breeding seabirds, including the endemic Desertas Petrel, which breeds only on Bugio, and they are the only breeding site in the islands for the Mediterranean Monk Seal.

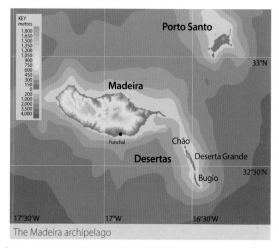

The Madeira archipelago

The final islands in the Madeira group are the Selvagens or Salvages. These windswept, uninhabited islands lie 280 km south of Madeira and are in fact closer to Tenerife (165 km to their south). They comprise two main islands and several islets; elevation rises to 163 m on Selvagem Grande. The islands are rocky and barren but hold an important population of seabirds, notably of White-faced Storm-petrels, and are home to resident wardens and scientists.

The Canary Islands

The archipelago of the Canary Islands consists of seven main islands and numerous smaller satellite islands and offshore rocks with a total surface area of some 7,490 km² (see pages 8–9 for detailed maps). For the purposes of this book, the 'Western Canaries' encompass the islands of El Hierro, La Palma and La Gomera; the 'Central Canaries' consist of Tenerife and Gran Canaria (although both, confusingly, are geographically within the Western Canaries); and the 'Eastern Canaries' comprise Fuerteventura and Lanzarote, together with the satellite

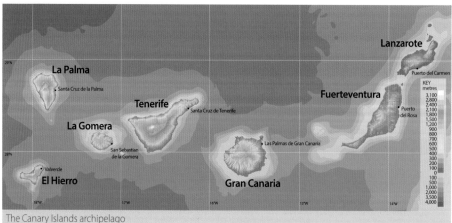

The Canary Islands archipelago

island of Los Lobos off north-eastern Fuerteventura and the Chinijo archipelago off northern Lanzarote, including the inhabited island of La Graciosa. The western islands are of more recent volcanic origin than the eastern ones – the westernmost island of El Hierro is only some 1.1 million years old, while Fuerteventura is thought to be about 17–20 million years old. As a result, the western and central islands are generally higher and steeper than the older and more time-eroded eastern islands. Tenerife is the largest island, at 2,034 km², and is also the highest, with the summit of Pico del Teide reaching 3,718 m. It is now the most populous island, with some 889,936 inhabitants, having recently overtaken Gran Canaria, which has some 838,400 inhabitants and is the third-largest island, at 1,560 km². Fuerteventura is the second-largest island, at 1,660 km², and has a smaller but increasing population of some 103,490 inhabitants. It is also the closest island to mainland Africa, some 100 km to the east.

Climate

Madeira and the Canaries are often known as the islands of eternal spring. They are located in the subtropics, so are warm year-round. They enjoy a typical Mediterranean climate, yet this is moderated at all times by the Atlantic Ocean, so they are never subject to the extremes of high and cold temperatures experienced on the adjacent mainland of North Africa. Average temperatures at sea level are remarkably constant year-round, typically ranging from 14° to 28° C, with hotter periods in the summer when the dry easterly Calima (Canaries) or Leste (Madeira) winds, often laden with dust, blow off the Sahara. Winds predominantly come from the north-east, particularly in summer, but westerlies associated with the passage of Atlantic depressions occur in late autumn–winter, bringing the bulk of the rain. Levels of precipitation are low in the Canaries, at generally less than 250 mm per year, but are higher on Madeira at around 600 mm per year. The Western and Central Canaries and Madeira receive much more rainfall than the Eastern Canaries and Porto Santo, as a result of their higher relief and their greater exposure to Atlantic storms.

There is also considerable local variation in climate, depending on aspect and elevation. Southerly slopes are typically drier and warmer than north-facing ones, and mean daily temperatures decline with elevation, such that Pico del Teide, for example, is often snow-capped during the winter months. On the higher islands rainfall typically increases with elevation but then declines again above 1,200 m. This is because the mountains force the north-easterly trade winds to rise up, cooling the air as they do so, which releases moisture in the form of clouds, forming a band around the mountains. Light rain often occurs at these elevations but rain also falls 'horizontally' in the form of fog, which is trapped by lichens and pine needles, condenses and then drips to the ground. Above 1,200 m, fog is less common, and the higher elevations become increasingly arid and cold, with freezing temperatures occurring at the highest levels on winter nights. Clouds passing over the mountain ridges quickly warm as they drop down the southern slopes, where they rapidly dissipate. This phenomenon can be very dramatic and is well worth looking out for on the upper southern slopes of the higher islands.

Maps of the Islands, including selected habitats and climate information

The maps below show the relief and simplified distribution of the remaining natural and semi-restored habitat (mirroring the broad categories described on *pages 10–17*) . Habitat and relief data for the Canaries are sourced from http://visor.grafcan.es/visorweb/. The temperature and rainfall charts show mean max and min temperature, total monthly rainfall and days of rainfall for islands as named. NB The islands are not in exact geographic position, but are set out topologically to match the species distribution maps.

Canary Islands (not to scale) showing relief and simplifed habitat distribution.

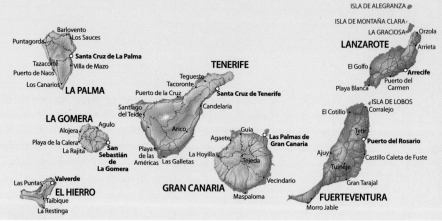

Western Canaries (WC)   Central Canaries (CC)

Madeira (not to scale) showing relief and simplifed habitat distribution.

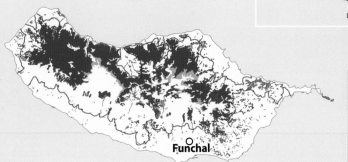

Funchal

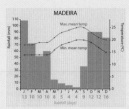

KEY

Relief	Canaries	Madeira
	metres	
	3,100	
	2,800	
	2,400	
	2,100	
	1,800	1,800
	1,500	1,650
	1,200	1,500
	900	1,350
	800	1,200
	700	1,050
	600	900
	500	750
	400	600
	300	450
	200	300
	100	150
	0	0

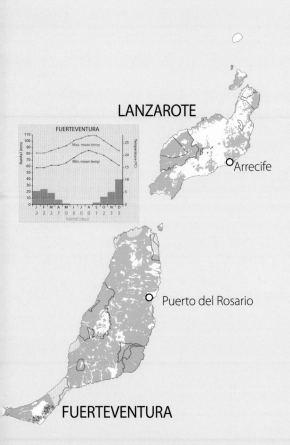

LANZAROTE

Arrecife

Puerto del Rosario

FUERTEVENTURA

Habitats

Subalpine arid scrub
Arid scrub
Pine Forest
Laurel Forest (including fayal-brezal)
Warmth-loving woodland
Desert (rocky)   Desert (sandy)
Man-made habitats

Protected areas (land)

Eastern Canaries (EC)

Habitats

There are 10 main types of natural habitat in the islands, including the open sea. All the terrestrial habitats have to a greater or lesser extent been altered by humans, either through direct alteration, such as clearance of trees and shrubs, or by more indirect means, such as the pernicious effects of grazing animals, including rabbits and goats, and of introduced exotic plant species. Over large areas, much of the original habitat has been lost entirely. Nonetheless the remaining habitats still support a diverse and often endemic flora, which in turn supports a very interesting range of animals, including many endemic species. Elevational zonation of the remaining native vegetation is still very marked on the higher islands and results from variation in rainfall patterns. Such zonation is easily appreciated as you drive up through the high central mountains of Madeira, Tenerife or La Palma. Generally, coastal areas are drier, and the height and lushness of vegetation increases with elevation, as the mountains create their own clouds and precipitation. On the highest peaks, there is a switch back to more arid habitats above the normal level of the clouds. Northern slopes are typically moister than southern ones, so the same habitat zones tend to occur at lower elevations there. Steep-sided valleys, being more sheltered from the wind and sun than more exposed slopes, create their own microclimates, which allow mid-elevation habitat zones to reach further down the slopes and higher habitat zones to reach further up the mountainsides.

Open Sea

Having risen directly from the ocean floor as volcanoes, the islands we see today are the tips of much larger undersea mountains. Consequently, the coastal waters drop rapidly away in depth at short distances from the islands – the sea floor in the Canary Basin just off El Hierro is some 4,000 m deep! Because of these great depths, oceanic cetaceans, seabirds and sea turtles regularly pass very close to each of the islands, which enjoy a diversity of species unparalleled in coastal Europe. Upwellings around the islands present rich feeding opportunities for both resident and migrant species. The coastal shallows have a chance to warm up in the summer, particularly on the more sheltered eastern coasts, and present excellent opportunities for snorkelling and diving. Many species of colourful sea fishes are present, some of which can be seen from shore in harbours and more sheltered coves.

Rock stacks east of Porto Moniz, Madeira.

Offshore Islets

There are a large number of offshore islets and stacks around the coasts of the larger islands. Some are too small and exposed to develop vegetation, but others are larger and harbour a fascinating flora and fauna, often including species that can exhibit different traits to their mainland counterparts. As these populations are often small, they are vulnerable to loss; unique forms of the Hierro Giant Lizard and Canary Islands Stonechat, for example, perished in the 20th century. However, many of the islets remain rat-free and, as such, provide vital refuges for large numbers of ground-nesting seabirds, most of which are otherwise restricted to the steepest slopes and cliffs on the main islands. These islets are also havens for the shy Mediterranean Monk Seal, which requires remote undisturbed caves on offshore islands in which to breed.

Intertidal Areas

Since the islands have such steep profiles, intertidal areas are rather limited in extent, particularly on the younger islands in the Western Canaries and Madeira. Rocky inshore reefs and rock pools provide feeding for a range of migratory shorebirds and egrets that are elsewhere more often associated with estuaries. On Fuerteventura, sheltered flatter shores hold pockets of salt marsh and saline lagoons that attract large numbers of shorebirds and gulls;

Saltmarsh, Costa Calma, Fuerteventura.

this habitat is replicated on several islands in man-made salt pans. Broad white-sand beaches on Fuerteventura and Porto Santo also support wintering shorebirds and terns.

Freshwater Wetlands

Owing to the widespread presence of naturally porous bedrock and low rainfall for much of the year, natural freshwater wetlands are very scarce on the islands. This situation has been exacerbated by the damming of many streams in their headwaters as a source of water for both drinking and irrigation. On the wetter northern slopes of the larger islands, a few streams run year-round; even on the drier islands, sheltered *barrancos* may hold small pools of water all year. All permanent water acts as a magnet for dragonflies and amphibians and for birds in search of a drink or a wash, while the zone of fringing vegetation in the moister environs of these areas is also rich in insects such as butterflies and moths, which in turn attract insect-eating birds and bats. Man-made water channels including the extensive *levadas* on Madeira are generally too clean and fast running for all but pioneer dragonfly species such as Red-veined Darter. However, man-made irrigation pools and reservoirs on all the islands act more like natural wetlands and are often very good places to look for wildlife, including breeding and wintering waterbirds.

Irrigation Reservoir, Rosa del Taro, Fuerteventura.

Desert

True stony and sandy deserts are largely restricted to the drier Eastern Canaries, although newer lava flows on the southern sides of the Western and Central Canaries can approach this habitat in terms of sparseness of vegetation cover. Until recently, there were extensive open sandy plains in southern Tenerife, but most of these have been lost to development and banana plantations. Some of the arid plains of the Eastern Canaries are used for low-intensity agriculture, but they retain much of the desert fauna. The desert areas can appear devoid of life at first glance, but a closer look reveals a wonderful array of indigenous drought-resistant plants, butterflies and reptiles and an exciting range of desert-dwelling birds that otherwise are restricted to the deserts of North Africa. These areas are fragile and easily damaged by overgrazing and by car tracks, so please stick to existing tracks to view the sensitive wildlife, using your car as a hide.

Sandy desert, Costa Calma, Fuerteventura.

Rocky desert, Triquivijate, Fuerteventura.

Subalpine Arid Scrub

On the highest peaks of Tenerife, La Palma, Gran Canaria and Madeira, an arid scrubby habitat exists in the dry and exposed conditions, which oscillate from very high daytime temperatures in summer to very cold temperatures at night and in the winter months. This is most marked in Las Cañadas del Teide in Tenerife, where the crater floor and walls are covered in species of broom and many other low-growing shrubby endemic plants. Above 2,700 m and up to 3,500 m on Pico del Teide, vegetation is dominated by a single species, the Teide Pansy. This is the most seasonal region of the islands, with plants flowering only from May to September and butterflies, other insects and reptiles active only in the summer months. On Madeira some high slopes are dominated by broom, while the highest peaks show much bare rock, with low-growing drought-resistant

Subalpine arid scrub, looking towards Mount Teide, Las Cañadas, Tenerife.

plants and stunted laurel trees in more sheltered gullies. Birds are scarce at these high elevations; Berthelot's Pipit and Plain Swift are the most common species, although on Madeira this is where Zino's Petrels nest.

Arid Scrubland

On the drier southern slopes of the Western and Central Canaries, a habitat of low, succulent scrub persists over large areas. Similar scrubby arid habitats occur in moister, more sheltered areas of the Eastern Canaries, although more richly vegetated areas are restricted to the less grazed hills, cliffs, mountains and upper sections of barrancos. Arid scrubland occurs widely on Porto Santo and more locally as arid herb-rich grassland on Madeira, most notably on the drier eastern headland of Ponta de São Lourenço. Rich in endemic plants, particularly where they have not been overgrazed by goats, these areas are excellent habitat for a wide range of butterflies and scrub-dwelling birds and for dragonflies in more sheltered spots. On the arid Eastern Canaries, clumps of tamarisks in the lower sections of barrancos are the closest

Arid scrubland, Punta de Teno, Tenerife.

habitat to native forest and attract both breeding *Sylvia* warblers and migrant songbirds.

Warmth-loving Woodlands

On the higher islands of the Western and Central Canaries, the arid scrubland becomes lusher at higher elevations (around 700 m on southern slopes and 100 m on northern slopes), giving way to a taller, denser and often tangled woodland comprising taller shrubs and small trees of flowering plant groups such as spurge, St John's wort and bindweed that on the mainland are only low-growing herbs. This is known as the warmth-loving (thermophilous) or dry woodland. In some areas, known as

Juniper-dominated sabinar woodland, El Hierro.

sabinar, this woodland is dominated by junipers. The famous Canary Islands Dragon Trees also grow in these woods, as do Canary Palms, particularly on La Gomera. Open rocky areas in these woods are full of wildflowers, which in turn attract a range of woodland-edge insects, such as butterflies, as well as a good range of woodland-edge birds. Unfortunately, these areas present a very equitable climate for growing crops, and as a result most of the original warmth-loving woodland habitat has long been replaced by terraced cultivation, for growing fruits, vegetables and chestnuts, and patches of native habitat are largely restricted to steeper slopes and barrancos. However, in recent years, as areas of agriculture have been abandoned in this zone, the warmth-loving woodland has shown signs of recolonising formerly cultivated ground adjacent to remnant woodland patches. This process is being actively encouraged in the Parque Rural de Teno on Tenerife, where a formerly cultivated plot of 54 ha is being planted with a selection of appropriate warmth-loving woodland species.

Warmth-loving woodland near La Palmita, La Palma.

Laurel Forest (Laurisilva)

Higher up the slopes, around 600–1,000 m elevation on the Canaries and 200 m (700 m in the south) to 1,300 m on Madeira, in the wettest areas grows the laurel forest. This forest is reliant on the regular cloud formation at these elevations to produce fog and light rain, which keeps the vegetation moist and rather cool. This type of subtropical cloud forest was widespread in mainland Europe between glaciations during the Tertiary period but has since been lost from the mainland due to climate instability. Much

Laurel forest interior, Anaga Mountains, Tenerife.

of the original forest on the islands was cut down for timber and to make way for agriculture. Laurel forest no longer occurs on the Eastern Canaries or Porto Santo, and precious little remains on Gran Canaria. However, large patches remain on Madeira, Tenerife and the Western Canaries. These remaining areas of laurel forest on the islands represent a precious relict ecosystem. They comprise a mix of different laurel species, often draped in luxuriant mosses that filter out water from the mist, which then drops to water the ground. Ferns are frequent in the damp understory, and a whole range of plants endemic to these forests flower in more sunlit areas at the forest edge, along track edges and on steep rocky slopes. The tallest and shadiest forest grows in the more sheltered and deeper-soiled valleys, while shorter and more thinly spread trees grow on the more exposed slopes, which often carry the most mosses and ferns. The laurel forest on the southern slopes is generally drier than that of the northern slopes, and different species tend to predominate on each. The higher levels of the laurel forest and areas of secondary growth are dominated by Tree Heath as well as, in the Canaries, Tree Gale, which together create the habitat known locally as fayal-brezal. Damp and dark, with a heavy smell of decomposing leaves, the laurel forest comes in sharp contrast to the sunlit habitats of lower levels. It is the home of the three endemic laurel pigeons and harbours most of the fascinating island subspecies of Common Chaffinch and, in the Canaries, the island subspecies of African Blue Tit. The tree heath areas are the favourite habitat of Tenerife Kinglet in the Canaries and Madeira Firecrest on Madeira.

Laurel forest, Los Tilos, La Palma.

Pine Forest

On the higher islands of Tenerife, Gran Canaria and La Palma (but not Madeira), the upper tree heath–dominated areas of the laurel forest give way to a belt of coniferous forest, at 1,200–2,000 m (down to 600 m on some northern slopes), dominated by the Canary Pine. At these elevations winters are too cold and fog is too occasional to support laurel trees. The pine needles and beard-like epiphytic lichens filter any moisture from the air and direct it to the soil. The tallest and densest pine forests grow on the lower northern slopes, and the trees thin out and become shorter with rising elevation as temperatures and moisture levels decline. The uppermost layer consists of widely separated, stunted small trees. The pine forest occurs in two ecologically different forms, according to its aspect.

Lichen-covered pine tree, La Palma.

Moist pine forest occurs on the north-facing windward slopes, and dry pine forest occurs on the south-facing leeward slopes. On Tenerife most of the taller pine forest was cut historically for building boats. However, there was a far-sighted programme of forest replanting in the mid-20th century to reinstate the complete ring of pine forest around Pico del Teide. Some of this planting extended to areas that would not have held pine forest originally, and some plantings were of non-native species of pines. However, most of the planting was done with native Canary Pines, and many of the non-native pine trees have now been removed. As a result of this replanting scheme, many of the regenerating woods we see now are rather dense and evenly aged, but they are slowly taking on a more natural character as they mature. Forest fires are not uncommon in the pine forest, but these generally pass through quickly and do not kill the trees. Much of the forest can appear rather uniform, and it can be rather bird-less. Hotspots for the Tenerife Blue Chaffinch, the Great Spotted Woodpecker and indeed other more widespread forest birds occur around picnic areas, where there is often a supply of water and additional food. The pine forest floor has fewer flowers than the other types of forest but is richest in flowers on sunlit rocky outcrops and in sheltered gullies.

Pine forest tree-line, above Hoya Grande, La Palma.

Man-made Habitats

Large swathes of the islands, including almost all of the southern side of Madeira below 700 m, have lost their original habitats. Much of the laurel forest and warmth-loving woodland was cut down for timber and to create agricultural plots, and much arid scrubland has been irrigated for cash crops such as bananas or developed for houses and hotel resorts. In their place, there is instead a range of man-made habitats, which can still hold some wildlife interest. Irrigation of the grounds of hotel complexes, golf courses and housing has created areas of lawns, flowering shrubs and trees, which attract woodland birds such as Common Blackbird and European Robin and often attract small migrating birds, particularly on the Eastern Canaries where such lush habitats were formerly rare. Butterflies such as the Monarch and African Grass Blue also find a home here, as do frogs, geckos, lizards and even some bats.

Chanelled river with laurel forest in the background, Machico, Madeira.

Huge areas of former warmth-loving woodland and laurel forest were cleared, terraced, irrigated and cultivated for a range of crops including grass/herb fodder, fruits, vegetables and chestnuts. Areas of native vegetation persist on adjacent rocky cliffs and in gullies, and together with the agricultural areas support a surprisingly rich fauna of birds, bats and insects, including higher densities of birds like European Goldfinch, European Greenfinch, Common Quail and Corn Bunting, than intact natural habitats do. On Madeira, large areas of the mid-elevation slopes have been planted with eucalyptus trees as well as with non-native conifers such as Maritime Pine. Smaller areas of such exotic woodlands also exist on all of the Canaries, particularly in wetter areas on Tenerife. Although clearly detrimental to native flora, such plantations can still harbour endemic birds such as Trocaz Pigeon and Madeira Firecrest, particularly where they are adjacent to laurel forest or where native forest remains in gullies.

Golf course with adjacent arid scrub, Gulf del Sur, Tenerife.

Agricultural terraces, Serra de Agua, Madeira.

Conservation

Because of the isolated volcanic environment, the number of species unique to the islands is very high, and they therefore have a very high conservation value. This is particularly true of the plants: some 10% of the 1,140 vascular plants on Madeira and 32% of the 2,176 vascular plants on the Canaries occur nowhere else on earth. Levels of endemism are also high among some of the invertebrate groups. For example, Madeira alone is home to over 160 species of spiders, of which around 25% are endemic, including one-third of those found in the laurel forest. The Canaries support a wide range of endemic reptiles, and both sets of islands support a small but fascinating array of endemic bird species and subspecies. Recent genetic work has shown that some forms previously treated as subspecies, such as the various island grayling butterflies, the two blue chaffinches and the Canary Islands Chiffchaff, are in fact endemic species. The changes have raised their conservation status further, and it is likely that other species may follow suit. The need for conservation is particularly pressing, considering that the endemic form of the Canary Islands Chiffchaff that formerly inhabited the Haria Valley area of Lanzarote quietly went extinct as recently as the 1980s, and a similar fate befell the La Graciosa form of the Canary Islands Stonechat in the early 20th century and indeed the Canary Black Oystercatcher of the Eastern Canaries around 1940.

Conservation area, Fuerteventura.

Analysis of bones discovered in caves on the islands has revealed the former presence of additional endemic species that were probably lost with the arrival of humans and their attendant dogs, cats, and rats, ca. 1,000–2,500 BC. These include the Long-legged Bunting and Slender-billed Greenfinch of Tenerife, both of which were essentially flightless and therefore easy prey for introduced predators. La Palma had its own endemic species of greenfinch, the Trias Greenfinch, which also had short wings but a much larger head and bill than the European Greenfinch, and presumably also succumbed with the arrival of humans on its island. Other long-lost extinct species include the Canary Islands Quail, remains of which have been found on El Hierro, La Palma, Tenerife and Fuerteventura; Hole's or Dune Shearwater from Fuerteventura; Olson's or Lava Shearwater from Fuerteventura and Lanzarote; and Madeiran Scops Owl from Madeira and Porto Santo. In order to prevent further extinctions of this nature, it is critical that the excellent conservation efforts currently being employed on the islands continue.

Fortunately, conservation has become a high priority on all the islands in recent years, and large areas of the islands receive various forms of protection. On Madeira, nearly all of the remaining laurel forest now lies within the Parque Natural da Madeira (56,700 ha, or 65% of the main island), which was established in 1982 and listed as a World Heritage Site in 1999. The park contains nature reserves, protected landscapes and leisure zones, which together restrict exploitation, including damaging agricultural practices. The protected areas also include natural reserves covering 2,322 ha in the Desertas and Selvagens Islands, partially protected nature reserves covering another 6,400 ha, and marine nature reserves at Garajau and Rocha do Navio.

The Canary Islands have four national parks: Parque Nacional del Teide on Tenerife, Parque Nacional de Garajonay on La Gomera, Parque Nacional de la Caldera de Taburiente on La

Palma and Parque Nacional de Timanfaya on Lanzarote. A recent addition is a network of 145 protected areas that cover some 40% of the total surface. The islands also host one World Heritage Site, La Gomera's Garajonay National Park, which was listed in 1980, and six Biosphere Reserves, one on each of the six main islands. The whole of El Hierro was designated a Biosphere Reserve in 2000, with the aim of pursuing only sustainable development on the island and achieving self-sufficiency in renewable energy. All of Fuerteventura was designated in 2009, with core conservation zones, buffer areas around existing developments and extensions to three miles out to sea on the east coast and five miles on the west. On Gran Canaria, 43% of the less-developed central and south-western uplands together with an extensive marine area off the south-west coast were designated a Biosphere Reserve in 2005. On Tenerife the biodiversity hotspot of the Anaga Mountains was designated in 2015. The Lanzarote Biosphere Reserve covers 42% of the island (including Parque Nacional de Timanfaya) and allows for the sustainable use of this land by managing tourism, protecting key species and supporting traditional activities. European Union–funded projects are increasingly undertaken to help conserve the key threatened species, including translocations to establish new populations in other parts of the species' former range.

Only time will tell whether current levels of protection will prevent further loss of natural biodiversity, particularly as the islands continue to face further development pressures and invasive alien species. Some habitats, such as the pine forest on the Western and Central Canaries, have been widely replanted in the past, and such plantations are becoming more biodiverse as they mature. The much-denuded warmth-loving woodland is beginning to make a comeback in some areas, as patches of cultivated ground are abandoned in the hills. However, other habitats, such as the arid scrub and desert-like plains in southern Tenerife, remain very vulnerable to further development, including the Montaña Roja nature reserve. These systems on Tenerife are already under great pressure, and the island has recently lost both Cream-coloured Courser and Lesser Short-toed Lark as regular breeding birds, and more recently the Trumpeter Finch also appears to have suffered the same fate. Other, currently unprotected areas may become more important as additional new cryptic species are identified by ongoing research and may require additional protection. Global climate change will exacerbate conservation problems, which is why it is very important that protected areas should be large and encompass a wide range of elevations in order to allow habitats and species to survive.

Changes away from more traditional forms of agriculture, such as the shift from small-scale crop-growing on arable land to more intensive raising of bananas, avocados, and similar cash crops, and indeed simple abandonment of former agricultural areas are presumably factors behind recent large-scale reductions in the populations of open-country seed-eating birds such as European Goldfinch, Common Linnet and Corn Bunting, as well as Rock Sparrow in areas lacking Spanish Sparrows. All of these species have declined greatly across the islands in recent decades and are increasingly difficult to find. Maintenance of low-intensity agricultural activities may be the key to retaining these species on the islands, which is particularly important for the endemic subspecies of Common Linnet.

Revegetated slopes, Porto Santo, Madeira.

Main wildlife sites

Each island has its own unique range of habitats and species, so all are worthy of exploration. There are many places that will reward a visit, but key sites for each island are listed briefly here.

Canary Islands (East to West)

LANZAROTE

Central Plains. The sandy plains west and north-west of Teguise are the best place to see the desert specialist birds such as Houbara Bustard, Cream-coloured Courser and Stone Curlew, which are perhaps easier to see here than on Fuerteventura because they are more concentrated. Trumpeter Finch and Lesser Short-toed Lark may also be seen by slowly driving the tracks and using your car as a hide.

El Jable plain, Lanzarote.

Haria Valley. The gardens, cultivated areas and scrub in this relatively moist valley are good for Atlantic Canary, the endemic subspecies of African Blue Tit, Common Linnet, European Greenfinch and Barbary Dove, as well as a range of butterflies including Greenish Black-tip, and Atlantic Lizard. The nearby Famara cliffs have both Eleonora's and Barbary Falcons as well as Corn Bunting and a wide range of endemic plants.

Salinas de Janubio. The salt pans and tidal lagoon here are wonderful places for birding; large numbers of shorebirds are present, including breeding Kentish and Ringed Plovers, and Black-winged Stilts in some years. Trumpeter Finch and Lesser Short-toed Lark also occur here, as well as Atlantic Lizard and East Canary Gecko in the walls.

Playa Blanca. The well-watered parks and hotel grounds attract a range of small migrant birds, and there are Great Grey Shrikes on the outskirts and egrets and shorebirds along the coast. The nearby headland of Punta Pechiguera offers good sea-watching, while the plain of El Rubicon north of the resort sustains Trumpeter Finch, Stone Curlew, Lesser Short-toed Lark and a few Houbara Bustards and Cream-coloured Coursers.

FUERTEVENTURA

Northern Plains. The dry rolling plains around El Cotillo and La Oliva are among the best areas to look for the desert specialists such as Houbara Bustard, Cream-coloured Courser, Black-bellied Sandgrouse and Stone Curlew. Try driving the tracks slowly early in the morning and stopping regularly to scan. Trumpeter Finch and Lesser Short-toed Lark are also common here, while Canary Islands Stonechat and Barbary Partridge can be seen at the head of the Fimapaire valley near La Oliva.

East Coast Barrancos. The must-see Canary Islands Stonechat is widespread and common in rocky valleys such as the Barranco de la Torre. This barranco also holds an introduced population of Gran Canaria Giant Lizard, as well as the native Atlantic Lizard and Eastern Canary Skink. The barrancos are also great places to look for dragonflies, including the recently arrived Violet Dropwing and Long Skimmer. The tamarisks are good for migrant warblers.

Central Hills. The hills and valleys around Betancuria are excellent for butterflies, including Fuerteventura Green-striped White and Greenish Black-tip, while the nearby valley of Las Peñitas has many Plain Tigers and a good range of dragonflies, including Tropical Bluetail. The Peñitas valley and the nearby gardens at Betancuria are also good places to see the endemic form of African Blue Tit, as well as Barbary Partridge, Laughing Dove, European Goldfinch, Sardinian Warbler and Barbary Ground Squirrel, although the former reservoir at the west end of the valley is now mostly dry except after heavy rain.

Las Peñitas valley in the central hills.

Reservoirs. The best remaining reservoirs on this arid island are at Los Molinos and at Catalina Garcia. Both hold good populations of wildfowl and waders, especially in winter, including Ruddy Shelduck and sometimes Marbled Duck. Los Molinos is also a good site for both Egyptian Vulture and Canary Islands Stonechat.

Jandia. This isolated peninsula holds a broad range of habitats that are home to all of Fuerteventura's special birds. The eastern section is particularly productive, as the plains

Barranco near Rosa del Taro, eastern Fuerteventura.

inland of Costa Calma are very good for all the desert birds, the planted trees at Costa Calma are excellent for migrant birds, the palms at Morro Jable hold breeding Monk Parakeet, the lagoons along the shore here are very good for waders and egrets, and there are several pairs of Barbary Falcons in the mountains.

GRAN CANARIA

Canary Pine Forest. The remnants of this once extensive forest occur in the central mountains, but other large areas have been replanted in recent decades and are slowly maturing. The island subspecies of Great Spotted Woodpecker is common and widespread. Plain Swifts feed over the canopy, while the endemic subspecies of Common Chaffinch, European Robin and African Blue Tit, plus wintering Song Thrushes, prefer moister areas with a thicker understory. More flower-rich open areas hold butterflies such as Canary Speckled Wood and Southern Brown Argus, plus the Gran Canaria Grayling in summer, and it is worth listening for the high-pitched squeaks of the Greater White-toothed Shrew in moister areas. The protected forest around Pajonales, Inagua and Ojeda is home to very small numbers of the endangered Gran Canaria Blue Chaffinch. Access to some of these areas is now restricted to assist the conservation of the blue chaffinch and its forest home, so please respect this.

La Cumbre. The massive caldera around Tejeda is an impressive sight. The last of the island's Common Ravens hang on here, as do Barbary Falcons, while Common Buzzards and Common Kestrels are more easily seen. The grazed rocky slopes around Artenara used to be a reliable site for Rock Sparrows, but these have become increasingly scarce, although Red-legged Partridge and European Goldfinch still occur, and Savi's Pipistrelles hunt through the town's central park on summer evenings.

Scrub on ash slope, Gran Canaria.

Laurel Forest. The infamous **Doramas Jungle**, which harboured the indigenous warrior leader of the same name in the late 15th century, once covered much of the island's northern slopes. Sadly, most of this forest is long gone, but the best remaining example is at Los Tilos and nearby Barranco de La Virgen in the north of the island, which contains many endemic plants, butterflies, including the Canary Speckled Wood, and the endemic subspecies of African Blue Tit, European Robin and Common Chaffinch. This area is also subject to a reintroduction project for Laurel Pigeon.

Canyons. Deep canyons such as Barranco de Guayadeque and Barranco de los Cernicalos have running water all year-round and are very good spots for endemic plants, as well as dragonflies such as Island Darter, butterflies such as Canary Blue, and Gran Canaria Giant Lizards.

Maspalomas. This busy resort at the southern tip of the island has a surprising range of habitats and species within easy reach. The tidal lagoon of La Charca holds a wide range of shorebirds and waterbirds, including breeding Kentish Plover and Common Moorhen, as well as feeding Plain and Pallid Swifts; it is best accessed early in the morning before it gets too disturbed. The nearby gardens and scrub hold Common Starling, Great Grey Shrike and Lesser Short-toed Lark, and there is the chance of migrants. Keep an eye out too for Eurasian Tree Sparrows here, their only breeding site on the islands. The arid scrub of the Ayagaures valley to the north supports the local subspecies of African Blue Tit as well as Common Waxbills and a range of butterflies and reptiles, including the Gran Canaria Giant Lizard.

Punta de la Sardinia. This north-westerly point is probably the best on the island for sea-watching, offering the chance of scarcer shearwaters and petrels among lots of Cory's Shearwaters. The point at Puerto San Nicolás can also be good, and the adjacent lagoon and scrub attract waders and small birds. The steep rocky gorge inland has Rock Sparrows, reptiles, dragonflies and sometimes waterbirds on its three small reservoirs.

Regenerating pine forest viewed from Pico de las Nieves, Gran Canaria…

…will help Gran Canaria's endemic subspecies such as Raven and the Great Spotted Woodpecker (*arrowed*).

TENERIFE

Las Cañadas del Teide. This arid, high-elevation crater skirting the peak of Mount Teide is full of endemic flowering plants in summer, which attract many butterflies, such as Canary Blue, Canary Grayling and Tenerife Green-striped White – the last found almost nowhere else in the world. Birds are few but include Berthelot's Pipit, Common Raven, Plain Swift, Great Grey Shrike and Barbary Partridge. The caldera is also home to some very tame Western Canaries Lizards.

Canary Pine Forest. This forest rings the central mountains and is home to Tenerife Blue Chaffinch and Great Spotted Woodpecker as well as Tenerife Kinglet and the endemic subspecies of Common Chaffinch and African Blue Tit. The well-marked picnic areas, such as those at Las Lajas north of Vilaflor and the Ramon Caminero recreation area, are the best places to search.

Pine forest near Vilaflor, Tenerife.

Laurel Forest. The best remnants of laurel forest are on the Anaga Peninsula and in the Teno Mountains. These hold good numbers of Bolle's Pigeon and smaller numbers of Laurel Pigeon, as well as the endemic subspecies of African Blue Tit and, in sunny spots, many butterflies such as Canary Islands Large White and Canary Brimstone. Remnant patches of forest on steep northern cliffs, such as those at Mirador La Grimona and Barranco de Ruiz east of Icod de los Vinos, also offer a good chance to see Laurel Pigeon.

The characteristic landscape of Las Cañadas del Teide, Tenerife, is home to much specialised wildlife.

Northern Cultivation and Warmth-loving Woodland. The mix of agriculture and patches of native woodland produces a rich assortment of wildlife. Birds such Atlantic Canary, African Blue Tit, European Robin and Blackcap are joined by European Turtle-dove, European Goldfinch and European Greenfinch and more locally by Corn Bunting and Common Quail. The open sunlit habitats are very good for butterflies too, and dragonflies occur along the streams.

Barrancos. Sheltered walks in places such as Barranco de Afur on the north coast and Barranco del Infernio in the south offer trekkers the chance of seeing a wide range of dragonflies, including Ringed Cascader and Red-veined Dropwing, as well as a range of butterflies, reptiles, frogs and the more common birds.

Freshwater Pools. The former hotspot reservoir at Punta de la Rasca is no longer accessible, but freshwater pools at Tejina, Guargacho, Bajamar and Embalse de Valle Molina are almost as good for waterbirds in winter and for dragonflies around the fringes. All pools are also worth checking at passage times for waders, swifts and possible swallows and martins feeding overhead, and drinking and bathing birds.

Golf Courses. Those at Amarilla and Golf del Sur present well-watered oases in an otherwise arid part of the island. They attract many small birds, Common Hoopoe and waders throughout the year but are especially good in winter for pipits, larks and wagtails, including a regular wintering Red-throated Pipit flock. Early mornings are best, and golfers always have priority.

Sea-watching Points. The best sea-watching points are at Punta de la Rasca in the south and at Punta de Teno in the north-west. Early mornings at either site should produce a good passing stream of Cory's Shearwaters, plus smaller numbers of the scarcer shearwaters and petrels.

LA GOMERA

Garajonay Laurel Forest. The extensive, lush laurel forest in Garajonay National Park is worth seeing in its own right, but it also harbours good numbers of Laurel and Bolle's Pigeons, Tenerife Kinglet and the endemic subspecies of African Blue Tit and Common Chaffinch, as well as small numbers of Eurasian Woodcock and Eurasian Sparrowhawk. Try El Cedro valley or the viewpoints from parking places on the roads nearby. El Bailadero trail is also very good for butterflies such as the Canary Red Admiral, while dragonflies including the scarce Ringed Cascader occur along El Cedro stream. The more open peak of Garajonay has great views and Barbary Partridge.

Lava plug with laurel forest, Garajonay, La Gomera.

Northern Slopes. The moist northern valleys inland of Agulo are a wonderful mix of small terraced fields and patches of tree heath and juniper. Laurel Pigeon is easily seen here, as is Barbary Partridge, Boettger's Lizard, Smooth Skink and a wide range of dragonflies and butterflies, including Gomera Grayling. Small reservoirs hold Common Coot, Common Moorhen and Stripeless Tree Frog, while very tame Common Chaffinches and Canary Islands Chiffchaffs can be photographed at the national park centre at Juego de Bolas.

Southern Slopes. The dry southern slopes clad in succulent arid scrub offer a real contrast to the north. Dry barrancos with patches of cropped ground around San Sebastian hold Spectacled Warbler, Berthelot's Pipit, Corn Bunting, Barbary Partridge and warmth-loving butterflies, and offer the chance of Trumpeter Finch and Rock Sparrow. Check the rocky cliffs for Barbary Falcon and Osprey.

The accessible southern slopes east of Playa Santiago., La Gomera.

Valle Gran Rey. The largely inaccessible cliffs in this very picturesque spot are the sole home of La Gomera Giant Lizard; it is hoped that the nearby captive breeding facility will one day open its doors to the public. This is also a good area for warmth-loving butterflies and the more common lizards.

LA PALMA

Northern Laurel Forest. La Palma has extensive and beautiful laurel forest covering much of the north of the island, where both Laurel Pigeon and Bolle's Pigeon are easily found. Try overlooks along both the upper and lower roads between Barlovento and Puntagorda, or

the barrancos at Los Tilos and Cubo de la Galga. Tenerife Kinglet and the endemic subspecies of Common Chaffinch and African Blue Tit are also easily seen at these sites as well as close to the man-made reservoir Laguna Barlovento, which also hosts gulls and a few ducks in winter. Red-billed Choughs are also present throughout much of the island, particularly on slopes with terraced agriculture. In summer the laurel forest paths have many Canary Islands Large Whites and Canary Brimstones, and dragonflies are seen in the barrancos. At higher elevations you may find the rare La Palma Grayling in summer.

La Cumbrecita. The volcanic cones and pine-clad slopes of this mountain dominate the island. Although birds are scarcer here, Red-billed Choughs, Common Ravens and Berthelot's Pipits frequent the slopes, and Spectacled Warblers occur in the subalpine scrub. In summer these rocky slopes host butterflies, such as Cardinal, Canary

A path through the laurel forest near Los Tilos, La Palma.

Skipper and Canary Blue, as well as many Western Canaries Lizards and, under the rocks, Tenerife Geckos.

Punta Fuencaliente. This southern point, with many shearwaters and petrels in summer, is excellent for sea-watching. The salt pans here are also good for wintering waders, and this is a likely spot for scarcer migrants. Some saltwater pools near the airport south of Santa Cruz de la Palma are also worth checking for waders, as is the reservoir at Puntagorda.

EL HIERRO

Northern Laurel Forest. The forests along the mountain ridge between Frontera and Sabinosa hold small numbers of both Laurel and Bolle's Pigeons, especially towards Sabinosa, as well as good numbers of Tenerife Kinglet, European Turtle-dove, European Robin, and the endemic subspecies of African Blue Tit and Common Chaffinch. The protected area north of the road between San Andrés and Valverde includes large patches of regenerating laurel forest, tree heath and pine forest, which hold Tenerife Kinglet, the island subspecies of African Blue Tit and Common Chaffinch, and the possibility of Laurel Pigeon. The quarry at La Albarrada is often flooded

Regenerating laurel forest near Ventejis, El Hierro.

in winter and is worth checking for waders, while sparsely vegetated volcanic slopes hold surprising numbers of Stone Curlews.

La Restinga. The southern point of the island is good for sea-watching and has some wintering shorebirds, including a tame group of Ruddy Turnstones that are fed daily in the street by locals during the winter. The harbour is very good for gulls, sometimes including more unusual species, and Common Ravens are commonly seen inland in the area around El Pinar and San Andrés. Keep an eye out too along the coast for Ospreys, which still breed here, but please obey warning signs in order to prevent disturbance to nest sites.

Reservoirs. Standing areas of fresh water are very scarce on the island, so even the man-made reservoirs at Frontera and Valverde attract waterfowl and waders in season, with the former particularly attractive to Nearctic waders in the autumn.

Cliffs. The inaccessible cliffs of La Fuga de Gorreta are home to Hierro Giant Lizards, but these lizards are easily seen at the captive breeding facility of Lagartario, just below the cliffs at Guinea. Mid-elevation grassy cliffs in the north of the island are worth searching for the very localised El Hierro Grayling.

El Sabinar. This remote area is worth visiting for the wind-sculpted junipers alone, but the flower-rich habitat is also good for butterflies such as Small Copper and Clouded Yellow, as well as some large Boettger's Lizards around the car park and large numbers of Common Ravens. Spectacled Warblers haunt the scrub, and the odd Corn Bunting still clung on in the small grassy fields here in 2017.

Wind-sculpted juniper, El Sabinar, El Hierro.

Madeira

Funchal. The small but lively capital is surprisingly good for
wildlife. The harbour attracts many gulls, terns, waders and
herons, while sea-watching from nearby headlands offers
shearwaters, petrels and dolphins. Many tour boats operate
from Funchal, providing closer views of the sea life. Visitors
who take a cable-car ride to Monte or the Botanical Gardens
have the chance of spotting Trocaz Pigeon, Madeira Firecrest,
Madeira Lizard, Perez's Frog and many butterflies.

Laurel forest slopes near São
Vicente, Madeira.

Parque Natural da Madeira. The wonderful laurel forest
of the central mountains and its endemic wildlife is a must-
see for visitors and is well served by a series of walking trails, often along the levadas. Well-
known locations are Ribeiro Frio north of Funchal, Boca de Encumeada and Ribeira de Janela,
but there are many other good locations to visit. Trocaz Pigeons and Madeira Firecrests are
surprisingly widespread and easily seen, even down to sea level at São Vicente. Pico do Arieiro
can be visited on guided trips at night to hear Zino's Petrel.

Ponta de São Lourenço. This arid, grassy windswept headland still has Rock Sparrow,
Common Linnet and European Goldfinch, as well as Berthelot's Pipit, and often attracts scarcer
migrants in spring, such as swallows and martins.

Ponta de Pargo. The open areas and fields of this western headland have Rock Sparrow,
Common Linnet, Spectacled Warbler and Red-legged Partridge, as well as butterflies and the
chance of migrant birds.

Porto Moniz. This is the premiere land-based sea-watching spot on Madeira. Watch from the
esplanade above the tidal rocky pools for shearwaters and petrels.

Porto Santo. This island is easily visited on a day trip from Funchal, although is worthy of a
few nights stay. Sea-watching for seabirds and cetaceans can be good from the ferry. Several
birds that are hard to see on Madeira, such as Common Hoopoe, Spanish Sparrow, Eurasian
Collared-dove and Red-legged Partridge, are common here. The pools at Tanque and the golf
course have Mallard, Mandarin Duck, Common Moorhen, Little Egret, waders, dragonflies and
Perez's Frog, and there is the chance of rarer migrant birds.

Desertas Islands. For the adventurous, these islands can be reached by small boat from
Funchal. They offer more seabirds, cetaceans and the chance to see Mediterranean Monk Seals.

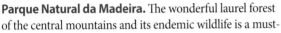

Ilhas Desertas, Madeira.

Wildlife-watching tips

Ecotourism is seen as an increasingly sustainable form of tourism in the islands and is one way of putting a value on the retention of natural habitats and species. Much wildlife can be seen by taking walks in the places suggested in *Main wildlife sites – pages 20–27*. This section gives some tips in order to help you maximise your encounters with the islands' wildlife. For watching cetaceans in particular and for seeking out particular endemic species, joining a local wildlife-watching trip is highly recommended.

An early start is normally a good idea, allowing you to see wildlife before the crowds arrive at popular spots, and early morning is often when birds are more active. On the higher-elevation islands, it is worth heading to the laurel forest early in the morning, as cloud cover often builds up during the day, hampering viewing and making walking less pleasant; however, always keep an eye on the clouds, as they can also clear in the afternoon. Stop at overlooks in the forest, where you can scan over the top of the tree canopy to see passing pigeons, raptors and swifts. Spend time at picnic sites, as many forest birds are accustomed to finding food and water in the presence of humans here and can be very tame. If the clouds descend, either head further uphill or head downhill to find the sun again. On many islands, heading into the direction of the wind will often lead you to a sunny area.

Timing of your visit is also important. Many species are present year-round in the islands' equitable climate, including all of the endemic land birds, reptiles and bats, as well as many of the dragonflies and butterflies. However, other species are more seasonal. Butterflies that live at colder higher elevations, including several of the endemic species, fly mostly in the warmer summer months, and reptiles are also less active in the mountains during the cooler winter months. On the other hand, some butterflies and dragonflies, particularly in the more arid Eastern Canaries, fly mostly during the cooler winter months. The winter is generally the best time for waterbirds and waders, while spring and autumn are best for migrant birds. There are

Cetacean watching, Madeira

always cetaceans and seabirds offshore, but different species can be seen at different times of year. Check through the species accounts to see which species you would like to see and time your trip accordingly. Trips to different islands at different times of year will always bring rewards.

Always look for wildlife wherever you go. Monarch butterflies may swoop over busy urban roundabouts, while African Grass Blues typically buzz low over well-watered hotel lawns. Inter-island ferries offer excellent opportunities for viewing seabirds, cetaceans and sea turtles, and it is worth timing your ferry trip for early morning or late afternoon, as more wildlife will be active at these times. On most islands there are dedicated whale- and dolphin-watching vessels, which can take you out on short trips to look for oceanic wildlife. On Madeira, there are also vessels dedicated to looking for the rarer seabirds, such as Zino's and Desertas Petrels. These are more expensive than the dolphin-watching vessels, as they travel further and use detailed local knowledge to track down the key birds, but are well worth it if you are a keen seabird-watcher. On land, local companies also offer guided trips for watching birds, butterflies, bats and general wildlife. These are all run by local experts and guarantee lots of good observations; they are particularly valuable if your time on the islands is short.

How to use this book

TAXONOMY AND NAMING

Each species account starts with a common name (the scientific name of each species can be found in a table on *pages 217–221*). The birds detailed in this book follow Birdlife International's species list, except where other regional authorities recognise certain subspecies to be separate species, namely Macaronesian Shearwater, Barbary Falcon and Tenerife Kinglet. The English bird names also follow Birdlife International's list except where there are generally accepted alternatives. The English names of other animals follow IUCN's list except where there are generally accepted alternatives.

ICONS

Each account features several icons. The numbers correspond to the adjacent photographic plate, allowing easy correlation of the text and photos. There are also icons for species that are endemic or introduced, and for those species that are considered threatened on the International Union for Conservation of Nature (IUCN) Red List – see www.iucnredlist.org for more information. The icons and codes are summarised in the panel to the right. NB Icons with a border refer to European status; icons without a border to global status.

DISTRIBUTION

Each species account includes a colour-coded map that is not a true geographically accurate range map, but instead shows a simplified island-by-island occurrence.
The colour codes are as follows:

LAND ▫ absent; ▪ resident; ▪ breeding; ▪ introduced (widespread); ▪ introduced (local); ▪ migrant; ▪ rare migrant; ▪ presumed extinct

SEA ▫ absent; ▪ present; ▪ rare

Status

E Endemic species
e Endemic subspecies
N Near endemic
I Introduced

IUCN Red List Status

CR Critically Endangered
EN Endangered
VU Vulnerable
NT Near Threatened
DD Data Deficient

Other icons

♂ male   ♀ female
s summer   w winter
b breeding   n non-breeding
i immature   j juvenile

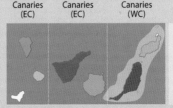

Eastern Canaries (EC)   Central Canaries (EC)   Western Canaries (WC)   Madeiran Islands

Birds

Despite their relative remoteness from the mainland, the volcanic islands of Madeira and the Canaries have been colonised by many species of birds since their formation. Migrating birds lost at sea would have found sanctuary on the islands, and some would have stayed, creating the distinctive avifauna that remains today. A total of 91 species currently breed more or less regularly on the islands, 45 species on the Madeiran islands and 85 on the Canaries, highlighting the smaller and more remote nature of the former group. The breeding birds include at least 10 species that are believed to have been deliberately or accidentally introduced by humans, of which four occur on Madeira and nine occur in the Canaries. The remoteness of the islands has allowed many of the birds to evolve in isolation into distinctive forms that differ from their mainland counterparts. Twelve extant species are endemic to these islands, occurring nowhere else on earth. Four species are endemic to Madeira, and seven are endemic to the Canaries, with one species (Plain Swift) breeding in both island groups. Endemics include such iconic species as the three laurel pigeons, Madeira Firecrest, Tenerife Blue Chaffinch and the Canary Islands Stonechat.

Recent studies have revealed that the resident chiffchaff of the Western and Central Canaries is a distinct species that differs consistently in structure, plumage and calls from the migratory forms that pass through the islands. The two island subspecies of blue chaffinches in the Central Canaries were split as distinct species in 2015. There are a number of highly distinct island subspecies, some of which, such as Stone Curlew and Houbara Bustard on the Canaries, may prove from ongoing genetic work to be distinct species in their own right.

An additional 72 species regularly visit the islands each year, passing through on spring and autumn migration or spending the northern winter in the more equitable climate. All 72 regular migrants and 91 breeding species that are likely to be seen are detailed here. A further 325 species had been recorded as rare visitors to the islands up to the end of 2017. Whilst these are much less likely to be encountered than the birds illustrated in this book, the 109 species that occur as regular migrants are listed on *page 212*. Odd lost migratory birds will occur on all of the islands from time to time, so it is worth noting and ideally photographing any bird that does not match those in this book, as it is still quite possible to find new species for the islands!

The African Blue Tit (*page 110*), with up to five distinct subspecies recognised in the Canary Islands, epitomises the concept of adaptive radiation, where new colonisers to a region diversify rapidly in terms of looks and preferred ecological niche. This process is particularly marked where a species colonises a cluster of islands. Famously, Charles Darwin studied this process on the Galápagos Islands but the Canaries show many similar examples.

1i

1

2n

2

2i

1 Common Tern L 33 cm | WS 82 cm

Breeds in very small numbers in the Canaries, mostly on El Hierro, La Palma and La Gomera, and more widely on Madeira and Porto Santo, but is also seen in larger numbers on passage, especially in the Eastern Canaries. Generally seen along the coast, but odd birds may hunt at freshwater sites. Smaller than Sandwich Tern, Common Tern has more obviously grey upperparts and upperwings bearing a blackish wedge near the tip. Adults have a full black crown in breeding plumage and rather bright red bill and legs. The very similar Roseate Tern and Arctic Tern pass through the islands in very small numbers, and the former breeds in tiny numbers on Madeira. Roseate Tern is much paler above, with a mostly black bill and very long tail streamers. Arctic Tern is slimmer and longer-tailed than Common Tern, with a darker red bill and grey-toned underparts. Typical calls of Common Tern include a repeated *kit* and a sharper *kreearr!*

2 Roseate Tern L 35 cm | WS 72 cm

Breeds annually in tiny numbers on islets off Porto Santo and regularly visits the coast of Madeira, particularly among Common Terns in Funchal Harbour. Overlooked or very rare on passage in the Canaries. Very similar to Common Tern but always looks distinctly whiter, with very pale grey upperwings bearing a narrow dark wedge near the tip and often a rosy flush to the chest on breeding adults. The adult bill can be all-black or show a red base, and the legs are rather long and bright red. Compared to Common Tern, the wings are shorter, resulting in a more rapid direct flight with less hovering when fishing, while the very long tail streamers impart an oddly long-tailed look in flight. The distinctive call is a far-carrying two-note *chi-vik.*

3 Sandwich Tern L 39 cm | WS 100 cm

This large tern is a fairly common passage migrant and winter visitor to the Canaries, gathering at times in particularly large numbers on Fuerteventura. It is also a winter visitor in small numbers to Madeira, where it was perhaps overlooked in the past. This is easily the largest tern on the islands. It feeds in bays and offshore around feeding dolphins and may also be seen roosting along the coast on rocks, piers and sandbars. Most birds seen are in winter plumage, when they show a white forehead, plus a black hind-crown and crest, while by March adults will show a full black crown. Generally appears much paler above than Common Tern, often whitish, with very long wings bearing slightly darker tips, a long black bill with a pale tip and black legs. Typical flight call is a harsh *kirrik!*

Nutrient-rich upwellings from deep waters close inshore harbour large numbers of small fish which provide rich feeding for terns around the islands.

1

1s

2s

3w

Zino's and Desertas Petrels are two near-identical species of petrel that visit their nesting areas at night and feed far offshore during the day. Zino's Petrel breeds only on the highest peaks of Madeira, while Desertas Petrel breeds only on Bugio in the Desertas Islands off Madeira. The birds breeding on Desertas were formerly considered conspecific with Fea's Petrel of the Cape Verde islands and perhaps the Azores, but recent work has revealed them to be a separate species. Recent tracking work has shown that Desertas Petrels scatter widely across the Atlantic when not breeding, with some birds feeding as far afield as the Gulf Stream off Florida and others along the Brazil Current off the eastern side of South America! Both of these species have small populations and are at risk of extinction, particularly Zino's Petrel, although both are subjects of targeted conservation efforts.

  Desertas Petrel L 35 cm | WS 90 cm

ENDEMIC TO BUGIO, DESERTAS ISLANDS

Slightly more numerous than Zino's Petrel, with some 120–150 pairs estimated nesting on Bugio in the Desertas Islands off Madeira in 2006–7. Young birds were formerly harvested for food by fishermen, but breeding success has improved since 1990, when Bugio was made part of a strictly monitored nature reserve covering the Desertas Islands. Desertas Petrel arrives on Bugio in late July and nests in burrows on vegetated plateau areas with deep soil and less commonly in rock crevices; young fledge in December–January. Birds of both petrel species can be seen off Madeira, including from sea-watching sites such as Porto Moniz and from the Porto Santo ferry, but best views can be had from specialised sea-birding boat trips out of Madeira. Birds of the two species are very rarely recorded at sea off the Canaries. This species is more or less identical to Zino's Petrel, but slightly larger, with a heavier bill and perhaps more pointed wing tips. Silent at sea but very vocal at nesting colonies, constantly emitting a guttural *gon-gon*, from which it received its local name, as well as a drawn-out wailing call similar to but deeper than call of Zino's Petrel.

  Zino's Petrel L 33 cm | WS 83 cm

ENDEMIC TO MADEIRA

Famously rediscovered nesting on the highest peaks of Madeira by local ornithologist P. A. Zino in 1969, this enigmatic petrel remains endangered despite ongoing conservation work to improve fledging success. It is restricted to nocturnal nesting in burrows on near-inaccessible grassy ledges at 1,600 m, and numbers of the species were slowly recovering through a conservation programme to reduce predation of chicks by Black Rats and cats. However, a disastrous forest fire in 2010 damaged the main nesting area and killed 25 young and three adult birds, leaving around 100 birds in the known population. Skilled conservation intervention allowed 45 pairs to nest the following year, but the species remains very vulnerable. With luck, birds can be heard and glimpsed at night on special guided visits to the nesting area during April–September, although better views can be had at sea. To all intents and purposes, this species is identical to Desertas Petrel, unless seen at the nesting sites or viewed at close quarters at sea in the presence of a Desertas Petrel. Zino's is very slightly smaller than Desertas Petrel, with a slightly less heavy bill and perhaps a slightly more rounded wing tip. Silent at sea but very vocal in the colonies at night, producing drawn-out ghostly wailing sounds, *ooo-eehhh, ooh-ho oeeeh*, not unlike the calls of a distant Tawny Owl.

Zino's and Desertas Petrels are the highlight of any sea-watch or boat trip around the islands, particularly Madeira, where they glide effortlessly over the waves.

Identification of Zino's and Desertas Petrels At sea they are essentially identical, appearing as fast-flying petrels, effortlessly shearing low over the sea, occasionally towering up higher before dropping back down again. They are superficially similar to the numerous and larger Cory's Shearwater but have strikingly dark underwings that contrast strongly with the whitish underparts of the body. The upperparts are grey with a dark bar across the lower back and coverts joining up with the darker wing tips to form a distinct 'M' pattern. The tail is strikingly pale grey by comparison. There is a darker mask through the eye and a moderately chunky dark bill. Identification features to separate these two species are still not fully understood, but close observations and photography at sea during targeted specialist boat trips from Madeira mark the way forward in this challenging ID conundrum.

Other seabirds As oceanic islands, Madeira and the Canaries boast a wide selection of breeding and migrant seabirds in their waters. Introduced predators such as Black Rats and cats have undoubtedly made huge inroads into the breeding populations that must have existed before humans arrived on the islands. Nevertheless, predator-free islets and islands remain as havens for more sensitive breeding birds, while other species, particularly larger birds such as Cory's Shearwater, seem able to maintain populations on the larger islands in more inaccessible locations such as sea cliffs and mountains. Many seabirds can be seen by conducting watches from coastal headlands, but better views can be obtained from inter-island ferry trips and even better views from dedicated seabird- and cetacean-watching trips. Sea-birding is a recently expanding area, and some migrant seabirds that are currently thought to be rare may prove to be more regular in the waters around both sets of islands.

1 Bulwer's Petrel L 27 cm | WS 70 cm

This graceful, mostly all-dark petrel is fairly common in the seas around all the islands from mid-April to October. The largest breeding colony, possibly in the world, with some 10,000 pairs, is on the Desertas Islands of Madeira, while smaller numbers breed in the Canaries, particularly on islets off Tenerife. Bulwer's Petrel is largely dark sooty brown, with very long, narrow wings bearing a fairly conspicuous paler bar across the mid upperwing, a plain brown underwing and a long, thin tapering tail. The flight pattern is distinctive: it twists and glides low over the waves with the wings held forward and bent back at the carpal. The very long wings make the bird look bigger than it really is, and the short neck and head look small as a result. Silent at sea but gives frequent dog-like yapping notes at night, *hroo hroo hroo*.

2 White-faced Storm-petrel L 20 cm | WS 42 cm

Breeds in tiny numbers on an islet off Lanzarote and in very large numbers on the Selvagens Islands north of the Canaries. May be encountered at sea on deepwater pelagic trips closer to the Selvagens, otherwise as a rare passage migrant off the main islands. A very distinctive storm-petrel, it is the only one with white underparts. Looks rather large for a petrel and has very long dangling legs and oddly broad, rounded wings that narrow towards the body. The back and upperwing coverts are grey, while the outer wing is blackish. The rump is paler grey and contrasts with the blackish tail. There is also a dark mask through the eye. Sails low over the sea on outstretched wings and then kicks off the waves with its long legs, often bouncing from side to side as it does so. Silent at sea but emits a long series of *koo* notes at night in the nesting burrows.

Bulwer's Petrels are quite easily seen around the islands in summer, particularly off Madeira, where the Desertas Islands hold perhaps the largest colony of this distinctive all-dark petrel in the world.

1 Madeiran Storm-petrel L 20 cm | WS 44 cm

Breeds on rocky islets off Lanzarote and Tenerife as well as on islets off Porto Santo and on the Desertas Islands. Some 300 pairs nest in the Canaries, and larger numbers nest on the Madeiran islands. Most birds in the Canaries nest in October to February, but some may also breed in the summer, while there are both summer and winter nesters in Madeira, which may represent different species. This is larger than European Storm-petrel, with longer wings and a longer tail that bears a notch at the end. It is essentially all black with a weak paler band on the upperwing and a bold white rump, which is normally broader than it is long. More purposeful in flight than European Storm-petrel, with a smoother flight action and longer zigzagging glides. Silent at sea but gives a whistled chattering call at night in the nest burrows.

2 European Storm-petrel L 16 cm, | WS 37 cm

A summer visitor to the Canaries breeding in small numbers on islets off Lanzarote, Tenerife and El Hierro, but also a passage migrant, when rare but perhaps overlooked off Madeira. This is the smallest petrel in the region and can be separated from other largely black white-rumped storm-petrels by the lack of an obvious paler bar on the upperwing, the presence of a narrow white band on the underwing and its generally blacker upperparts. The flight action is also distinctive, being more fluttery and busier than that of other larger storm-petrels. Silent at sea but gives a long purring sound at night from its burrows followed by a hiccupping grunt, *chuk*.

3 Wilson's Storm-petrel L 17 cm | WS 40 cm

Formerly considered to be a vagrant, but observers on dedicated seabird-watching trips in recent years have found this species to be a regular summer visitor to seas surrounding both the Canary and Madeiran islands. Very similar to Madeiran and European Storm-petrels, it is essentially black with a white rump. However, it is intermediate in size between these two species, lacks the white underwing line of European Storm-petrel and has a conspicuous pale panel on the upperwing. Close views reveal a square-ended tail, long legs that project well beyond the tail tip and yellow webbing on the feet. The wings are evenly curved on the leading edge and rather straight on the hind edge, lacking the obvious bend at the carpal joint of the longer-winged Madeiran Storm-petrel. Like other storm-petrels, Wilson's is silent at sea. It is the most numerous and widespread seabird in the world.

The **White-faced Storm-petrel** (*page 38*) appears marginally larger than other storm-petrels, its distinctive plumage and preference for deep waters make it a sought after bird.

1 Cory's Shearwater L 53 cm, | WS 122 cm

This large shearwater is widespread and often abundant around all coasts from mid-February to early November and breeds on all the islands, including inland on cliffs and barrancos, as well as on offshore islets, with particularly large numbers on Alegranza off Lanzarote. This is generally the most numerous seabird viewed from sea-watching points or from boat trips around the islands, so it is worth studying well as a means to helping you pick up scarcer species. It is a large bird, greyish brown above and white below, with a small white band across the upper-tail coverts and a dark tail. The large bill is mostly pale yellow with a darker tip, and the pale bill base can be seen at great distances in good light. The flight action is slow and relaxed, with the long flexible wings held slightly forward and bent back as well as bowed from the carpal joint to the tip, and it often glides for long periods without flapping the wings. Birds look alternately grey-brown and white as they glide from side to side. Very noisy at night in colonies, which can often be close to cliff-top hotels, giving frequent harsh wailing screams, *car-ooogh* or *car-ooo-wah*.

2 Manx Shearwater L 32 cm, | WS 78 cm

Breeds commonly on Madeira, in small numbers in N Tenerife and fairly recently discovered breeding in moderate and possibly larger numbers on the Western Canaries. Present around all coasts from February to September but scarcer around the Eastern Canaries. Very similar to Macaronesian Shearwater but a little larger and longer-winged, with more pointed wing tips. The upperparts are a little browner black, but more useful ID pointers are the larger amount of black on the face and the broader dark wing tip and trailing edge on the underwing. The flight action is also subtly different, with a shorter series of wingbeats on straight wings followed by longer glides. In stronger winds birds merely glide, switching from one side to the other and often arcing up high into the sky before dropping back down again. Noisy at night in breeding colonies, giving a series of raucous coughing and cackling calls with drawn-out crooning notes; e.g., *kak-kak-kitch-ach*.

3 Macaronesian Shearwater L 28 cm, | WS 62 cm

This small seabird is also known as Barolo Shearwater and is present most of the year around all coasts. It is commoner around Madeira and Porto Santo, where it breeds in good numbers on islets off Porto Santo and on the Desertas, than in the Canaries, where it breeds in small and declining numbers on offshore islets and on some of the larger islands including Tenerife. In the Canaries it is most often seen in August–October, particularly off the Western Canaries and Tenerife. It is a very small shearwater with a rapid flight action involving a long series of stiff, flapping wingbeats followed by a short glide. This species is blacker above than Manx Shearwater, with more white on the face, and has shorter and more rounded wings. The head is also rounder and is often jerked upwards in flight. Sometimes encountered in small rafts in the daytime quite close to the shore. At night in colonies it produces a rhythmic series of high-pitched laughing calls, *car-KEY-cukcukcar-hoo*.

Cory's Shearwater is the most numerous seabird in the islands for much of the year and groups of them are easily seen off most coasts and from inter-island ferries.

1 Red-billed Tropicbird

L 48 cm excluding tail projection of 45 cm | WS 110 cm

An exciting sight, this tropical-looking seabird has become an increasingly regular visitor to waters around the Canaries, and odd pairs have bred in recent years in holes in steep sea cliffs on several islands, with as many as eight pairs nesting at one site on Fuerteventura in 2016. Although currently present only in very small numbers, this species is very conspicuous and is therefore included here. It is a largely white bird with a black panel on the outer wing, a black eye stripe and narrow black bars across the upperparts and upperwing coverts. Adults have a pointed, bright red bill and very long, white central tail streamers, which render them unmistakable. Immatures have a yellowish bill and lack the tail streamers. Birds often fly high on stiff wingbeats, like Sandwich Terns, and will hover before plunge diving. Typical call is a loud shrill whistle; will also cackle in display flights.

2 Great Skua   L 56 cm | WS 136 cm

A scarce but regular passage migrant to seas around all the islands, particularly off Madeira in recent years. This is a large, rather gull-like seabird, but note its all-dark-brown colour, relieved only by prominent white flashes at the base of the flight feathers. Some young birds can be more reddish brown in colour, while some adults can be paler sandy brown, but all show the white wing flashes and usually a darker crown. Compared to young gulls, Great Skua is heavier-bodied and rather short-tailed, with a thick neck and a chunky dark bill. It is a bruising pirate of a bird that will often chase other seabirds relentlessly to steal their prey, and indeed it will also capture and kill other birds as large as Northern Gannet! Will soar high above the sea on straight wings and also often sits on the sea, where it floats high and buoyantly. Generally silent away from breeding grounds.

3 Northern Gannet   L 93 cm | WS 173 cm

This large distinctive seabird is a regular winter visitor and migrant to seas around both Madeira and the Canaries, although it is rarely seen in large numbers. Adults 3 are largely white with boldly contrasting black wing tips and a yellowish wash to the head. Immatures 3i resemble adults but start off brown with white spots in their first year, and the amount of white increases with age until adult plumage is reached, usually after the fourth year. The large size with long narrow wings, characteristic high gliding flight and spectacular plunge dives are distinctive. Birds can be seen at sea from headlands or from boats, and the mostly white plumage of adult birds is distinctive even when observed at great distance. Generally silent at sea away from breeding colonies.

The Nrthern Gannet's contrasting plumage stands out against a dark sea – even at a great distance.

3i

1

2

3

3i

3RD-YEAR

3i

2ND-YEAR

Birds of fresh water Both Little Egret and Cattle Egret have recently started breeding regularly on Lanzarote and Fuerteventura, and Little Egret also now breeds on Tenerife; it is perhaps only a matter of time before they spread further in the Canaries as breeding birds. Both are successful and adaptive species whose ranges are expanding in Europe. Grey Herons have occasionally bred on the islands, but they are also great wanderers and are regularly present and very noticeable because of their large size. Black-crowned Night-heron and Purple Heron are both regular migrants, particularly on the Eastern Canaries in spring, and the former now breeds in very small numbers on Tenerife and Gran Canaria. Eurasian Spoonbill regularly winters in small numbers in the Canaries, while the very secretive Little Bittern now breeds in tiny numbers on Tenerife.

Natural freshwater sites are very limited on all of the islands, owing to their generally steep nature and the damming of most streams at source to provide drinking water. However, dams have created artificial wetlands on many islands, and these are a magnet for ducks, Common Coots, Common Moorhens, and other waterbirds. Moorhens and coots breed in small numbers on some islands. The handful of breeding ducks is greatly outnumbered by passage and wintering ducks.

1 **Little Bittern** L 35 cm | WS 118 cm

A scarce but regular migrant in the Canaries, particularly in spring on the E islands, rarer on passage on the Madeiran isles. Has recently been recorded breeding regularly near Bajamar on Tenerife. This very small heron is easily overlooked as it skulks in the dense emergent vegetation of marshes and pools. It creeps up reed stems and flies with quick, jerky wingbeats. Males ♂ have a black crown, a black back and black wings bearing a buff-white patch on the upperwing coverts, which is striking in flight. The underparts are buff. Females ♀ and immatures are duller, with brown-streaked backs, but still show paler upperwing patches, although these are streaked darker in immatures. Breeding males give a monotonous repeated barking *kough*, and birds in flight may give a croaking *cerack*.

2 Black-crowned Night-heron L 61 cm | WS 95 cm

This small, stocky dark heron is a regular passage migrant to the Canaries, particularly on the E islands in spring, when small groups can occur, but its occurrence is more irregular on Madeira. It has also bred in tiny numbers in recent years on both Tenerife and Gran Canaria. Largely nocturnal, it feeds at freshwater margins and also coastal pools at night and roosts in trees during the day. Often seen heading off to feeding areas at dusk, in flight it looks stocky-bodied, with a short tail, rather short, blunt wings and a short bill that is angled downwards. Adults are largely grey with a black crown and a black mantle. Immatures 2j , 2i are largely brown, spotted buff above, and paler below, bearing darker streaks particularly on the chest. In flight gives a harsh frog-like *kwark!*, which is quieter and shorter than call of Grey Heron.

2j

2i

2

1 Grey Heron L 95 cm | WS 160 cm

This large, long-necked and long-legged heron is a common passage migrant and winter visitor to the Canaries and the Madeiran islands. Some birds are present year-round, and it may occasionally breed. Grey Herons hunt for fish along the shoreline and at freshwater sites, where they will also take frogs and small birds. This is a large, mostly grey heron with darker grey flight feathers and whiter underparts. Close views reveal a large, pale dagger-like bill, black plumes over the eye on adult birds and black streaks down the long neck. Younger birds are greyer below and show a dark crown. Flying birds reveal large wings held strongly bowed and moved in slow beats, with the long legs trailing behind and the neck often held tucked in. Typical flight call is a harsh, loud, far-carrying *kar-aark*.

2 Purple Heron L 80 cm | WS 130 cm

A scarce though regular migrant in the Canaries, particularly in spring, but only a rare migrant to Madeira. Usually feeds at freshwater wetlands, where it prefers to hunt from cover, although also seen along coasts on migration. Very similar in shape to the more numerous Grey Heron, Purple Heron is slightly smaller and appears slimmer-necked and slimmer-headed, with a longer and finer bill. The wings are also a little slimmer, and it tends to have a rather jerky flight. It always looks darker and browner than Grey Heron. Adults show reddish brown on the head, neck sides, thighs and upperwing, while the back is dark grey. Immatures appear all ochre-brown with darker mottling above and show darker stripes on the face and throat. Purple Heron gives a gruff, short monosyllabic *crek* call in flight.

3 Little Egret L 60 cm | WS 100 cm

A common winter visitor and passage migrant in the Canaries, where increasing numbers are present all year, Little Egret now breeds regularly on Lanzarote and Fuerteventura and has also recently bred on Tenerife. It is a regular visitor to Madeira, where it occurs in all months. Typically feeds alone or in loose groups along the shoreline, often in rocky pools and in harbours, but also feeds around freshwater pools and dams inland. Breeds in trees in the Eastern Canaries. A slim all-white heron, separated from Cattle Egret by its long, fine dark bill and black legs with contrastingly bright yellow feet. Mostly silent, except for the occasional harsh *aarrrk* call when flushed, but gives a wider range of hoarse guttural notes at breeding colonies.

4 Cattle Egret L 50 cm | WS 93 cm

Regular on passage and in winter in the Canaries, with increasing numbers of birds now breeding regularly on Fuerteventura and Lanzarote, but only a scarce and irregular visitor to Madeira. Birds often feed in dry habitats such as lawns or areas grazed by livestock, although also in wetter areas such as marshes and pools. Another small mostly white heron, best separated from Little Egret by the shorter, thicker bill, which is yellow in adult birds **4n** but dark in juveniles, and by the paler grey or yellowish legs. Breeding adults **4b** also show orange tones to the crown, mantle and breast. Gives a light croaking *cruk* in flight and also a gruff *crick-crek*.

❶ ① Sacred Ibis L 70 cm | WS 118 cm

Small numbers of this large distinctive bird have started breeding recently in the Jandia area of Fuerteventura, most likely from former captive stock. Odd pairs have also bred on Lanzarote, and others have been seen on Gran Canaria and Tenerife, and it could spread further. Prefers open, often wet ground for feeding but perches and nests in trees. An unmistakable bird: adults have largely white plumage except for long black feathers in the wings, which give them a black rear end when perched and black wing tips in flight. The bare head and neck are black, as are the legs. The black beak is long and down-curved like that of a curlew. Young birds lack the tail plumes and have a mottled head and neck. Gives a harsh croak in flight but also a range of squeals and moans at the nest. The smaller, all-dark Glossy Ibis is mostly a rare visitor to the Canaries, but released birds have also bred occasionally on Fuerteventura.

② Eurasian Spoonbill L 85 cm | WS 120 cm

Only a vagrant to Madeira but a scarce migrant and winter visitor to the Canaries, where it can occur in small groups and some birds may remain for long periods. Typically favours shallow, sheltered open waters including tidal pools but also occurs along rocky shores in the Canaries. All-white and heron-like, it is larger than the two egrets, has all-black legs and typically flies with the neck outstretched rather than tucked in like the egrets. The large dark bill with a spoon-shaped tip is diagnostic, although it is often tucked out of sight on roosting birds, on which the slight hind-crest of adults and ochre breast patch of adult breeding birds is helpful. Feeds with the bill held open in the water, swinging the head from side to side to catch small fish, crustaceans and molluscs. Generally silent.

3 **Common Moorhen** L 29 cm

A regular but localised winter visitor to all of the Canary Islands
and to Madeira and Porto Santo. Breeds in very small numbers
at sites on Fuerteventura, Gran Canaria, Tenerife, La Gomera
and La Palma and has recently started breeding on Porto Santo.
Favours areas of fresh water, including small marshes and ephemeral pools, as well as reservoirs, dams
and permanent streams. Similar to Common Coot, but it is smaller and does not dive. It also has browner
upperparts, an upturned tail with a white underside, a white line along the side of the body, and on the
head a red frontal shield and bill with a yellow tip. Like Common Coots, Common Moorhens will also
feed on grassy banks adjacent to wetlands, when their long green legs and unwebbed toes are revealed.
A noisy waterbird, it is often heard calling when hidden from view in marshy vegetation. Typical calls
are a gurgling *keyorr!*, a sharp *kick-eck!* and a repeated *crek, crek, crek.*

NT 4 **Common Coot** L 38 cm

A regular but localised winter visitor to all the islands; some
birds remain to breed on Tenerife, La Gomera, Gran Canaria and
Fuerteventura in the Canaries and more recently on Porto Santo.
Favours open areas of fresh water such as reservoirs, irrigation
dams and man-made golf-course ponds, where it will also feed on adjacent grassy banks. A plump, largely
dark grey diving waterbird with a blacker head, a bold white shield on the forehead and a white bill.
Immatures have a darker bill and a whitish throat and lack the white shield. The legs are long and green,
with large lobed toes, which aid in swimming underwater. Often nods it head as it swims; it jumps up to
dive, resurfacing quickly and buoyantly. Very vocal, giving a frequent very loud *pitt!* as well as a repeated
croaky *crooke.*

1 Northern Shoveler L 48 cm

A regular winter visitor in small numbers to the main Canary Islands except El Hierro and La Gomera, but only a very rare winter visitor to Madeira. Very much tied to freshwater sites, particularly dams and reservoirs where there is some fringing vegetation, although may occasionally occur on the coast on migration. Both sexes have a remarkably large, rounded bill and a short neck, which gives them an oddly front-heavy look, although this is less obvious when the bill is largely submerged during feeding. The striking male ♂ has a dark green head, a dark back and vent contrasting with otherwise white underparts, which bear a large chestnut patch on each side, and an obvious pale blue forewing patch in flight. Females ♀ are browner, mottled darker like female Mallard, but look for the outsize bill and in flight a bluish-grey forewing panel bordered white below. Not very vocal; males will give a nasal *tuck-tuck* when flushed, while females give a more muffled *kerr-esh*.

2 Mallard L 55 cm

This widespread dabbling duck has declined as a winter visitor to the Canaries, where it is now scarce. Conversely, it has recently started breeding regularly on Porto Santo. A very familiar duck of freshwater wetlands; on Porto Santo especially frequents man-made lakes near the airport and at the golf course. Males ♂ have a distinctive glossy green head separated from a purple-brown chest by a narrow white collar. The rest of the body is variably grey, with a black rear end, orange legs and a white-edged blue speculum in the wing. Females ♀ and young birds are brown, mottled darker, with a darker crown, a dark line through the eye and an orangey or yellowish bill, but still show the white-edged blue speculum in flight. If in doubt, check for adult male bird nearby. Gives classic, rather loud *quack* calls.

VU 3 Marbled Duck L 40 cm

This rare duck, which formerly bred on Gran Canaria in the 19th century, started breeding again on the dams and reservoirs of Fuerteventura in the 1990s, and odd birds have remained there and more recently on Gran Canaria. Frequents shallow freshwater bodies such as dams but will also sit well away from the water's edge in shade. A rather small, slim dabbling duck, it is sandy brown, bearing many paler blotches and a darker area through the eye and on the ear coverts. The bill is dark and rather long. The pale wings show no clear plumage features in flight other than slightly darker tips and a paler rear edge to the inner wing. Generally silent.

1 ♀

1 ♂

2 ♀

2 ♂

3

1 Eurasian Wigeon L 50 cm

This midsize dabbling duck is a scarce but regular winter visitor
to the Canaries but is very rare on Madeira. Frequents freshwater
bodies such as dams and reservoirs, although it will also use tidal
pools. As with many ducks, the brightly coloured male is easily

identified, whereas the drabber female is more difficult. Males ⬤♂ have a chestnut head with a paler
yellow forehead; the breast is pinkish, and the rest of the body is grey with a black rear end. In flight, the
upperwing shows a bold white area on the inner wing contrasting with the blacker flight feathers. Females
⬤♀ are a rather uniform rusty-brown colour, although some can be greyer. They do not show a white
patch on the upperwing in flight, which instead is rather grey, although they do show a whiter belly and
a short, pointed tail. Females are larger than female Common Teal, have a shorter neck and show a steep
fore-crown, which gives them a rather round-headed appearance. Typical male calls are a loud whistled
whee-ooo and a more snorting *ra-carrr*, while females give a repeated *carr carr ...* in flight.

2 Common (Eurasian) Teal L 36 cm

This small dabbling duck is a fairly common and regular winter
visitor to the Canaries but is a scarcer migrant to Madeira and
Porto Santo. It favours freshwater wetlands, including dams and
reservoirs as well as small temporary pools. Much smaller than

Eurasian Wigeon. Males ⬤♂ have a brick-red head bearing a thick dark green patch through the eye, a
buffy dark-spotted breast and a grey body bearing a bold white horizontal line along the side and a rich
yellow triangle on the vent. Females ⬤♀ are rather nondescript brown, mottled darker, but are much
smaller than other similarly plumaged ducks. Close views reveal a darker crown, a dark line through the
eye and a blackish bill, which often has an orangey base. Flies very fast on narrow, pointed wings, and
both sexes show a white-bordered green speculum on the wing. Males give a high whistled *treeel* and *trip-
trip*, while females give very weak quacking notes that are higher pitched than those of Mallard.

❶ 3 Mandarin Duck L 45 cm

This attractive compact duck recently escaped from captivity
on Porto Santo, where it has established a small feral breeding
population on the island's pools and reservoirs; odd birds
occasionally appear on nearby Madeira. It does not occur in the

Canaries. Drakes ⬤♂ have a broad white stripe over the eye forming part of a fluffy crest behind the
large head, erect bronzy-orange 'sails' towards the rear, a red bill and bronzy-orange, combed whisker-
like feathers along the sides of the face and neck. Females ⬤♀ and juveniles are olive grey with white
spectacles, a thin white line leading behind the eye and pale spotted flanks. It swims and dabbles like
other ducks but will also perch in trees and nests in tree holes. Mostly silent, but the alarm call is a shrill
whistle, and females also produce low clucks.

1 ♂　1 ♀

2 ♂　2 ♀

3 ♂　3 ♀

1 Tufted Duck L 43 cm

This small, short-bodied diving duck is a regular winter visitor to
all of the main Canary Islands except Lanzarote and La Gomera,
sometimes occurring in small flocks, but is very rare on Madeira.
Frequents freshwater bodies such as reservoirs and dams, even
steep-sided concrete-lined tanks, where it dives for freshwater invertebrates. Males ♂ are largely glossy
black with boldly contrasting white side panels and a long drooping crest on the hind-crown. The bill
is pale blue-grey with a darker tip, the eyes are yellow, and a bold white stripe shows in the upperwing
in flight. Females ♀ and immatures are duller and browner but still usually show diffusely paler
flanks, yellow eyes and a hint of a tuft on the hind-crown. The rare North American Ring-necked Duck
sometimes occurs with Tufted Ducks, especially on Tenerife and Fuerteventura; watch out for a pale band
on the bill, grey flanks on the male and a paler spur of feathers at the front of the flanks on both sexes.
Tufted Ducks are generally silent, but females may give a growling *krrr* call.

VU 2 Common Pochard L 46 cm

This midsize diving duck is a regular winter visitor to the
Canaries, where it can occur in small flocks, although it has
declined in frequency recently; it is very rare in winter on
Madeira. Found on freshwater dams and reservoirs, where often
occurs alongside Tufted Duck. The striking male ♂ has a dark reddish head and a black breast and
vent, which contrast with the otherwise pale grey plumage. Females ♀ and immatures are a rather
nondescript greyish brown, lacking distinctive features, although like the male they show a darker chest;
they have diffuse paler head markings and somewhat mottled upperparts. They are paler than female
and immature Tufted Ducks and show a different profile, with a longer bill that slopes up seamlessly to
join the slope of the forehead, reaching a smoothly peaked crown that lacks any hint of a crest. Common
Pochards are generally silent away from breeding areas.

3 Ruddy Shelduck L 64 cm

Formerly just a vagrant in the region, this large orange-brown
duck started breeding at man-made reservoirs on Fuerteventura
in 1994 and has since become a common breeding bird in those
sites and elsewhere on the island, where flocks of over 200 birds
have been recorded in recent years. Odd pairs have also bred recently on Tenerife and Gran Canaria.
It is confined on all islands to man-made wetlands and adjacent areas, including golf courses. An
unmistakable duck, it is the size of a small goose and has quite long legs, a longish neck and rather long
narrow wings. It is largely dark orangey brown in colour, with a paler head, and shows boldly contrasting
black and white wings in flight, with a white inner wing contrasting with black flight feathers on both
upper- and underwing surfaces. Males show a narrow black collar in breeding plumage. Gives goose-like
honking calls, *agh-ung* and *ang*.

Ducks

1♂

1♀

2♂

2♀

3

57

Waders include some of the longest-distance migrants in the world, so they are well equipped for the sea crossings to and from the islands. Numerous wader species pass through the islands, often in quite large numbers on passage, while smaller numbers winter around the coasts and at freshwater sites. Only six species breed on the islands: the bizarre crepuscular wood-haunting Eurasian Woodcock; the plains-dwelling Stone Curlew and Cream-coloured Courser (dealt with under 'Desert Birds'); the Little Ringed Plover and Kentish Plover, which breed locally in small numbers at dams and on sandy coasts, respectively; and the recently recolonising Black-winged Stilt.

① Grey Plover L 28 cm

A common winter visitor to the Canaries, where a few remain all year; very scarce or perhaps overlooked on Madeira. This large, sturdy plover frequents both sandy and rocky coasts. Often rather wary, it moves slowly and deliberately on rather long legs. It has a large head and a short, sturdy dark bill. In non-breeding plumage ① it is mostly grey, spangled darker above and whiter on the belly, but is most distinctive in flight, when it reveals black armpits, a bold white wing bar and a white rump. In breeding plumage ① it is much more striking, becoming mostly black below, with spangled black and white upperparts and a bold white stripe over the eye extending down the neck and broadening on the breast sides as a shawl. The typical flight call is a haunting *pee-you-eee*.

VU ② Northern Lapwing L 30 cm

A regular but declining winter visitor in small numbers to the Canaries and Madeira, although less frequent on Porto Santo. This distinctive crested plover occurs in small flocks along the shore but also in open agricultural areas and plains with short vegetation. A pigeon-size wader, it has unusually rounded wing tips and a long wispy crest on the hind-crown. No other wader has the combination of bronzy-green upperparts contrasting with a black breast band, a black crown and black face markings. The rest of the underparts are white, except for the rich rusty vent. In flight the wings look blackish above with a white tip, and the white tail has a black tip. In winter plumage birds are a little duller, with pale fringes to the feathers above, but still show the same overall pattern. The characteristic plaintive *pee-wit* call accounts for its old name, Peewit.

③ Black-winged Stilt L 38 cm

A former breeder and regular passage migrant in small numbers to the Canaries, Black-winged Stilt has recently started breeding again regularly on the Salinas de Janubio salt pans of Lanzarote and irregularly in small numbers at inland wetland sites on Fuerteventura, Gran Canaria and Tenerife. It is a very rare visitor to Madeira. An unmistakable wader, it has almost ludicrously long, thin pink legs and a very thin black bill. Adult males ① are black above on the wings, back and head, with contrastingly white underparts, while females ① and immatures are browner grey above and show less darkness on the head. In flight, the white of the tail extends in a V-shaped wedge up the back, and the legs extend well past the tail. Largely silent except near the nest, where it gives a repeated shrill *kyick, kyick, kyick* and a louder grating *creet creet* when alarmed.

1b

MOULTING OUT
OF BREEDING
PLUMAGE

1n

2

3♂

3♀

59

1 Ruddy Turnstone L 22 cm

This rather dumpy short-legged wader is the commonest
shorebird in the Canaries, occurring in good numbers on passage
and in winter, with some birds remaining all year; also a regular
winter visitor to Madeira and Porto Santo. This species is most
at home on rocky shores and breakwaters but will also feed on
sandy beaches and on beachside lawns. In winter plumage the
very dark upperparts and black breast band contrast with the
white underparts. The bill is short, dark and wedge-shaped, and
the short legs are orange. Highly distinctive in flight, when a bold
pattern of white on black is revealed, including a white tail base, a
white central back and white wing bars. In breeding plumage **1b**
the upperparts are richly orange brown with blacker markings,
and there is a bold black pattern on the otherwise white breast
and face. Gives a chuckling *tuk-tuk-tuk* call in flight and also a
yelping *teuw*.

2 Kentish Plover L 16 cm

A resident breeder, Kentish Plover is fairly common although
localised and probably declining on Lanzarote and Fuerteventura,
very localised on Gran Canaria and almost extirpated on Tenerife,
where it is now restricted to the El Médano area, although small
numbers can also be seen throughout on passage. A few pairs also breed on Porto Santo.
Very much tied to sandy beaches and salt pans for nesting, where vulnerable to human
disturbance, although occasionally visits the edges of inland reservoirs and dams.
Slightly smaller, thinner-billed and longer-legged than Ringed Plover, with a rather
short rear end and a rather large flat-topped head. Always appears paler and less
well marked than Ringed Plover and shows black or dark greenish-grey legs. Males
in breeding plumage **2♂** have a rusty hind-crown and a black line through the eye.
Immatures and non-breeding birds **2n** are duller, and all plumages show small dark
patches on the breast sides rather than a complete breast band. Kentish Plover shows a
bold white wing bar in flight like Ringed Plover but also white sides to the tail base.
Gives a range of calls including a soft *bit*, a more plaintive *bewit* and a harder *prrrr*,
sounded in alarm.

3 Little Ringed Plover L 16cm

Resident in small numbers on Fuerteventura, Gran Canaria and Tenerife and occasional on passage elsewhere in the Canaries. Also occasional on Madeira, where it has bred. In contrast to Ringed Plover, this species is much more tied to fresh water, where it breeds on the fringes of permanent man-made reservoirs and dams, although it will also use salt pans and can be encountered along sheltered sandy coastlines during passage. It is a little smaller and slimmer than Ringed Plover, with slightly longer legs that are duller pinkish or grey-brown and a slimmer all-dark bill. In flight, shows plain wings above without an obvious pale wing bar. Adults in breeding plumage show a bold yellow eye ring, and the lower edge of the face mask is usually rather pointed. Typical calls are a down-slurred piping *pew* and a more strident *prii* given in alarm.

4 Ringed Plover L 18cm

A common winter visitor and passage migrant in the Canaries but only occasional on Madeira. Mostly found on sandy coasts and salt pans but will also visit freshwater margins. Plumper and slightly larger than the other two small brown 'ringed' plovers, Kentish and Little Ringed. Easily told from the other two species if seen well by the bright orangey legs and a prominent pale wing bar in flight. In breeding plumage **4b** the breast band and facial mask are boldly black, while the bill base is bright orange. Non-breeding birds **4n** are duller, with a darker bill and grey-brown breast and head markings, although the legs remain orange. A handy ID tip is that the lower edge of the eye mask is rounded, whereas it is pointed on Little Ringed Plover. The typical call is also distinctive, a soft rising *koo-weep*, but it will also give a more piping *peep* in alarm.

1 Sanderling L 20 cm

A common winter visitor and passage migrant in the Canaries, where a few are seen in the summer months 1b , and a regular winter visitor to Madeira and Porto Santo. Generally prefers sandy beaches, where groups follow waves in and out while feeding with a rapid running gait like clockwork toys. Will also visit salt pans and roost on rocky coasts. These are quite stocky birds that generally look much paler than other waders, being mostly pale grey above and white below, with contrasting black legs and a stout black bill. Immatures in autumn show a more contrasting pattern of black spangles above, with a dark central crown and a smudgy dark line through the eye. The typical flight call is an emphatic short liquid *plit* or *kwip*.

1n

1b

1n

2 Little Stint L 15 cm

A regular passage migrant in small numbers to the Canaries, where a few birds winter; rare or under-recorded at such times on Madeira and Porto Santo. Occurs at both freshwater margins and more sheltered coasts, including salt pans, often mixing with other small waders such as Dunlin, when Little Stint's smaller size becomes readily apparent. A very small wader, it normally shows distinctive white stripes forming Vs on the upperparts, particularly on the more numerous juveniles in autumn. The bill is short, straight, and spiky compared to that of Dunlin, and the face and breast are whiter, making stints appear paler than Dunlin. Confusable with Sanderling but much smaller and finer-billed, and juveniles are browner above. The typical flight call is a short high-pitched *stit*, which is quite unlike the calls of other small waders

2n

2b

VU **3** **Curlew Sandpiper** L 20 cm

A regular passage migrant in small numbers to the Canaries, where odd birds are recorded in winter; even more occasional at such times on Madeira and Porto Santo. It frequents both freshwater margins and sheltered coasts, including salt pans, often mixed in with other small waders, particularly Dunlin. Always appears a little larger than Dunlin, with longer legs and a longer, more smoothly down-curved bill that ends in a fine tip. The striking breeding-plumaged adults **3b** are largely brick red, speckled darker above. The more numerous juveniles in autumn show a peachy wash on the chest, a prominent whitish line above the eye and rather uniformly scaled upperparts with darker feather centres and neat pale buff fringes. In all plumages, Curlew Sandpipers show a bold, clean white rump in flight, unlike Dunlin, and they tend to feed in deeper water with more of a drilling action. Generally less vocal than Dunlin; the typical call is a short jingling *chirrip*.

4 **Dunlin** L 19 cm

This small wader is fairly common on passage in the Canaries, wintering in smaller numbers, and is a scarce but regular visitor to Madeira and Porto Santo. It feeds along sheltered shores on both sandy and rocky substrates, including salt pans, but will also appear at freshwater margins. It is a starling-size wader with a mid-length, slim, slightly downturned bill. Birds in winter plumage are rather plain grey above and white below, with a dark line through the eye. Breeding-plumaged birds **4b** show a diagnostic black belly patch and rich rufous upperparts. Autumn immatures **4i** are browner, with a gingery wash on the head and upper breast, pale V-shaped lines of feathers on the mantle and upper side of the wing and normally bands of dark black spots on the sides of the otherwise white belly. The typical call is a harsh, high-pitched buzzing *shrreeet*.

1 Common Redshank L 28 cm

This slim, noisy midsize wader is a regular passage migrant to the
Canaries; smaller numbers appear in winter there and on passage
in Madeira. It frequents both sandy and rocky shorelines and
will also feed along freshwater margins on passage. This species'
key features are its long, bright red legs (orangey red in immatures), red bill base, bold white hindwing
patches and pointed white rump. In summer plumage it is brownish above, with a streaked breast and
flanks, while in winter plumage it is more evenly grey-brown. A noisy, alert wader, it is quick to take flight
with a musical *tyeu!*, a sad-sounding *tee-hoo-hooo* or, when alarmed, a persistent yelping *kyip-kyip-kyip*.

2 Spotted Redshank L 31 cm

A regular passage migrant in small numbers to the Canaries,
where odd birds can occur in winter; very rare on Madeira.
Generally prefers freshwater margins and pools but will also
appear on more sheltered coasts, particularly in spring, when it
may occur in small groups. Breeding-plumaged adults **2b** are highly distinctive, being largely black in
colour, with paler spotting above and on the hind underparts. Immatures and winter-plumaged birds **2n**
are more like Common Redshank but are subtly longer-legged and have a longer finer bill with a slight
droop near the tip. Adults are greyer than Common Redshank in winter and show a prominent white line
in front of the eye. They are most distinctive in flight, however, when they reveal a white cigar-shaped
rump patch and all-dark wings lacking the bold white hindwing flash of Common Redshank. The flight
call is also diagnostic, a strong quick *chew-it!*

3 Greenshank L 32 cm

This pale, elegant wader is a regular passage migrant to all
the islands and winters in small numbers in the Canaries. It
frequents both sandy and rocky shorelines and will also feed along
freshwater margins. Larger than Common Redshank, Greenshank
has pale grey-green legs and a longish upturned bill with a pale blue-grey base. It always looks rather pale,
with greyish upperparts and a whiter head and underparts. In flight, the wings look uniformly dark grey
and contrast with a long white wedge that runs up the back from the pale tail. A vocal bird, especially in
flight, when it gives a musical ringing trisyllabic *tyeu-tyeu-tyeu*.

1n

2n

2b

3

1 Common Sandpiper L 19 cm

A common passage migrant and winter visitor to the Canaries; fairly common at such times on Madeira and Porto Santo. Appears in widespread ones and twos, rather than flocks, along both rocky and sandy shores as well as at freshwater wetlands, including pools in otherwise dry barrancos. A very active bird, it habitually bobs its rear body up and down on landing and after other movements, and while in flight low over the water the wings appear to freeze briefly on some downstrokes. On the ground it appears rather long-bodied and long-tailed with quite short greenish legs and a mid-length dark bill. Dark brown above and on the chest, it has a contrasting white belly with a narrow extension forming a white gap before the closed wing. Unlike Green and Wood Sandpipers, it shows a dark rump and a distinct white wing bar in flight. A very vocal bird, it frequently calls a descending whistled *tswee-tswee-tswee-tsweu* as well as a drawn-out whistled *wheeeep* in alarm.

2 Green Sandpiper L 22 cm

A regular passage migrant and winter visitor in small numbers to the Canaries; more occasional at the same times on Madeira and Porto Santo. It shows a distinct preference for freshwater wetlands, including small ditches and streams as well as reservoir edges. Larger and darker than Common Sandpiper and more robust than Wood Sandpiper, with shorter legs and a subtly longer bill. Largely dark grey above and on the chest, with a short white line reaching the eye, it has contrastingly white underparts that are sharply divided from the dark chest. In flight it looks very dark above, with a bold square white rump above a broadly banded tail, and shows dark underwings. Often first seen when flushed up from a ditch, when the upperpart pattern recalls that of a large House Martin, calling a clear whistling *clueet-wit-wit*.

3 Wood Sandpiper L 20 cm

A regular passage migrant in small numbers in the Canaries but rare there in winter and on Madeira. Like Green Sandpiper, it prefers freshwater margins but will also occur on sheltered coastal pools. Much slimmer and more elegant than Green Sandpiper, with longer legs and a shorter fine bill. Rather brown-looking above, it is prominently speckled paler and has a bold whitish line over the eye contrasting with a dark crown. The legs are a bright yellowish green, and the bill is dark. In flight the white rump contrasts with the browner upperparts (although much less so than on Green Sandpiper) above a narrowly barred tail, while the underwing is pale. Will bob its rear body up and down when agitated. Flight call when flushed is a quick high-pitched *chiff-if-if*.

1

2

3

1 (Red) **Knot** L 25 cm

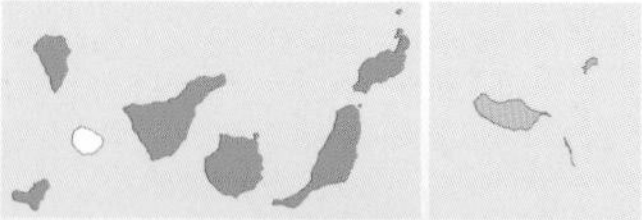

A regular passage migrant and winter visitor in small numbers to the Canaries and in even smaller numbers to Madeira and Porto Santo. Will occur at both freshwater margins and along coasts, including salt pans, often in small groups that feed separately from adjacent small waders. It is a rather portly looking wader with relatively short legs and a rather short, thick, straight bill. Always looks larger than other small waders such as Dunlin. Breeding-plumaged adults **1b** are mostly orangey red, but more frequent are the mostly pale grey winter-plumaged adults **1n** and juveniles, which both show a pale line over the eye and a pale whitish rump patch in flight. Fresh juveniles show a rich peachy wash to the underparts and neater pale feather fringes above. Typical flight call is a soft nasal *knet* or *knet-knet*.

1b

1n

2 **Ruff** L 29 cm male, 23 cm female

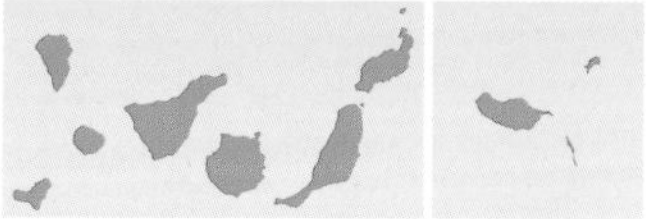

A regular passage migrant in small numbers to the Canaries, where odd birds winter from time to time; even more occasional at such times on Madeira and Porto Santo. This rather variable wader favours freshwater wetlands such as dams and reservoirs. Males are much larger than females, but both share a large-bodied/small-headed look and a rather long neck and a mid-length bill that is slightly decurved. Juveniles in autumn are plain buff below, with neat dark scaling above, while adults in winter plumage **2n** are rather plain pale grey-brown with some darker feather centres above. Adults often show a pale narrow white area around the bill base, and some males may show some white on the head and neck; the more exotic breeding plumage is unlikely to be seen on the islands. The bill is usually dark but can show a brighter base, while leg colour varies from greenish in juveniles to orangey red in adults. In flight the wings appear rather dark above with a thin and rather diffuse pale wing bar, whereas the white sides to the tail base are more distinctive. Generally silent.

2n

3 **Common Snipe** L 26 cm

This cryptic wader is a regular passage migrant and winter visitor
in small numbers to the Canaries but is more uncommon and
localised in winter on Madeira and Porto Santo. It frequents the
margins of freshwater wetlands and pools, where it often hides
in grasses or other marshy cover, although it will also wander out into the open to feed. A dumpy brown
wader with a very long straight bill and short legs, it creeps about on bent legs and drills rapidly in the
mud in search of worms and other invertebrates. There are bold black and pale stripes on the head, and
the body shows a complicated pattern of dark bars and paler stripes intermingled with more gingery
tones above and a white belly. The wings look dark in flight, with a thin white trailing edge to the inner
wing, while the gingery tail shows a white border. The typical flight call is an abrupt harsh *cetch*.

4 **Eurasian Woodcock** L 36 cm

This curious crepuscular woodland wader is a resident breeder
on Madeira and in the Western and Central Canaries and is an
occasional migrant in the Eastern Canaries. It has declined in
recent years on the islands, although it remains fairly common on
La Gomera. It feeds among leaf litter in woodland and is rarely seen unless flushed by chance during the
day or, more frequently, when it performs aerial territorial 'roding' displays at dusk. This a large, squat,
dark brown wader with a rather long, straight bill, dark bars across the head and a complex pattern of
brown, black, white and chestnut above, including a bright gingery rump. When roding, males fly in a
straight line above the trees at dusk, with the head held high, on broad wings with odd double wingbeats,
emitting four grunting notes followed by a loud high-pitched sound, *korr-korr-korr-korr, Pissp!*

1 Bar-tailed Godwit L 38 cm including bill of 9 cm

A regular passage migrant and winter visitor to the Canaries, particularly the E islands, but only a scarce passage migrant on Madeira and Porto Santo. Frequents both sandy and rocky shores and more rarely may appear at freshwater margins, particularly on migration. It is a large wader with a very long, slightly upcurved bill and mid-length legs. In winter plumage **1n**, the bill is distinctly two-toned – fairly bright pink at the base with a darker tip – while the legs are always dark. Winter birds are brownish grey with darker feather centres above, giving a streaked effect, and they show a distinct pale line above the eye. Flight reveals a bold white rump patch extending up the back and a barred tail. Breeding-plumaged adults are cleanly brick red (male) or peachy (female) below. In flight, the similar Black-tailed Godwit always shows a bold white wing bar contrasting with black flight feathers, a square white rump and a black tail. Bar-tailed Godwit's typical flight calls are a harsh nasal *kee-vik* and a shorter *kik*.

VU 2 Black-tailed Godwit L 40 cm including bill of 9 cm

A regular passage migrant in small numbers to the Canaries, where occasional birds winter; rare but increasing autumn–winter records from Madeira and Porto Santo. Rather more tied to freshwater wetlands than Bar-tailed Godwit but will also occur along the shore, particularly on passage. More elegant than Bar-tailed Godwit, with longer legs and a slightly longer, largely straight bill. Winter-plumaged adults **2n** are rather plain grey with a thin white line over the eye, while juveniles show an orangey-buff neck and browner upperparts that are coarsely dark-spotted. Breeding-plumaged adults are brick red on the head, neck and breast, but unlike Bar-tailed Godwits they always show dark barring on the belly and flanks. At a distance they can be hard to separate from Bar-tailed Godwit, until Black-tailed Godwit's bold white wing bars, square white rump and solidly black tail are seen in flight. Its flight call is a nasal *kee-kee*.

VU **3** **Eurasian Curlew** L 55 cm including bill of 12 cm

A regular but scarce passage migrant and winter visitor to
the Canaries, particularly in the E islands, and occasional
at such times on Madeira. Frequents both sandy and rocky
shores, although it can also appear at freshwater margins and
on plains inland, particularly on passage. A very large wader,
it is much bigger and longer-billed than Whimbrel. Like
Whimbrel, it is largely brown, with darker streaks and bars,
and shows a pointed white rump and darker wing tips in
flight. The head is rather plain, lacking the bold markings
of Whimbrel. The bill of adult Eurasian Curlews is very
long and evenly decurved along its whole length.
If still in doubt about the ID of a distant bird,
listen for the haunting fluty *curr-lee!* call,
which is very different from the
whinnying call of Whimbrel.

4 **Whimbrel** L 42 cm including bill of 8 cm

A common passage migrant and winter visitor to all islands;
some birds remain all year. This curlew-like wader feeds
along both sandy and rocky shorelines, as well as on nearby
grasslands including lawns, and may also occur at freshwater
margins and inland pastures on migration. Whimbrel is
a large wader with a long, strongly down-curved bill and
mid-length blue-grey legs. It is a rather uniformly grey-
brown bird, streaked and mottled darker, with rather bold
blackish lateral crown stripes separating a boldly paler
central crown and a dark stripe to the eye. The superficially
similar Eurasian Curlew is much larger and longer-billed
than Whimbrel; it lacks bold dark head markings and has
a very different call. Whimbrel's typical flight call is a rapid
whinnying *pupupupupupu.*

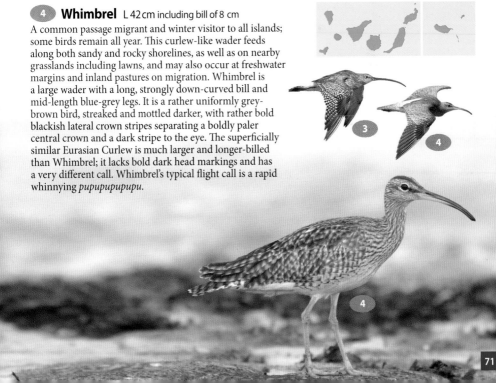

Birds of the desert The barren lava deserts and dry plains of Fuerteventura and Lanzarote can appear devoid of wildlife, but careful scanning from roads and tracks, particularly early in the morning and towards dusk, will reveal a range of specialist birds that thrive in this seemingly hostile terrain. Many of these birds, particularly the bustards, are very sensitive to disturbance so are best viewed by using your vehicle as a hide along existing tracks.

NT ① Cream-coloured Courser L 22 cm

This species formerly bred on Gran Canaria and breeds only very occasionally now on Tenerife, but it remains widespread on Lanzarote and Fuerteventura. Watch for it in the same places as Houbara Bustard on the Eastern Canaries. A beautiful wader of dry barren plains, it hunts for insects by running along the ground. Elegant and long-legged, it has a uniform sandy colouration that blends easily into the background but is unmistakable if seen well. Close views reveal fine black lines bordered with white extending from each eye and meeting on the bluish-grey nape. The slim black bill is slightly decurved. The flight feathers and underwings show much black in flight. Emits a frequent *wit* call in flight. Breeds early in the year; eggs and chicks appear as early as February.

e ② Stone Curlew (Eurasian Thick-knee) L 42 cm

2 endemic subspecies: E and C Canaries | W Canaries

A widespread and locally common resident of dry open areas, breeding on all of the main Canary Islands, Stone Curlew is particularly widespread on the drier E islands and is increasingly localised on the W and central islands. It is only a vagrant on Madeira. This large and unusual wader is most active from dusk to dawn but can also feed during the day. Extremely well camouflaged, it has pale brown upperparts with darker streaking and a white underside. The large eye is yellow. A white bar bordered black on the wing is particularly striking in flight, when the black wing tips are also visible. The birds walk stealthily or run with the body held horizontally to the ground and the head hunched into the neck. They can be hard to see but are often very vocal, especially at night, giving a range of loud whistling *Cur-lee* notes, including a mournful rising series of loud whistled *klur-LEE* notes in display. Birds from the Canaries are smaller and genetically distinct from mainland birds and may represent a different species. Birds from the Eastern Canaries have a sandy-pink ground colour, while those from the Western and Central Canaries have a paler ground colour; both are more heavily streaked below than mainland birds.

EN ③ Black-bellied Sandgrouse L 36 cm

Locally common on dry plains in Fuerteventura, particularly in the Jandia area in the south and in the El Cotillo area in the north, and very scarce on Lanzarote. Unmistakable, as it is the only sandgrouse present, it is a chunky ground-dwelling bird with very short legs and a short tail. Birds are often seen in flight, when the striking black belly and outer wing contrast with the white underwing and pale sandy upperparts. If seen well, the male ①♂ has a grey head and breast with a bright orange throat and golden-brown tones above. The female ①♀ is duller and more evenly speckled with black on sandy brown above and on the head and breast. In flight, the profile is stocky-bodied with broad-based wings and a very short tail. It has a far-carrying bubbling flight call, *churr-urr-urrr*.

Black-bellied Sandgrouse are most often seen in flight.

1

2

EAST

Birds from the Central and Western Canaries are paler than those from Lanzarote and Fuerteventura.

3♀

3♂

Game birds Three species of traditional game birds are found on the islands, and all are still hunted to a lesser or greater extent. Barbary Partridge was introduced historically to the Canaries, where it is now naturalised, whereas the similar Red-legged Partridge has been introduced to Madeira and Gran Canaria for hunting purposes. Common Quail are resident breeders that are more easily heard than seen. Quail also arrive in variable numbers as migrants, depending on breeding success elsewhere, and seem to be less common than formerly, particularly on Madeira.

1 Common Quail L 17 cm

A scarce resident breeder on Madeira and Porto Santo and a widespread breeder in fluctuating numbers on all main islands in the Canaries. Prefers areas of long grass and agricultural crops for breeding. Larger numbers arrive to breed on the Canaries after rains, which create larger areas of suitable habitat, particularly on the moister N sides of the islands. Quail lurk in dense habitat and are rarely seen. Fortunately the males frequently emit a loud, moist *whep-or-whip!* call, which betrays their presence. Flushed birds appear very small and buffy brown, flying straight and low on long straight wings with rapid wingbeats before quickly dropping back into cover. Closer views reveal a small buff-brown bird with both dark and paler streaks on the flanks and upperparts. The male has a black throat and the female a pale throat.

❶ 2 Barbary Partridge L 33 cm

Breeds on all the main islands in the Canaries except Gran Canaria, where some are occasionally released for sport shooting and it is replaced as a breeding bird by Red-legged Partridge. It does not occur on Madeira, and an introduction to Porto Santo failed. Breeds in more open habitats such as agricultural fields, patchy scrub, thinly wooded areas and rocky hillsides. Widely hunted and often hard to approach but remains widespread and locally common, with numbers in some areas bolstered by releases. A typical plump ground-dwelling game bird, Barbary Partridge has a light grey face, throat and breast, and a reddish-brown band spotted paler across the neck and a dark stripe down the centre of the crown. Like Red-legged Partridge, it is rusty-brown above and has bold dark bars on the flanks. Frequently calls with a throaty *cut-chuk, chuk*, which once known quickly betrays its presence.

❶ 3 Red-legged Partridge L 33 cm

Breeds only on Gran Canaria and Madeira, where it has been introduced and continues to be regularly released for hunting; also released from time to time on Tenerife. It is widespread but uncommon in more open habitats at both low and high elevations on the two islands where it occurs. It does not generally occur on the same islands as Barbary Partridge, but if seen well it can be distinguished by the white throat, black line through the eye and a black breast band that runs into lines of spots below. Richer brown above than Barbary Partridge, it lacks the central dark crown stripe of that species, although it shares the bold dark barring on the flanks. Has a loud and repeated territorial call consisting of rhythmic hoarse repeated notes, *ka-chak-chak!*

(African) **Houbara Bustard** L 60 cm

NT

Endemic subspecies: Fuerteventura and Lanzarote

The dry plains of Fuerteventura and Lanzarote are home to a large and protected population of Houbara Bustards. Canarian birds are smaller and darker than North African birds and belong to a separate subspecies. These are very large, slim, long-necked, long-legged birds that strut across the plains; yet despite their large size, they can be amazingly hard to spot. Their mostly grey-brown colour with extensive darker mottling above helps to camouflage them against the background. The most striking features are a thin black line down the side of the neck, a plainer grey throat and a whiter belly. Bustards are much larger than the superficially similar Stone Curlew and have a relatively smaller head and eye by comparison. They look huge in flight, like a very large owl, with broad, well-fingered wings. The outer wing is black and bears a striking white patch near the tip. They rarely call, but like all bustards, the male has an impressive display in which he hides his head within his plumped-up plumage and can appear very turkey-like.

1 ♀

1 ♂

Birds of prey The islands are home to a small selection of birds of prey ranging from the very large Egyptian Vulture to the diminutive Common Kestrel. Most of the resident species are now racially distinct from their mainland counterparts and are worth looking at closely. The island forms of Common Kestrel and Common Buzzard are common and widespread and will be seen most days if looked for. The island form of Eurasian Sparrowhawk is also widespread, although more restricted to wooded habitats for breeding. The island form of Egyptian Vulture has, sadly, declined in recent years, but it can still be seen on Fuerteventura and with luck on Lanzarote. Red Kites were formerly common and widespread breeders in the Western and Central Canaries but were lost by the late 1960s, probably to widespread use of pesticides; there are plans to reinstate the species on Tenerife. Several migratory raptors, such as Black Kite, Montagu's Harrier and Marsh Harrier, are fairly regular passage migrants in the Canaries but are much rarer on Madeira.

e **2** **Egyptian Vulture** L 60 cm | WS 165 cm

Endemic subspecies: Fuerteventura and Lanzarote

Once widespread in the Canaries, this large and spectacular bird of prey has declined greatly and is now restricted to Lanzarote and Fuerteventura, with more birds remaining on the latter island, although even there it is declining. Breeds on cliff ledges but can be seen anywhere on the two islands as well as on adjacent islets such as Los Lobos and Alegranza. An unmistakable, mostly dirty-white vulture with black flight feathers and a white wedge-shaped tail. The cere and bare skin on the face are yellow. The head is small, and the bill is long, for probing into carcasses. Immatures start off brown, slowly moulting and attaining the white adult plumage over five years but at all ages retain the distinctive wedge-shaped tail and long broad wings with fingered tips. The birds on the Canaries belong to a recently identified subspecies, larger than those on the mainland and with more rusty tones within the white feathering. Largely silent, Egyptian Vulture will whistle and grunt when agitated.

1 CANARIES

1 MADEIRA

2

3im

e 1 **Common** (Eurasian) **Buzzard** L 53 cm | WS 128 cm

2 endemic subspecies: Canaries | Madeira

A common resident breeder on all of the Canaries except Lanzarote, where it is now extirpated. A common breeder on Madeira, but less common on Porto Santo and no longer breeds regularly on the Desertas Islands. Generally breeds on cliffs but can be seen soaring over all habitats from sea level to mountaintops. By far the commonest large soaring bird of prey on the islands, it has broad, rounded, fairly long finger-tipped wings, a rather stocky body, a short neck and a fan-shaped tail when spread. Birds vary in plumage but are generally dark grey-brown above and whiter below with various dark streaks and bars. The endemic subspecies on the Canaries is a little smaller and paler, with more distinctly streaked underparts. Typical call is a far-carrying mewing *pee-yay!*, often given in flight.

1 CANARIES

2 Osprey L 60 cm | WS 160 cm

Formerly bred throughout the Canaries but has declined and
is now reduced to fewer than 30 pairs breeding on Lanzarote,
Tenerife, La Gomera and El Hierro; however, it also occurs
sparingly on passage, when it visits all of the Canaries. Very rare
on Madeira. A large raptor that breeds on sea cliffs, Osprey is typically
seen hunting along the coast for fish. It is dark brown above and mostly
white below, except for a dark band across the chest, darker barred
flight feathers and a dark tail, and the white head bears a thin
dark mask through the eye. The wings are very long and often
rather bowed in flight. Osprey hovers slowly over water and
plunges to catch fish with its talons. Mostly silent but gives
a sharp *kew-kew-kew* alarm call, as well as yelping calls
in display.

3 Black Kite L 54 cm | WS 145 cm

A scarce but regular passage migrant to the Canaries, particularly
the E islands, but very rare on Madeira and in winter. Has recently
bred on Gran Canaria. Black Kite can occur anywhere but
particularly in more open areas near the coast. An all-dark-brown
medium-size raptor, it has long broad wings and a shallowly forked tail,
which is often twisted to aid flight. The tail fork can disappear when the
tail is spread. There is usually a pale panel on the underwing at the base
of the primaries. Overall uniformity of colour separates this species
from the similar-size Common Buzzard, and its lack of contrasting
pale crown and throat separates it from female and immature Marsh
Harrier. Typical call is a whinnying *pee-ee-ee-ee*.

1 **Eurasian Sparrowhawk** L 35 cm | WS 70 cm

Endemic subspecies: Western Canaries and Madeira

A fairly common resident breeder in the Western and Central Canaries but only a scarce passage migrant in the Eastern Canaries; a scarce resident breeder on Madeira. Favours wooded habitats for nesting but can be seen hunting anywhere from sea level to mountaintops. Glides at height on short, straight, round-tipped wings, showing its long, square-ended barred tail, which helps separate it from the falcons. The smaller male **1♂** is blue-grey above, with rusty-barred white underparts, while the larger female **1♀** is grey-brown above, with grey-barred white underparts and a more distinct white eye stripe. The endemic breeding subspecies is darker above and has thicker barring below than the migrant forms seen in the Eastern Canaries. Hunts low for small birds, at speed, through trees and built-up areas. Often silent but gives a loud, sharp repeated *cek-cek-cek* when alarmed.

2 **Montagu's Harrier** L 45 cm | WS 111 cm

A scarce but regular passage migrant to the Canaries; very rare on Madeira. Normally hunts over open habitats such as plains, agricultural areas and salt pans. Montagu's Harrier is a much more rakish bird than Marsh Harrier, with very long, thin wings, a slim body and a long narrow tail, which give it an oddly buoyant, tern-like flight. Adult males **2♂** are mostly a rather pale grey with darker wing tips, a paler grey outer wing and a dark bar across the base of the inner wing. The white rump is less obvious than on the darker brown female **2♀**, which also shows the diagnostic dark band across the base of the inner wing. Immatures appear a little darker brown above than females and show striking, plain golden-chestnut underparts. Generally silent away from breeding areas.

3 **Marsh Harrier** L 49 cm | WS 127 cm

A scarce but regular passage migrant and winter visitor to the Canaries; very rare on Madeira. Typically hunts for birds and mammals over wetlands but will also hunt over drier plains and agricultural areas. Similar in size to Common Buzzard but has a slimmer body, a longer tail and slimmer wings, which are held in a shallow V when soaring. Males **3♂** look very three-coloured in flight, with a brown body and upperwing coverts contrasting with paler grey tail and bold black wing tips. Females **3♀** are more uniformly dark brown, with a contrasting paler creamy-yellow crown, throat and variable forewing patch. Immatures are like females but often show a more golden-toned crown and throat and lack the pale forewing patch. Largely silent away from breeding areas.

1♂

1♀

1♀

2♂

2♀

3♂

3♀

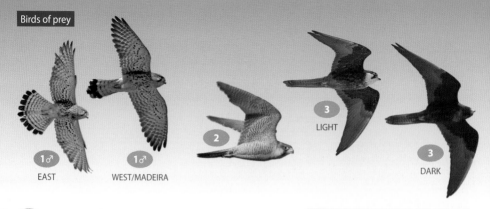

1♂ EAST   **1♂** WEST/MADEIRA

2

3 LIGHT

3 DARK

e **1** **Common Kestrel** L 32 cm | WS 70 cm

2 endemic subspecies: Western Canaries and Madeira | Eastern Canaries

A common resident breeding bird throughout the Canaries, Madeira and Porto Santo. Birds breeding in the Eastern Canaries are smaller and paler than those elsewhere and males lack the heavier spotting below and darker heads of birds from the other islands. This small falcon occurs in all habitats from sea level to mountaintops, breeding on cliffs, in trees and on buildings. Frequently seen hovering in one spot on rather long, pointed wings and with the long tail fanned. Chestnut above with darker spotting, darker wing tips and a dark band near the tip of the grey tail. Males 1♂ have grey heads, and females 1♀ have brown crowns and are less rusty above. Both have pale buffy undersides with darker spotting. Common Kestrels are quite vocal birds, giving a fast series of sharp *kee-kee* … notes.

1♀ EAST

1♀ WEST/MADEIRA

1♂ WEST/MADEIRA

2 Barbary Falcon L 36 cm | WS 88 cm

This large resident falcon breeds in small but increasing numbers throughout the Canaries; it is only a vagrant to Madeira. Barbary Falcons breed on ledges on sea cliffs and in mountains but can be seen hunting almost anywhere in the Canaries. Breeding numbers have increased markedly since the 1990s, particularly along the main barrancos on Tenerife. This is a large stocky falcon with pointed mid-length wings and a medium-length tail. Not as agile or as long-tailed as Eleonora's Falcon, it lacks the dark underwings of that species. Adults are blue-grey above, with darker wing tips, a rufous nape and a dark band towards the tip of the tail. The underparts are pale buff with a rusty wash. Young birds are browner grey above and show dark streaking below but retain the dark moustache of adult birds. Gives a fairly high-pitched, repeated, scolding *ryehk, ryehk, ryehk* call. The similar Peregrine Falcon, a rare winter visitor to the Canaries, is larger, darker above and whiter below and has a more evenly dark-barred tail.

3 Eleonora's Falcon L 38 cm | WS 94 cm

Breeds only on rocky islets off the N coast of Lanzarote but regularly seen hunting in N Lanzarote and more occasionally as a passage visitor to other islands in the Canaries. Only a vagrant to Madeira. A slim, long-winged and long-tailed falcon, it spends much of its time on the wing and nests in colonies on rocky cliffs, where present May to September. Highly variable plumage: some adults are all dark brownish grey, while others have dark-spotted, warm buff underparts, a white throat and cheeks and a dark moustache. All, however, show black underwing coverts, which are diagnostic. Gives a nasal *kyea, kyea, kyea* call.

Dark form birds are very striking.

Owls Only two species of owl occur regularly on the islands. The widespread and familiar Barn Owl breeds on both island groups, whereas the Long-eared Owl is restricted to the Canaries. Neither owl is likely to be seen except in car headlights at night, although the loud unearthly calls of Barn Owls may be heard at night.

e **1** **Barn Owl** L 34 cm

2 endemic subspecies: Eastern Canaries | Madeira

A common resident on Madeira and Porto Santo but more patchily distributed in the Canaries, where it is fairly common on Tenerife and Lanzarote, scarcer on Gran Canaria, Fuerteventura and El Hierro, and only a scarce non-breeding visitor to La Gomera and La Palma. Uses most habitats on Madeira, where it will nest in ruins and outbuildings. More confined to nesting in small caves in cliffs and barrancos in the Canaries, hunting over agricultural areas, although also occasionally seen in larger towns. Largely nocturnal in habits on the islands but an unmistakable long-winged owl if seen well. Often appears very white below when seen in car headlights, especially on Madeira where birds are generally paler below and darker above than elsewhere, whilst birds of the endemic Eastern Canaries subspecies have darker buff undersides and a buff-washed face. The eyes are dark and are set in a distinctive white or whitish heart-shaped facial disc. The upperparts are a buffy grey-brown, spotted darker; they are darkest in the Eastern Canaries and palest in the Central Canaries. The typical calls are a repeated drawn-out, ghostly shriek, *shhreeee!*

1
EAST

e **2** **Long-eared Owl** L 36 cm

Endemic subspecies: Canaries

The Long-eared Owl does not occur on Madeira, but it is a common resident on all the Canaries except Fuerteventura, where it is rare. Found in almost all habitats, from arid coastal areas to mountaintops and parks and gardens in towns. However, it is largely nocturnal and rather quiet so is generally seen only when found roosting in trees in daylight hours or glimpsed in headlights at night. A slim long-winged owl, it is most easily separated from Barn Owl if seen well by its finely streaked and speckled grey-brown plumage above and below, often prominent ear tufts and rich orange eyes. Birds from the islands are smaller and darker, with heavier streaking, than those from elsewhere. The flight is rather slow and wavering, and the upperwing reveals a yellowy-buff patch at the base of the flight feathers. Does not call very often, but males establish territories with a deep repeated *whoop* note, and begging juveniles regularly call with a rusty-gate-sounding *pee-eh!*

Swallows, martins and swifts Barn Swallows and two species of martin are regular passage migrants through the Canaries and may be seen in some numbers there, especially in spring. All are more occasional on Madeira, although the conditions that bring Barn Swallows are equally good for the martins, so any groups of Barn Swallows encountered should be checked for other species.

1 Sand Martin L 12 cm

A regular visitor to all of the Canaries, particularly in spring; only a rare visitor to Madeira. This small brown martin can occur anywhere, aerial feeding in insect-rich areas, particularly over wetter habitats, and often occurs with Barn Swallows. It is smaller and more compact than Barn Swallow, with a shorter and less deeply forked tail. Close views reveal grey-brown upperparts and a diagnostic grey-brown breast band across the otherwise white underparts, creating a neat white chin patch. Has a rapid and light flight with very little gliding. The gravelly grating call, *Trrrshh!*, is quite unlike that of other swallows and martins.

2 (Northern) House Martin L 14 cm

A common passage migrant to all of the Canaries, particularly in spring; more occasional on Madeira. Another aerial feeder that will hunt for insects over most habitats, it will often join flocks of Sand Martins and Barn Swallows. Smaller, shorter-winged and shorter-tailed than Barn Swallow, it has a small tail fork resulting in a different flight style – it often glides in slow curves through the air on straight wings. It is blacker above than Barn Swallow and more contrastingly white below. The bold white rump patch is very striking in flight and is diagnostic. Typical flight call is a rolling *prrrit*, which is less grating than that of Sand Martin.

3 Barn Swallow L 18 cm including 6 cm tail projection

A common visitor to all of the Canaries, particularly in spring, Barn Swallow has occasionally bred on Gran Canaria at least; it is more occasional on Madeira. It hawks for insects over most habitats, and flocks will often mix with martins. Flies rapidly and strongly with clipped beats, often passing low backwards and forwards over the same patch of ground or water. It is longer-winged and longer-tailed than martins, with a deeper tail fork and longer tail streamers. Entirely a rich, glossy blue-black above, it has a distinctive brick-red throat and forehead separated from the whiter underparts by a dark blue-black band, although at a distance the head and throat can simply look dark. The overall pattern is most similar to House Martin, but Barn Swallows have a dark throat and lack a bold white rump, and white stripes are revealed on the upper side of the tail when it is fanned. Males have a delightful twittering song given in flight; the species' alarm call is a sharp *viit!* and often indicates the presence of a bird of prey. Barn Swallows winter in S Africa and undertake one of the longest migratory flights of any land bird.

Plain Swift L 15 cm | WS 38 cm

ENDEMIC TO CANARIES AND MADEIRA

This is generally the commonest swift and breeds in large numbers on all the islands. Many leave to spend the winter months in North Africa, so it is commonest in summer, although smaller numbers remain throughout the year. Occurs in all habitats from the coast to mountaintops, feeding lower on damp cloudy days and high in the sky on clear days. Subtly smaller, thinner, finer-winged and longer-tailed than the other swifts, it has a deeper tail fork and an even more flittering flight. Good views reveal rather dark plumage with a less obvious white throat than on the other swifts. The call is perhaps a little higher-pitched and harsher than that of other swifts, but the difference is hard to judge.

Common Swift L 18 cm | WS 43 cm

A rare breeder on Gran Canaria and Lanzarote, and probably breeding in small numbers on Tenerife, but a regular passage migrant through the Canaries, particularly in spring, when it can be numerous; occasional on passage in Madeira. Can occur in any habitat but like Pallid Swift favours rocky gorges when breeding on the islands. Very similar to Plain Swift but slightly larger, broader-winged and shorter-tailed, with a slightly less flittering flight. It shows a cleaner white throat than Plain Swift if seen well; and is darker, shows less contrast and has finer-tipped wings than Pallid Swift. The calls are typical high-pitched *shreeee!* screams.

Pallid Swift L 17 cm | WS 43 cm

Breeds on Madeira and probably Porto Santo, as well as on most of the larger Canaries except La Gomera and La Palma, although it occurs on all of the islands from time to time. Generally rare or rather localised and normally outnumbered by Plain Swift. Occurs in all habitats but favours rocky gorges at lower elevations for nesting. This is the largest-looking of the three all-dark swifts, with a stockier body, broader blunt-tipped wings and a shallower tail fork. It is also the palest of the three swifts, with a larger white throat patch and more white on the lores and forehead. Given good views, a contrast can be seen between the paler inner wing and darker outer wing, which is not shown by the other species. The calls are a little deeper than calls of other swifts and sound more two-noted as they drop in pitch.

Alpine Swift L 22 cm | WS 55 cm

A regular passage migrant in very small numbers in the Canaries; only occasional on passage on Madeira. This is much the largest and most distinctive swift. Often occurs with other aerial-feeding swifts but may also be seen alone, when its larger size is less apparent. The large wings and body result in a slower wing action with deeper wingbeats. The upperparts are paler and browner than those of other swifts. The most obvious feature is the pure white belly patch, which no other swifts show; it is obvious even when seen at a distance, although the smaller white throat patch is often hard to make out. The overall pattern may recall Sand Martin, but that species is a much smaller bird and lacks the scythe-like wings. Alpine Swift sounds very different to other swifts, emitting a loud, drawn-out twittering *titititititititi …* , which often slows and drops in pitch towards the end.

Identification of Swifts The swifts of the islands are very similar and pose a major identification hurdle. The near-endemic Plain Swift occurs only here and in adjacent parts of North Africa and is generally the commonest swift, although numbers drop considerably in the winter. Focus on subtle differences in overall size, tail length, wing shape and colouration, especially if different species are seen together, or simply enjoy the rapid flight and calls of these aerial masters!

Laurel pigeons Isolation has allowed three endemic species of pigeon to evolve on the islands. A fourth species, an endemic form of Common Woodpigeon, was formerly common on Madeira but became extinct around the turn of the 20th century. Known as laurel pigeons, the three remaining pigeons are very much tied to the remaining native laurel forest and tree heath habitats, although they may be found outside of these areas following good breeding years or when natural food is scarce, and on Madeira they may still cause problems for local farmers at such times. All three laurel pigeons were formerly thought to have globally threatened populations, but following habitat protection and restoration, as well as control of illegal hunting, their numbers have increased and they are currently secure.

E **1** ### Laurel Pigeon L 38 cm

NT

ENDEMIC TO WESTERN CANARIES

Formerly thought to be very rare, this species has been brought back in good numbers through conservation work. The largest populations are on La Palma and La Gomera, but it also occurs on the N slopes of Tenerife, particularly in the Teno Mountains, and in very small numbers on El Hierro. Since 2012, birds have also been released in Barranco de La Virgen as part of a reintroduction project on Gran Canaria. Birds prefer mature laurel forest but also occur in degraded laurel forest, in Canary Pine woods, in pockets of warmth-loving woodland and in areas of tree heath almost down to sea level, and they are now easily seen in good habitat, particularly in steep areas of more open natural woodland. This is the most distinctive of the three species, easily told from the others by its pale grey tail with a broad white tip, which contrasts strongly with the sooty-brown upperwings and dark vinaceous underparts. It is slightly larger than Bolle's Pigeon, with rather short wings, which give it a slower flight. Birds often fly high above the canopy with a lazy flapping flight, and they are not overly shy. Laurel Pigeon has a distinctive call comprising a series of quite loud, deep *hoo* notes; it carries far down valleys and can be hard to pinpoint.

E **2** ### Bolle's Pigeon L 36 cm

ENDEMIC TO WESTERN CANARIES

Conservation work has brought this formerly rare species back in good numbers, and it is easily seen in good habitat, particularly in and around tall dense laurel forest at higher elevations. It is commonest on La Palma, Tenerife and La Gomera, with smaller numbers on El Hierro. The species also bred on Gran Canaria until about 1889, by which time most of the laurel forest there had been destroyed, and a reintroduction project is being planned. Bolle's Pigeon is very similar to Trocaz Pigeon, but confusion is impossible because the latter is found only on Madeira. Like Laurel Pigeon, Bolle's Pigeon is largely dark in colour and is best identified by the darker tail bearing a central pale grey bar and, if seen from above, by the two-toned wings consisting of a paler grey inner wing contrasting with a blackish outer wing. It is slightly smaller and dumpier than Laurel Pigeon and often flies very fast just above the canopy. The call consists of a quiet Common Woodpigeon–like cooing, which does not carry far in the dense habitat.

E **3** ### Trocaz Pigeon L 40 cm

ENDEMIC TO MADEIRA

Currently found only on the main island of Madeira, this species was lost from Porto Santo as the laurel forest there was cleared, and it became rare on Madeira through habitat loss and hunting. Protection of the remaining 15% of laurel forest within the Parque Natural da Madeira since 1993 and stronger control of hunting have brought the bird back in good numbers. It favours laurel forest at mid elevations in the north of the island but also occurs in remaining pockets of habitat in the south, even close to Funchal. Birds can also be seen flying around and perching on sparsely forested cliffs, even close to the sea, particularly in the morning, although it remains a relatively shy bird. It is very similar to Bolle's Pigeon of the Canaries and was formerly treated as the same species. However, it is a little paler grey above, generally with a silvery-grey neck patch, and in flight the paler grey upperwing shows greater contrast with the black flight feathers. It also has a longer tail with an even more prominent pale tail band. The call is rather like a Common Woodpigeon's cooing, although it is rather quiet and does not carry far.

Doves Five species of dove occur regularly on the islands. They are smaller than the endemic pigeons, and all but one tend to avoid the dense laurel forest, preferring instead more open and bushy habitats often close to human habitation. Two species, Eurasian Collared-dove and Laughing Dove, are recent colonists from the mainland, while Barbary Dove has been introduced to the Canaries from North Africa.

1 Eurasian Collared-dove L 32 cm

This small sandy-brown and grey dove is a recent colonist of the Canaries and Porto Santo but remains a vagrant on Madeira. This species expanded rapidly across Europe in the 20th century from its original E Asian range. It is now a common resident in more built-up areas of lowlands, particularly where there are gardens and parks, of all the main Canary Islands and Porto Santo, and it is probably only a matter of time before it colonises Madeira. The plain sandy-brown body and greyer wings and blacker flight feathers are distinctive, as is the frequently uttered monotonous call, *coo-coo-cooh!* Adults also show a thin black half-collar bordered white on the hind-neck.

2 Barbary Dove L 30 cm

This N African version of a collared-dove breeds in the Sahel region. It has been introduced to the Canaries, where it breeds locally on all the main islands except El Hierro. Barbary Dove looks very like Eurasian Collared-dove, but these species often occur in mixed groups, and its smaller size, shorter tail and generally paler tones stand out. Some birds are a very pale sandy brown, which makes them easy to spot, but others are much more like the collared-dove, in which case Barbary Dove's darker tail with a more contrasting pale tip should be looked for. Fortunately the call is highly distinctive; unlike the three-part collared-dove call, it consists of two parts: a short *cook* followed by a long, rolling *rrrrrrooooo!*

3 Rock Dove L 33 cm

The familiar Feral Pigeon, which has descended from Rock Dove, is common in more built-up areas on all the islands. Birds closely resembling purebred Rock Doves are still found in more remote areas of all the islands, particularly around sea cliffs, in barrancos and on rocky mountain slopes. However, even here they can show signs of hybridisation with Feral Pigeons, and true Rock Doves are increasingly hard to find among the flocks. Classic Rock Doves show a darker blue-grey head and neck, a paler grey mantle, upperwings and underparts and a bold white rump patch in flight. There is normally a metallic green patch on the neck, as well as two prominent black bands on the wings and a black band on the tip of the mid-grey tail. Has a rather mournful cooing *trrruoo-u* call.

VU 1 European Turtle-dove L 27 cm

Unlike the other doves, which are resident, European Turtle-doves are migrants; they winter in the Sahel region of sub-Saharan Africa and return to breed on all of the main islands beginning in March. Turtle-doves prefer dense bushy cover and inhabit natural wooded habitats as well as man-made ones, so are found at all elevations, in contrast to Eurasian Collared-dove. Their numbers have declined in recent years. The species is widely hunted across it range and is shy, so is most often located by its oft-repeated deep purring call, *turrrrrr, turrrrr*. Usual views are of a slim, fast-flying dove. If seen well, however, it is much more colourful than the collared-dove, with bright orange-brown edges to dark-centred feathers on much of the upperwing, which contrast with the pale grey head and pinkish breast. The flight feathers are darker grey, and the tail has a striking pattern of bold narrow white tips banded black at the base.

2 Laughing Dove L 25 cm

This small dove has recently established breeding populations on Fuerteventura and Lanzarote that are thought to represent natural colonisations from adjacent parts of North Africa. It now also breeds on Gran Canaria, La Gomera and El Hierro, possibly as a result of escapes from captivity. Birds have also been sighted recently on both Tenerife and La Palma, where colonisation also seems likely, and very rarely on Madeira. A rather tame bird, it frequents built-up areas with palms and other trees. It is a plainer and darker bird than European Turtle-dove, showing uniform dark brown upperwings and a pinkish head and neck with a delicate black and ochre gorget on the lower throat. The tail is longer than that of the turtle-dove but shows a less striking pattern in flight, with large white patches at the sides but only limited black at the base. The distinctive laughing call is a series of six to eight coos: *coo-coo-KU-KU, coo-coo!*

There are impressive captive aviary collections of a wide range of parrots and parakeets on both Madeira and the Canaries. Whether these were the sources of currently wild-living populations of parakeets on the islands is not clear, but two species have now become established, while five other species, the Budgerigar, Cockatiel, Black-hooded Parakeet (Nanday Conure), Senegal Parrot and Yellow-crowned Amazon are seen from time to time in built-up areas of Tenerife, particularly Santa Cruz and Puerto de la Cruz, and may breed there on occasion.

❶ ③ Ring-necked Parakeet L 40 cm
including 20 cm tail projection

This is the most widespread parakeet in the islands, with breeding groups well established on Lanzarote, Tenerife, Gran Canaria and probably Fuerteventura, as well as a recent population in Funchal on Madeira. The species breeds in temperate areas of Asia, so the mild climate of the islands appears to suit it. Birds favour parks and gardens in built-up areas, where they nest in tree holes and often perch high in the tallest trees. This is a bright green midsize parrot with a very long, graduated tail with bluish central feathers. Close views reveal a large red beak and on the male a black chin, a narrow pink collar and pale grey neck sides. The female has a shorter tail than the male and lacks the head and neck markings. Ring-necked Parakeets are most often revealed by their loud, harsh *ke-ak* calls, given in flight and when perched.

❶ ④ Monk Parakeet L 33 cm

This parakeet from Argentina has established breeding groups on Tenerife, Gran Canaria and Fuerteventura, and has also bred on La Palma. Monk Parakeet favours parks and gardens with tall trees in built-up areas where it can build its huge stick nests. It is the only parrot in the world to build stick nests, which are communal, with separate entrances for each pair. Monk Parakeet is similar to Ring-necked Parakeet, being mostly green, but is smaller and has a slightly shorter tail. Close views reveal a pale greyish face and breast, a pinkish bill and a yellow band on the lower chest. Like Ring-necked Parakeet, it is very vocal, giving a range of chatters, squawks and screeches.

Colourful birds This group of midsize colourful birds includes the widespread and bizarre-looking Common Hoopoe, the two endemic subspecies of Great Spotted Woodpecker that inhabit the mountain forests of the Central Canaries, the gaudy European Bee-eater, the more familiar Common Cuckoo, the endemic subspecies of Great Grey Shrike that lives in open areas on the Eastern and Central Canaries, the recently introduced Red-vented Bulbul and the brightly coloured but elusive Eurasian Golden Oriole, which turns up in the Eastern Canaries on passage.

Great Spotted Woodpecker L 22 cm

2 endemic subspecies: Tenerife | Gran Canaria

The only woodpecker to occur on the islands, it is resident on Tenerife and Gran Canaria only, where it occurs in native and replanted Canary Pine forest above 500 m elevation. It is rather scarce and localised, although gradually spreading on Tenerife as the plantations mature, but is more common on Gran Canaria, where it also occurs in palm groves, chestnut and almond plantations and even eucalyptus groves. A midsize black and white woodpecker, it has mostly black upperparts, a white patch in the closed wing and black-and-white-barred flight feathers. The crown is black, and the male ♂ shows a red patch on the nape. Both sexes have a bold red vent. Gran Canarian birds are paler below and have longer bills than those from Tenerife. The typical call is a sharp *kik!*, often repeated, which carries far through the trees, as does the drumming sound made by territorial birds tapping on tree trunks.

1 ♀

1 ♂
TENERIFE

1 ♂
GRAN CANARIA

2 **European Bee-eater** L 28 cm | WS 47 cm

This highly attractive bird is a regular passage migrant in the
Canaries, especially in spring, when it can occur in small flocks, while
it is a scarce migrant on Madeira. Hunts for bees and other insects
in flight over open areas, but will frequently perch conspicuously on
bare tree branches or on roadside wires, when it appears slim and
long-tailed, with a long, fine, slightly curved bill. Adults of this lovely,
colourful bird are rich chestnut above, with yellow on the mantle
sides and throat, and the underparts are sky blue. Juveniles in autumn
are duller and a little greener above but still show the same basic
pattern. In flight, these bee-eaters show long, pointed wings and long,
pointed central tail feathers. They attract attention with their throaty
proop, proop calls.

3 **Common Hoopoe** L 27 cm including 4 cm bill

A common resident on Porto Santo and the Eastern Canaries and a scarcer
resident on the Central and Western Canaries; rare on Madeira. Also
commonly appears as a migrant in spring in the Canaries, especially the
E islands. Favours areas with short grass or open ground, such as golf
courses, agricultural areas, open scrub and even parks in towns.
A highly distinctive bird, it is unmistakable if seen well. The bill is
long and decurved, and the body plumage is largely pinkish-brown.
An erectile crest bears black marks, the wings are boldly black-and-white
patterned and the black tail bears a single white band. The wings are
broad and blunt, inducing a floppy, butterfly-like flight. Hops jerkily
on the ground. Wary, it has a habit of disappearing from view.
Rarely calls, but the onomatopoeic song is a three-note *oop-oop-oop*.

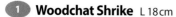

1 Woodchat Shrike L 18 cm

This colourful, dumpy-looking shrike is a regular passage migrant to the Canaries in spring, when it can appear in large numbers, particularly on the E islands, but it is much scarcer in autumn. It is very rare on Madeira. Occurs in more open habitats with bushes, such as agricultural areas, bushy plains and hotel gardens, and will often perch in the open on wires. Smaller and shorter-tailed than Great Grey Shrike, it has a relatively large head and a rather chunky body. Adults show a bright chestnut hind-crown and nape, a black face mask and black upperparts bearing bold white patches on the wing and rump. The underparts are contrastingly white. Often rather silent on passage but will give a harsh *vi-vi-vi* … in alarm.

e 2 Great Grey Shrike L 25 cm

Endemic subspecies: Eastern and Central Canaries

A fairly common resident on Fuerteventura and Lanzarote but scarce and local in the drier S arid zones of Tenerife and Gran Canaria and in Las Cañadas del Teide on Tenerife. Does not occur in the Western Canaries or Madeira or Porto Santo. Inhabits open bushy country, such as dry *Euphorbia* scrub, abandoned agricultural land and lava flows with scattered bushes, and the edges of cultivated land and golf courses. A slim, midsize, long-tailed bird, it habitually perches on the tops of bushes and rocks, on the lookout for its prey of reptiles, small rodents and large insects, which it often stores for later consumption by impaling them on thorns or on barbed wire. Grey above, it has a bold black eye mask, black wings with small white markings and a long black tail tipped white. The underside is washed pale grey, with a whiter throat, and the large beak is grey. Birds on the Canaries are smaller and darker grey above than those on the mainland. Varied calls include a harsh *shree* and a softer *kerr-clee*; the complex song of the male is a mixture of squeaks, clicks, chatters and whistles.

3 Common Cuckoo L 34 cm

A fairly regular passage migrant in the Canaries, where it is most often observed in spring; it is very rare at such times on Madeira. This familiar long-tailed bird can occur almost anywhere and will perch in the open on overhead wires and similar structures, but it more often frequents cover, such as woodland, parks and gardens. The male is grey above and on the chest and has dark barring on the white belly and vent. Females can be similar or have rufous plumage with dark barring above and below. Autumn juveniles show a mix, with both grey and rufous tones above, and usually have a white patch on the nape. In flight, Common Cuckoos can look very like Eurasian Sparrowhawk and are often mobbed by small birds, but note the very long, slim tail, strongly pointed wings and quick wingbeats with the wings held below the body. The familiar *cuc-koo* call of the male often betrays its presence in spring.

2

1

2

3♂

1 Red-vented Bulbul L 20 cm

This exotic thrush-like bird from the Indian subcontinent has recently established a breeding population on Fuerteventura from escaped or released cage birds. It frequents areas with trees, such as hotel gardens, town parks and shelter belts, with hotspots in La Lajita and towns such as Corralejo. It is a perky, upright and rather bold bird with a slight crest on the hind-crown. Looks rather dark when perched, with a black head and a grey-brown body with paler scaling, while the vent is conspicuously red. In flight, it reveals a bold white rump and a white tip to the otherwise blackish tail. The typical call is a cheery *be-quick-quick!* The closely related Red-whiskered Bulbul has bred recently at Los Realejos on Tenerife, and attempts are being made to prevent it from spreading further.

2 Common Starling L 21 cm

This familiar cosmopolitan bird breeds very locally on Tenerife (La Laguna) and Gran Canaria (Maspalomas) and is a widespread if declining winter visitor to all of the Canary Islands and occasionally to Madeira. Prefers open habitats in towns and villages but also frequents sea cliffs and agricultural areas, where it often feeds around livestock. It is a largely black bird in summer plumage but with green and purple glossy sheens and a pointed yellow bill. It has a more upright stance and shorter tail than the superficially similar Common Blackbird. In winter 2n the bill is dark and the dark plumage is heavily sprinkled with paler yellowish-white spots. The very varied range of calls includes a buzzy *churr* and a long, whistled *steeh*. The song is amazingly mimetic, full of the calls and songs of other birds, mammals and even man-made objects such as trilling phones, car horns and sirens!

3 **Golden Oriole** L 23 cm

A regular migrant in small numbers, particularly to the Eastern
Canaries in spring, but very rare on Madeira. This thrush-like
bird is drawn to trees and cover on migration, often appearing in
the well-watered gardens of hotels, although it can be surprisingly
elusive for such a brightly coloured bird. Males 3♂ are bright yellow with contrasting black wings, a
largely black tail and a reddish beak. Females 3♀ and immatures are a rich yellowy green above, with
yellower flanks and vent, plus a whiter breast and belly bearing fine dark streaks. Males have a very
distinctive fluty whistled song, *wheee-wooo!*, but birds can also give a harsh jay-like *vheeek!*

Chats, redstarts, wheatears and thrushes This group of perching birds includes some of the finest resident songsters on the islands, as well as a very special endemic chat and several passage and winter migrants. The resident breeding robins and blackbirds are rather different from their mainland counterparts and reward close scrutiny. Ongoing genetic studies of the robins of the Central Canaries may yet prove the existence of up two distinct species there.

1 Common Redstart L 14cm

A fairly common passage migrant in the Canaries, especially in the Eastern Islands in spring; much scarcer on Madeira. Favours scrub on migration and is also found in cultivated areas and hotel gardens. A robin-size bird, it has a distinctive habit of perching upright and shivering its red tail. Males ♂ are unmistakable, with a black face, white fore-crown, grey upperparts and an orangey-red breast. Females ♀ and immatures are duller and browner above but retain orangey tones below and still show a reddish tail and rump. Typical calls are a plaintive *hweet* often followed by a harsh *tuc!*

2 Black Redstart L 14cm

A scarce though regular passage migrant and winter visitor to the Canaries but very rare on Madeira. Can occur in a range of habitats from rocky cliffs and barrancos to agricultural areas, gardens and villages. Very similar in shape and behaviour to Common Redstart, including the habit of shivering its rusty-red tail, but it is often rather shy and has a habit of disappearing. Males ♂ are distinctive, as they are largely dark grey with a whitish underbelly and wing flash, with orangey red confined to the undertail and tail. Females ♀ and immatures are more like Common Redstart but are always greyer; rather uniform smoky grey above and below, they lack the browner tones above and orangey tones below of Common Redstart. Black Redstart is often rather quiet, but the typical call is a sharp whistled *sist*, with ticks added when alarmed – e.g., *sist-tick-tick.*

3 Northern Wheatear L 15cm

A fairly common passage migrant in the Canaries, in both spring and autumn, but only occasional on Madeira. A ground-dwelling chat, it favours open areas such as cultivated fields, bare arid ground, lawns and beaches, where it hops deliberately with an upright stance. Males ♂ are distinctive, with blue-grey upperparts, a black face mask, black wings and a rich pink-buff throat and chest. Females ♀ and immatures are duller and browner. All show a bold white rump and tail base in flight, contrasting with a black tail tip and outer central tail. Calls include a whistled *hit* and a clicking *chack.*

1♂ 1♀

2♂ 2♀

3♂ 3♀

1 Whinchat L 13 cm

A fairly common passage migrant in the Canaries, especially in the Eastern Islands in spring, but very rare on Madeira. Occurs in more open habitats, such as scrub, cultivated areas and edges of hotel gardens. It is a plump, short-tailed chat with a bold pale stripe over the eye. Males ♂ are more brightly coloured, with a rich orangey-buff throat and breast and a more contrasting head pattern. Females ♀ and immatures are a duller buff below but retain a broad pale stripe over the eye. Males have small white patches in the wing, which are most obvious in flight, and both sexes show white sides to the tail base. Compare with Canary Islands Stonechat. Common calls when alarmed are a soft *you-tek* or *you-tek-tek*.

E 2 Canary Islands (Fuerteventura) Stonechat

NT

L 12 cm

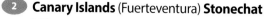

ENDEMIC TO FUERTEVENTURA

This is an endemic chat found only on Fuerteventura, although a separate subspecies formerly inhabited the islets of Alegranza and Montaña Clara off the N tip of Lanzarote, and birds from Fuerteventura still occasionally stray to S Lanzarote. It was down-listed from endangered to near-threatened status by IUCN in 2010, as recent surveys have found the species to be more common than previously thought (750–1,300 pairs in total). This handsome chat is quite widespread on the island in open bushy habitat, including scrubby hillsides, barrancos and the edges of cultivated land. Perching on bushes and rocks, it looks like a cross between Whinchat and Common Stonechat with a longer and finer bill. Males ♂ are darker brown above than Whinchat, with a darker brown head bearing a short fine white line over the eye. Key points to look for are the white throat and white half-collar, plus the all-dark tail and rump in flight. Females ♀ and immatures ♀i are paler and lack a paler stripe over the eye. Common calls are *sit, chut-chut* or a combination of these notes; the male's song is a scratchy *bit, beezee, beezoo*.

3 Common Stonechat L 12 cm

A scarce and irregular winter visitor to the Canaries, particularly the E isles, but only a rare migrant to Madeira. This species favours the same open areas with scattered bushes as the similar Canary Islands Stonechat, which can cause ID issues on Fuerteventura. It has a similar habit of perching prominently on bushes, rocks and fences. Compared with Canary Islands Stonechat, the male Common Stonechat ♂ has a blacker head lacking a white line over the eye, more extensive orange on the underparts and an obvious white rump in flight. Females of the two species are even more alike, but female Common Stonechat ♀ again shows more extensive orange tones below, as well as a more obvious pale patch at the base of the wing and a warmer-toned rump. The typical call is *wist, track-track*, which is very similar to call of Canary Islands Stonechat.

1 ♀

1 ♂

2 ♀

2 ♂

3 ♀

3 ♂

1 Common Blackbird L 25 cm

Endemic subspecies: Canaries and Madeira

This familiar bird is very common on all of the Canary Islands and on Madeira but is oddly scarce on Porto Santo. Found in all habitats from sea level to high mountains, it is particularly numerous in areas of native forest and scarce in more open arid areas. Males ♂ are all black, with a bright orangey-yellow beak and eye ring, while females ♀ are browner, with paler underparts and a whiter throat. Birds on the islands are smaller than those of the mainland and have a slightly longer bill and shorter wings. Males are blacker than mainland males, and the females are darker and have a more restricted white patch on the throat. Typical call is a harsh *chak*, often given in succession when alarmed, plus a thin *tsee* note. The song of the male is a beautiful relaxed series of warbles and fluty notes, which drifts through the trees and on calm spring mornings is a very distinctive sound of the native woodlands.

2 Ring Ouzel L 24 cm

Small numbers of this migratory thrush winter regularly in Las Cañadas on Tenerife, on Fuerteventura and possibly elsewhere in the Canaries, but it is only a vagrant on Madeira. Wintering birds feed mostly on juniper berries, so their distribution is tied to the presence of fruiting juniper trees. They have recently been found to winter annually in Las Cañadas, and searches should be made of juniper-rich habitat elsewhere in winter. Similar in size and shape to Common Blackbird, but males ♂ show a distinct white crescent on the chest, a dark tip to the yellowish bill and pale grey fringes to the flight feathers. Females ♀ and first-winter birds are browner and more scaly above, show a reduced pale breast crescent and have a duller bill, but like males they retain distinctive pale edges to the flight feathers. Typical call sounds like two stones being knocked together, *Tuck*; birds also produce a more rattling chatter.

3 Song Thrush L 22 cm

Song Thrush is a regular winter visitor to the Canaries, recorded on all the main islands, although more common in the Eastern Canaries, and is rare on Madeira and Porto Santo. Favours areas with cover, such as cultivated areas, gardens and parks, where it can forage on the ground, as well as native woodland. A midsize thrush, it is rather smaller, shorter-tailed and more round-bodied than Common Blackbird. Plain brown above, it is white below, washed with buff and heavily spotted with black. The orangey-buff wing linings can be seen in flight, but it lacks the deep red tones on the flanks and the bold white eye stripe of Redwing. The typical calls are a sharp *zit* and a more chattering *chock, chock*. The male's varied song of repeated phrases is regularly given early in the morning in the winter quarters.

NT **4 Redwing** L 21 cm

An irregular winter visitor to the Eastern Canaries and Tenerife, although more birds are seen in some years and it may be overlooked. Favours bushy cover such as gardens, parks and dense vegetation including aloe groves. Similar to Song Thrush in size and colouring of upperparts. However, Redwing shows a bold white line over the eye and a dark moustache line if seen well, plus diagnostic deep reddish flanks and underwings. A rather wary bird, it flies up in small groups on approach, emitting a characteristic high-pitched *zeeep* call in flight. It also has a scolding *trrrt* note and a more muted *chuk, chuk* call.

1♂

1♀

2♀

2♂

3

4

The Robins of Madeira and the Canaries The robins show rather marked differences between the islands and highlight another case of potential speciation in action. The most distinctive robins are from Gran Canaria and Tenerife, which are believed to be derived from the earliest robins to colonise the islands some 2 million years ago. Gran Canarian birds have slightly shorter wings than those on Tenerife but otherwise look very similar. However, large differences in their DNA and vocalisations suggest that birds on these islands represent two distinct subspecies or possibly even species. Robins breeding on La Gomera, La Palma, El Hierro and Madeira are more similar to European birds and are thought to have arrived more than recently, while those seen on Fuerteventura and Lanzarote are purely mainland birds, either wintering or stopping off on their passage flights between Europe and North Africa.

European Robin L 14cm

2 endemic subspecies: Madeira and Western Canaries |
Gran Canaria and Tenerife [+ migrant subspecies from Europe]

A common resident breeder on Madeira and the Western and Central Canaries but only a scarce winter visitor to the Eastern Canaries and Porto Santo. Prefers densely vegetated areas, particularly native forest, but also breeds in scrub, thickets and gardens. The robin is a familiar bird with a rich orangey face, throat and breast, olive-brown upperparts and a paler belly with a thin blue-grey line bordering the edge of the orange breast. Birds from Tenerife and Gran Canaria are larger, with a more restricted and redder breast patch, a broader blue-grey margin to the breast, typically a more distinct eye ring, and are darker brown above and whiter below. European Robin is a wary bird but not overly shy. The usual call is a sharp hard *tick!* The beautiful song of descending, trembling warbles and trills usually starts with a few higher clear notes; it often betrays the presence of birds in dense habitat.

1
MADEIRA

1
TENERIFE

1
GRAN CANARIA

Flycatchers Two species of flycatcher are regular migrants through the Canaries, particularly Lanzarote and Fuerteventura, where E winds in autumn sometimes bring large numbers of both species at the same time, allowing for nice comparisons.

2 **Spotted Flycatcher** L 14 cm

A regular migrant to the Canaries, particularly on the E islands in autumn, where it can be quite numerous, but a very rare visitor to Madeira. Likes to perch on fence posts, rocks and walls in open areas of scrub, gardens and edges of cultivated fields. A slim, long-winged and rather long-tailed bird, it is plain dull greyish brown above and paler below, with faint streaks on the chest and the crown, plus a beady dark eye set in a plain face. More distinctive is its habit of sitting upright on exposed perches and sallying out to catch flies before returning to the same perch. Calls are soft and easily missed but include a shrill *zee* and, when alarmed, a *hwee, tuk-tuk*.

3 **Pied Flycatcher** L 13 cm

A regular migrant to the Canaries, particularly the E islands in autumn, where it can be quite numerous, and a rare but perhaps overlooked visitor to Madeira. Favours trees and bushes in open areas, from which it will sally out to catch flies, but is often less obtrusive than Spotted Flycatcher. Smaller and more brightly coloured than that species, it is mostly white below in all plumages and has darker upperparts, black in males and grey-brown in females and immatures. All plumages show a bold white wing patch and white edges to the tail base, which catch the eye, particularly in flight. The typical calls include a persistent *pik* when alarmed as well as a quieter *tek*.

African Blue Tit is a resident breeding bird throughout the Canaries, but birds on the different islands (shown opposite) show subtle plumage and vocal differences and are considered distinct subspecies. The birds on the Eastern Canaries are very similar to those in adjacent North Africa, but those inhabiting Tenerife and La Gomera and those on Gran Canaria are each rather different, and further separate distinctive subspecies are found on the westernmost islands of El Hierro and La Palma. All are well worth seeking out, as they represent an excellent example of speciation in action. Recent research suggests that the two W subspecies, the subspecies from Gran Canaria, the subspecies from Tenerife and La Gomera, and the subspecies from the Eastern Canaries could represent as many as five new species!

ⓔ African Blue Tit L 11·5 cm

Up to 5 endemic subspecies: El Hierro | La Palma | Tenerife and La Gomera | Gran Canaria | Fuerteventura and Lanzarote

A resident breeding bird throughout the Canaries with as many as five subtly different subspecies occurring across the islands.

African Blue Tit is common and widespread in the Western and Central Canaries but is scarcer and very localised on the drier Eastern Canaries, since it favours trees and tall scrubby habitat, including tree heath, laurel and pine forest, parks, gardens and taller arid scrub. Very similar to European Blue Tit, which does not occur on the islands, it differs in being more boldly coloured: a deeper indigo blue above, with blacker head markings, and a richer yellow below. As is seen with many other endemic island birds, the bills are also longer than those on mainland forms. Birds on the E islands ('Fuerteventura [or Ultramarine] Blue Tit') are paler and greyer above and show a distinct paler wing bar. Those on La Palma ('Palma Blue Tit') and El Hierro ('Hierro Blue Tit') show some greener tones on the mantle, and La Palma birds show a white belly. Birds on La Gomera and Tenerife ('Tenerife Blue Tit') have the darkest slate-blue upperparts and lack a wing bar when adult, while the very similar-looking birds on Gran Canaria ('Gran Canaria Blue Tit') give subtly different high-pitched trilling calls like those of European Serin. All also give a wide range of churring calls and rather metallic songs comprising repeated notes, which differ subtly between the islands. Birds on La Palma have the most distinctive repertoire and can sound more like Great Tits!

GRAN CANARIA – Very similar to Tenerife but with a slightly different call

LANZAROTE + FUERTEVENTURA – Paler and greyer mantle with a distinct pale wing bar; yellow belly

EL HIERRO – Greener tones on the mantle; yellow belly

TENERIFE + LA GOMERA – Dark slate-blue mantle; adults with no wingbar; yellow belly

LA PALMA – Some green tone on mantle; white belly

Just two species of crow breed on the Canary Islands; none breed on Madeira. There are no ID challenges here, unlike on the mainland, as the smaller and highly distinctive Red-billed Chough is oddly restricted to La Palma, and the more widespread Common Raven is much larger and has an all-black bill.

 ### Red-billed Chough L 39 cm

Near-endemic subspecies: La Palma [+ NW Africa]

The occurrence of this bird as a breeding resident on La Palma in the Canaries and on no other islands in the area is a real geographical quirk. The nearest populations are in the mountains of Morocco. Occasional birds stray to Tenerife and La Gomera, and their bones have been found in caves on both islands, but attempts to re-establish the species on Tenerife have so far failed. This distinctive species remains common on La Palma, where it can occur almost anywhere from coast to mountaintops, although it avoids dense laurel forest and is most common on terraced slopes. A midsize all-black crow, with glossy black plumage bearing a green sheen above, it has bright red legs and feet and a long, down-curved bright red beak when adult. Immature birds have a yellower-hued bill. The wings are broad throughout their length and show strongly fingered tips. Choughs often travel and feed on the ground together in sociable groups of up to 150 birds and can be rather approachable. They frequently call to each other a far-carrying *kee-arrr* or a cutting *chiach*.

Common Raven L 64 cm

Endemic subspecies: Canaries

Resident on all of the Canary Islands, Common Raven is
now very localised on Gran Canaria and increasingly scarce
on Tenerife, La Palma and La Gomera, but it remains more
numerous on Fuerteventura and in particular on El Hierro.
It is a vagrant to Madeira. Can occur anywhere from sea level
to mountaintops but particularly favours rocky cliffs and
barren mountainsides. A very large, all-black crow-like bird,
it is easily identified in the absence of other similar crows
on the islands. The bill is heavy and black, and the tail is
distinctively wedge-shaped in flight. The typical flight call is
a honking *pruk pruk*, although island birds also give a diverse
range of calls, including quacking notes and a two-toned
derr-do call that mainland birds do not give. The ravens of
the Canaries are smaller than those on the mainland and
show some brown on the neck, which together with the
different calls suggest they may one day be considered a
separate species.

Endemic crests The islands are home to two endemic species of crests, which originate from wandering continental birds that were able to evolve on the islands in isolation. On Madeira, ancestral Firecrests have evolved into a distinctive island form, while on the Western Canaries and Tenerife, ancestral Goldcrests have become the Tenerife Kinglet, although some authorities still regard this as only a subspecies of Goldcrest.

E **1** **Tenerife Kinglet** L 9 cm

ENDEMIC TO WESTERN CANARIES
2 subspecies: Tenerife and La Gomera |
El Hierro and La Palma

These tiny birds inhabit natural forest habitats on Tenerife, La Palma, La Gomera and El Hierro, including pine and laurel forest, but are particularly numerous in the tree heath zone on moister N slopes. The birds on La Palma and El Hierro are now considered to be a separate subspecies. Pairs are easily located by their high-pitched trilling calls, but they can be difficult to see in the dense bushy habitat. Very similar to Goldcrests of mainland Europe, they are moss green above, with an orange (male) or yellow (female) central crown, but are a darker pinky buff colour below. In addition, the black borders to the gold crest join on the forehead, and together with the pale lores impart a more spectacled look. As on Madeira Firecrest, the bill is longer than that of mainland birds, presumably as an adaption to island living. The calls are a Goldcrest-like, high-pitched *zree-zree-zree*, and the high-pitched trilling song is also Goldcrest-like but tends to be shorter.

E **2** **Madeira Firecrest** L 9 cm

ENDEMIC TO MADEIRA

This tiny brightly coloured bird is common in the remaining areas of native laurel forest and tree heath on Madeira, although it does not occur on nearby Porto Santo. It can also be found feeding within eucalyptus plantations in the hills and among low coastal shrubs on the N coast. Pairs constantly give a range of high-pitched *tseep* and *wheez* calls, which attract attention to the rapidly moving birds, which are often quite tame. Compared to mainland Firecrests, Madeiran birds have much shorter white eye stripes, which form white goggles around the dark eyes. They also have more black in the closed wing and a longer bill and legs imparting a leaner look. They are moss green above and show a rich orange crown and a golden patch on the side of the neck. The song, rather similar to that of Goldcrest, is a short, fairly high-pitched *see-see-see-sit-sit-sit*, unlike any other song in the Madeiran woods.

Leaf warblers Five species of similar-looking leaf warblers, including an endemic species, occur regularly in the Canary Islands, whereas only three species are scarce and irregular visitors to Madeira. The absence of resident chiffchaffs on Madeira is in striking contrast to their abundance on the Western and Central Canary Islands. All the islands' species are small, fast-moving greenish-coloured warblers that hunt for insects in bushes and trees.

3 Wood Warbler L 12 cm

The most distinctive of the five leaf warblers on the islands, Wood Warbler is a regular passage migrant in the Canaries, particularly to the E islands, where it favours well-watered parks and hotel gardens. This is the largest-looking leaf warbler, and its stocky body and very long wings give it a short-tailed look. The underparts are rich yellow from chin to breast, sharply demarcated from the cleanly white belly. There is a bold yellow stripe over the eye and a cleanly marked dark line through the eye onto the ear coverts. The upperparts are a rich moss green with bright yellowy-green fringes to the wing feathers and tail. Wood Warbler is most similar to Willow Warbler but easily separated if seen well by combination of features given above. The typical distinctive call is a sharp *tsip*, quite different from the calls of the other leaf warblers.

4 Western Bonelli's Warbler L 11 cm

A scarce but regular passage migrant on the Eastern Canaries but very rare on the other Canary Islands and on Madeira. Like other migrants, this warbler is drawn to bushes and trees, so on the arid Eastern Canaries typically appears in the lush planted grounds of hotels, parks and nearby windbreaks. Slightly smaller than Willow Warbler, it has a rather bland-looking, pale face pattern showing a pale eye ring and a weak pale line through the eye. Far more striking are the gleaming silky-white underparts, which contrast strongly with the bright yellow-green wings, rump and tail, and the duller olive-green mantle and crown. Seen from behind this species can look like Wood Warbler, until the absence of yellow on the throat and face can be seen. Gives a loud, emphatic two-toned and up-inflected *du-EEF* call, like a hypercharged Willow Warbler.

1 Common Chiffchaff L 11 cm

Common Chiffchaff is a regular spring and autumn migrant in small numbers to the Canaries, occasionally appearing in large numbers under the right conditions; it winters in small numbers, particularly on the Eastern Canaries. Very scarce and irregular on Madeira. Common Chiffchaff is most readily separated from the resident Canary Islands Chiffchaff on Fuerteventura and Lanzarote – because the latter does not occur there! Like all leaf warblers it favours areas of trees and woody shrubs, and lone birds can occur even in isolated trees in lava desert. Common Chiffchaff is smaller and shorter-winged than Willow Warbler and usually browner/duller in tone, with a less well-marked pale line over the eye, making the pale eye ring more conspicuous. The legs are usually black. The typical call is a soft single *hweet*.

 ### 2 Canary Islands Chiffchaff L 10 cm

ENDEMIC TO WESTERN AND CENTRAL CANARIES

Formerly treated as an island subspecies, this distinctive form has recently been given species status. Resident on the Western and Central Canaries including Gran Canaria, this is a very common and widespread bird found wherever there are trees and shrubs, with the exception of the driest arid-zone areas. An isolated form inhabited the moist Haria Valley of Lanzarote but became extirpated there in the 1980s. Canary Islands Chiffchaff is very similar to Common Chiffchaff but is even darker brown above and darker buff below and has a more prominent buffy line over the eye, a longer and slightly down-curved bill, oddly short wings and longer legs that are often paler than those of Chiffchaff (i.e., not black). The short wings are typical of resident island birds that do not need to migrate long distances, and they give the birds a distinctly longer-tailed look than Common Chiffchaff. Calls include a typical Common Chiffchaff *hweet* but also a distinctive harsh *chik*; the song is often much louder, more explosive and more variable than the usual monotonous *chiff-chaff, chiff-chaff* song of Common Chiffchaff.

3 Willow Warbler L 12 cm

This species is a regular passage migrant in the Canaries, occasionally appearing in very large numbers under the right conditions, whereas it is very scarce and irregular on Madeira. The same size as Wood Warbler, it is less stocky and has slightly shorter wings, giving it a longer-tailed look, although the wings are still longer than those of the chiffchaffs. Willow Warbler is olive green above and has a yellowish wash on the face and chest but lacks the clearly demarked separation from the paler belly shown by Wood Warbler, and it also lacks the sharply defined face pattern of that species. Duller individuals are best separated from chiffchaffs by the paler pinkish legs, longer wings and by voice. Male Willow Warblers give a haunting descending cadence of notes in song, very different from the monotonous *chif-chaff* of chiffchaffs, but this song is rarely heard on the islands. The typical call is a whistled rising *hooo-eeet*, distinctly longer and more two-toned than the *hweet* given by chiffchaffs.

Sylvia **warblers** These warblers lurk in dense scrub and seem confusing at first glance. However, most have a habit of showing themselves, and males are readily separated if watched closely and their calls and songs are heard. Females and immatures are often harder to identify, so focus on the ID tips given below and look out for nearby male birds.

1 Garden Warbler L 14cm

This very plain warbler is a scarce but regular passage migrant in the Canaries, particularly on the E islands in spring, whereas it is extremely rare, or perhaps overlooked, on Madeira. Another denizen of dense scrub, this one tends to be more furtive than the other island *Sylvia* warblers and rarely gives good views. When seen, it appears to be a rather plump, plain olive-brown warbler, lacking any distinctive features – and its nondescript plumage is a distinctive feature in its own right. The bill is short and dull grey. The dark eye is set in a plain face with a faint pale eye ring, a weak pale line through the eye and a slightly greyer neck side. Fortunately, this skulking bird often gives away it presence with a series of clicking calls, *check, check, check* … , particularly when alarmed, which are less harsh and softer than those of Blackcap.

e 2 Blackcap L 14cm

Near-endemic subspecies: Western and Central Canaries and Madeira [+ S&W Iberia; NW Africa]

A common resident bird of bushy and wooded habitats on Madeira and the Western and Central Canary Islands; occurs more locally in winter on Fuerteventura and Lanzarote. Often first detected by its *tack!* contact calls, the male also has a varied and melodious song. These are rather stocky, grey-looking warblers with browner-grey upperparts. Males have distinctive black caps, while females and immatures have reddish-brown caps. Compared to Sardinian Warbler, Blackcaps are rather short-tailed, stocky and more uniformly coloured, lacking white in the outer tail. Blackcaps frequently skulk in shrubberies and low cover but will also emerge into the open and climb high into trees, where they feed on berries as well as insects. Resident birds are a little smaller and darker than the migratory birds seen in the Eastern Canaries.

3 Sardinian Warbler L 13cm

Endemic subspecies: Canaries

A resident warbler of dense taller scrub, common in the Western and Central Canaries but more localised to areas of suitable bushy habitat, including tamarisk thickets, in the drier Eastern Canaries and absent from the Madeiran islands. Rather restless, like Spectacled Warbler, it will often reveal itself. Frequently calls with a hard *sek!*, very similar to call of Blackcap, but fortunately also often gives a distinctive machine-gun-like chattering call. The rattling song of the male is similar to that call – and is sometimes given in flight. Compared to Blackcap, the male is a slimmer, longer-tailed bird with more extensive black on the head that contrasts with a white throat. Close views reveal a bold red ring around the eye. The dark grey tail has bold white corners and is often fanned in flight. The duller female is more like Spectacled Warbler (*page 120*) but is larger, has a red (not white) eye ring and is drabber, with a grey head and a medium-brown wing lacking the rusty tones of Spectacled Warbler.

1 Spectacled Warbler L 12 cm

Endemic subspecies: Canaries and Madeira

A shy resident bird common in drier habitats on the Western and Central Canary Islands and particularly numerous and

widespread on Lanzarote and Fuerteventura; rather localised in such places on Madeira, although more widespread on Porto Santo. Occurs in low bushy habitat in more open, drier areas, including salt marshes and subalpine scrub, and has a habit of revealing itself. The common call is a buzzing rattle; the male's fast, warbling song is often given in song flight. The male ♂ is a richly coloured bird with a blue-grey head, white throat, pinkish underparts and a bright rusty wing. The female ♀ is duller but retains the rusty wing. When seen well Spectacled Warblers, with their intermediate-length tail and oddly short-looking wings, are clearly smaller than Sardinian Warblers and Blackcaps. The white eye ring stands out and is a useful ID character.

2 Common Whitethroat L 14 cm

This species does not breed on the islands but is a regular and fairly common migrant in the Canaries, especially the E islands. Feeds in bushes and low trees but is not especially shy and is generally quite easy to see. Rather similar in appearance to

Spectacled Warbler, but a larger, more robust bird with obviously longer wings and a thicker bill. The larger size imparts slower movements than the quicker, nervous movements of Spectacled Warbler. The rusty wing panel is less complete than on Spectacled Warbler, with obvious black-centred feathers near the top. The male ♂ lacks the black area between the eye and bill of male Spectacled Warbler. Typical calls are a sharp but soft *tak* and a distinctive *churr*.

3 Subalpine Warbler L 12 cm

A scarce but regular passage migrant in the Canaries, particularly on the E islands in spring, and extremely rare in spring on Madeira. This is a slim warbler with a relatively short tail compared to similar species. Spring males ♂ are very distinctive,

with lead-grey upperparts, a brick-red throat leading to rufous underparts and a white moustache. Females ♀ retain a white moustache but are less brightly coloured, with a grey head, browner-grey upperparts, a pinkish-buff throat and whiter underparts. Unlike other similar warblers they also show a distinct pale eye ring, and they lack the rusty wing panel of female Spectacled Warbler. The typical call is a dry *tek*, not unlike that of Lesser Whitethroat, although often repeated rapidly in a long series. Migrant males may sing in spring, often doing so in song flight, like Spectacled Warbler. The song consists of a random, rippling mix of rather high-pitched twitters and squeaks, which is less rattling than that of Spectacled Warbler.

1♂

1♂   1♀

2♂   2♀

3♀

3♂

Wagtails, pipits and larks This group of birds includes the boldly marked and often colourful wagtails as well as a suite of small brown streaky birds that at first glance can appear confusingly similar. You can enjoy these birds for what they are or you can seek out the subtle differences in shape and plumage that tell them apart. Remember that some birds will always have to be left unidentified, particularly those seen only distantly or against the light. Instead, focus on trying to identify those birds that show well in good light and take photos to help you. The more you watch common species such as Berthelot's Pipit, the easier it will be to spot something different.

1 Grey Wagtail L 18 cm

2 endemic subspecies: Madeira | Canaries

This handsome yellow and grey bird of streams and other freshwater areas is common and widespread on Madeira and scarcer on Porto Santo. It is widespread and quite common in the larger Western and Central Canaries but only a rare visitor to El Hierro and a localised winter visitor to Fuerteventura and Lanzarote. Birds in the Western and Central Canaries are darker and richer yellow below than continental birds, while those in Madeira are even darker above, have a less pronounced supercilium and show less white in the outer tail. A striking bird, Grey Wagtail has slate-grey upperparts and rich yellow underparts, which are more extensive on the male. The male 1♂ has a black throat, whereas the female 1♀ has a white one. Both sexes have very long tails, which they constantly wag as they feed on the ground. The high-pitched *tsip* call attracts attention, as does the high trilling song, and both cut through the background noise of running water.

EUROPEAN SUBSPECIES

Migrant Grey Wagtails from the continent, are paler than the resident island subspecies.

1♂

BLUE-HEADED (EUROPE)

The blue-headed subspecies of Yellow Wagtail could be mistaken for a Grey Wagtail.

2♂

2 Yellow Wagtail L 16 cm

A regular passage migrant to the Canary Islands, where it can occasionally appear in large flocks given suitable E winds. Yellow Wagtails favour coastal wetlands as well as flat grassy areas, cultivated areas and edges of pools. In breeding plumage they are essentially yellow below and greenish above, with bold white edges to the blackish tail, which is noticeably shorter than the tails of the other two wagtails. Males 2♂ can have a blue-grey or yellow head, depending on their subspecies, whereas females have duller greener heads. Immatures in autumn, duller still, are olive brown above, with yellow tones below often limited to the vent. The call is a sharp *tseet* or a fuller *swee-eet*.

3 White Wagtail L 18 cm

A regular winter visitor in small numbers to all the Canary Islands and to Madeira. Birds frequent open areas, particularly near water, including beaches, lawns, golf courses and environs of swimming pools. Easily separated from Grey Wagtail by its entirely black, grey and white plumage lacking any obvious bright yellow tones. Young birds 3i can show a dirty-yellowish wash on the face and breast, but this never approaches the intensity of the yellow of Grey Wagtail. Male birds show more black on the crown and on the chest, and this increases in extent in late winter as birds adopt breeding dress. Regularly wags its tail as it feeds on insects on the ground, but the tail is not as long as that of Grey Wagtail. The common calls are a single *sit*, a sibilant *tslee-wee* and a more sparrow-like *chisik*.

Wagtails

1♂
MADEIRA

1♀
MADEIRA

2♂
BRITAIN AND ADJACENT
CONTINENT

2♀

3

3i

123

E **1** **Berthelot's Pipit** L 14 cm
ENDEMIC TO MACARONESIA

The common and widespread pipit of the islands, it favours
more open, drier, uncultivated habitats at all elevations. On the
Madeiran islands it is more frequent at higher elevations and on
drier coastal headlands and is most common on Porto Santo. It
is frequent in the Canaries and is particularly numerous on the
drier Eastern Canaries and in the drier S parts of the Central
and Western Canaries. It is a rather pale, streaky greyish bird
with a bold whitish line over the eye and a finely streaked chest.
Compared to Red-throated Pipit, the mantle is largely unstreaked
and the legs are placed further back on the belly, imparting a
front-heavy look. The common call is a sharp rolling *tslreee*;
the male repeats this call in an energetic song often given in
undulating flight.

2 **Red-throated Pipit** L 14 cm

A breeder from the high Arctic tundra, it regularly winters in
small numbers in open grassy habitats on the S side of Tenerife
(Golf del Sur and Amarilla Golf); odd birds appear on passage
and in winter elsewhere in the Canaries, but it is very rare on
Madeira. Similar in size to other pipits, adult birds have variable amounts of reddish
pink on the face and throat, spreading to the breast in breeding plumage. **2b** In all
plumages they are more boldly streaked than other pipits, with boldly contrasting black
and white stripes on the mantle and heavy black streaking on cleanly white underparts
below, particularly on the flanks. The call is a high-pitched drawn-out *speeeez!*, higher-
pitched and longer than call of Tree Pipit.

NT **3** **Meadow Pipit** L 15 cm

A scarce but annual winter visitor to the Canaries, especially in December–January and on the E islands, but not recorded on La Palma or El Hierro, although easily overlooked. Favours open areas of rough grassland and cultivation but will also feed on lawns. A little larger than Berthelot's Pipit, it has more centrally placed legs, giving it a different stance, and it walks with a characteristic jerky gait. More olive brown above and darker-looking than Berthelot's Pipit, it lacks a bold eye stripe, which creates a plain-faced look. The bill is small and rather thin compared to other pipits. The best ID feature may be the voice, a distinctive high-pitched, repeated thin *tseep* or *pheet* call, which is often given as birds take flight.

4 **Tree Pipit** L 15 cm

A regular migrant in the Canaries, particularly in spring on the E islands; odd birds remain in winter. Birds feed on the ground like most pipits, but Tree Pipits are also happy to spend time perched in trees and particularly favour open areas with scattered trees or shelter belts such as hotel grounds. Tree Pipit is a little larger than Meadow Pipit, with a more robust bill, a more marked pale line over the eye, a dark line through the eye and a more substantial pale area below the face. There is also usually more contrast between the buffy-toned breast bearing heavier dark streaks and the white belly, as well as finer streaks on the flanks. Tree Pipits are often less approachable than Meadow Pipits and will fly up into trees emitting a hoarse drawn-out *spiz* call.

1 Tawny Pipit L 17 cm

This large pale pipit is a scarce but regular passage migrant in the Canaries, particularly in spring, but is very rare on Madeira. Tends to favour open sandy areas such as plains, golf courses and agricultural fields but will also occur on lawns and on beaches on migration. A large, slim, almost wagtail-size pipit, it has rather plain sandy-brown plumage, unlike all the other pipits on the islands, which show extensive dark streaking. Spring adults are largely unstreaked above and below and instead show a marked pale stripe through the eye that is bordered dark below and darker wing feathers fringed paler buff. The call is a House Sparrow–like *tchlip* or *chup*.

2 Eurasian Skylark L 17 cm

A regular winter visitor to all of the islands, although more frequent on Porto Santo than on Madeira and more common in some years than others. Feeds on the ground in open areas of short grass, cultivation and semi-desert. It is a sandy grey-brown bird with prominent dark streaking on both the whiter breast and the browner upperparts. It is much larger and longer-winged and has a longer, finer bill than Lesser Short-toed Lark. Usually shows a fairly conspicuous crest, although this can be flattened. Gives a variety of dry rolling calls, such as *preeet*, rather different from the buzzing call of Lesser Short-toed Lark. The beautiful song is rarely heard away from breeding areas.

3 Short-toed Lark L 14 cm

A scarce but regular passage migrant on Tenerife and the
Eastern Canaries, where it can occur in flocks but is easily
overlooked or misidentified; a very rare migrant on Madeira.
Occurs on barren plains as well as on cultivated lands and salt
marshes – i.e., the same places as Lesser Short-toed Lark.
The two species are very similar, but if seen well Short-toed
Lark tends to be paler and generally shows no streaking on the
white underparts, with often just a dark mark on the breast
sides, and only limited streaking above. It also has a rather
more pointed bill and a less 'cute'-looking face. The typical
call is a dry *drit*, which is very similar to that of Lesser Short-
toed Lark.

e 4 Lesser Short-toed Lark L 14 cm

2 endemic subspecies: N Tenerife (probably extinct) |
S Tenerife (probably extinct), Gran Canaria and Eastern Canaries

A common and widespread resident breeder on Lanzarote
and Fuerteventura but increasingly scarce and local on Gran
Canaria and recently extirpated on Tenerife due to habitat
loss. Does not occur in the Western Canaries or on Madeira.
Favours open dry grasslands, cultivated areas, salt marshes
and semi-deserts and can form large flocks out of the breeding
season. A small lark, it hops about rapidly on dry ground. It is
largely sandy grey-brown above and whiter below, with quite
distinct dark streaking on the breast and less obvious streaking
above. The N Tenerife subspecies (presumed extinct) was
more rufous brown above and more rusty cinnamon on the
chest. The head is rather rounded, giving it a 'cute' expression,
and the bill is rather short and stocky. Plumage-wise it is
rather similar to Eurasian Skylark, but it is much smaller and
shorter-winged and has a stubbier bill. The typical call is a dry
buzzing *drrrd*, not unlike that of a Sand Martin. The variable
twittering song is full of mimicry so is hard to describe.

Sparrows and buntings One bunting and four species of sparrow occur on the islands; refreshingly, the cosmopolitan House Sparrow is restricted to a small colony persisting on the docks of Las Palmas on Gran Canaria. Spanish Sparrow has slowly colonised the islands since the 19th century and has seemingly forced Rock Sparrow into more remote areas, although the former remains very localised on Madeira, where Spanish Sparrow is still very rare. Eurasian Tree Sparrow is confined to the S tip of Gran Canaria.

① Eurasian Tree Sparrow L 13 cm

Occurs only on Gran Canaria, where it breeds locally in parks, gardens and agricultural holdings on the S tip of the island from Puerto de Mogan in the west to Sardina in the east, centred on the Maspalomas area (i.e., at the opposite end of the island to the House Sparrows!), although with odd breeding records further north at Agaete and El Troncón. A slightly smaller, neater sparrow than Spanish Sparrow, Eurasian Tree Sparrow has similar plumage in both sexes. Like Spanish Sparrow, Tree Sparrow has a chestnut cap, but it is separated from the brown of the back by a thin whitish collar. It also shows a neat black spot on the white ear coverts, a neat black chin and richer, brighter brown upperparts and lacks the black chest and heavy black streaking of Spanish Sparrow. Tree Sparrow typically nests under roofs, in holes in buildings and on electricity pylons. Gives a typical sparrow *churp* but also a distinctive cheery *soo-wit* and a rattling *tett, tett* in flight.

○ ② House Sparrow L 15 cm

Introduced

Occurs only on Gran Canaria, where it breeds only on and around the docks at Las Palmas in the NE part of the island. Odd birds travel on ships from time to time and have occasionally been recorded on Madeira, although the species has never bred there. The same size as Spanish Sparrow, with which it will hybridise, the familiar male ②♂ House Sparrow is best identified by its grey crown, grey (not white) cheeks and dirty-grey underparts lacking prominent dark streaks. Females ②♀ and immatures are essentially identical to Spanish Sparrows – so always look for male birds. A social bird that is very much a commensal with humans, House Sparrow typically nests under roofs and in holes in buildings. In it groups gives typical sparrow calls such as *churp, chirrup* and a softer *swee* note.

③ Spanish Sparrow L 15 cm

This is the common widespread sparrow on the Canary Islands and on Porto Santo but remains largely restricted to the Caniçal area of Madeira. It is abundant in built-up and farmed areas but is largely absent from densely wooded habitats and has declined recently on Tenerife. Males ③♂ have chestnut caps, whitish cheeks and much black on the breast, which runs down the flanks in streaks; the back is also heavily streaked black. Females ③♀ are duller and paler and look very much like female House Sparrows. Birds nest in colonies in buildings, under bridges and in trees. Calls are a range of metallic harsh *churp* notes.

1

2♀ 2♂

3♀ 3♂

1 Rock Sparrow L 16cm

Once a common and widespread breeder, Rock Sparrow is now
very localised on Madeira and Porto Santo. It has also declined
steadily recently in the Western and Central Canaries, as Spanish
Sparrows have spread across the islands and as agricultural
practices have changed. It is becoming increasingly hard to find anywhere in the
Canaries, and on Tenerife it is now largely confined to Teno Alto in the north-west.
A large chunky sparrow, it favours remote open rocky areas with grasses, such as
cliffs, mountains and hill slopes, although it is still also found around agricultural
areas in hill villages, where it may perch on roadside wires. It used to occur in large
flocks outside of the breeding season. The robust body, chunky pale bill and rather
long tail are distinctive, as is the rather variegated plumage pattern and the fact
that the sexes appear similar. Close views reveal broad black stripes on the
crown sides, a paler central crown stripe and a broad pale line behind
the eye. The whitish underside is heavily streaked dark grey as
are the browner upperparts. Bold white spots near the tip
of the undertail can be conspicuous in flight. The typical
calls include a loud, drawn-out nasal *tseee-ooo-eee*
and a shorter *voo-ee*.

2 Corn Bunting L 18cm

Although not a sparrow, this chunky bunting is included here
because it is rather sparrow-like in appearance. Corn Bunting is
a resident breeder and partial migrant throughout the Canaries,
although it was always more widespread in the W and central
islands than in the E islands. It does not occur on Madeira. It has declined
greatly in recent years with changes in agriculture, and on Tenerife is now
largely confined to cultivated areas in the north, while there are few recent
records from La Palma or El Hierro. Corn Bunting particularly favours arable
crops but also occurs in open areas, whether agricultural or not. This is a large,
stocky, rather large-headed bunting that often sits up on wires or on walls and
flies with dangling legs. It is a rather nondescript bird, grey-brown above with
darker streaks and paler below with darker streaks on the chest and throat.
The rather short tail lacks any white. There is a neat pale eye ring around the
eye. More distinctive is the song, which consists of *tuk tuk, zik zik*
notes, followed by a jangling *zczcrisssss*, like the rattling of a
bunch of keys. Other calls include a short *bit* and a
more metallic *tsrit*.

Finches This group comprises a wide range of small perching birds with chunky bills designed for seed-eating, ranging from the tiny introduced Common Waxbill of the grassy lowlands to the large endemic blue chaffinches of the high-elevation Canary Pine forests of the Central Canaries. The group also includes the numerous and widespread Atlantic Canary, whose trilling song is such a special feature of the islands, as well as a range of other colourful and attractive species. Special mention must be made of the endemic subspecies of Common Chaffinch, showing subtle differences in male plumage between the islands, which nicely demonstrate evolution in action. European Serin has recently colonised parts of Tenerife and Gran Canaria, while European Goldfinch and Common Linnet are declining due to changes in agricultural practices.

e 3 Common Linnet L 13 cm

3 endemic subspecies: Madeira | Western and Central Canaries | Eastern Canaries

3♂
MADEIRA

3♂
EAST

Linnets occur on all the Madeiran and Canary Islands. However, the Madeiran subspecies has declined in recent years on Madeira and Porto Santo, where it is now rather local. Linnet populations are also declining throughout the Canary Islands as a result of recent changes in agriculture, and this bird is becoming increasingly hard to find on many islands. A midsize, slim and long-tailed finch, it is mostly found in more open and agricultural lowland areas but can occur at all elevations and in most habitats except dense laurel forest. Often mixes with other finches, especially European Goldfinches and Atlantic Canaries, outside the breeding season. Males 3♂ are distinctive with their pinkish breast and forehead, grey face and plain chestnut-brown upperparts. Females 3♀ are duller and streaked below but retain chestnut-brown upperparts, although these are also duller and streaked. Both sexes show a pale whitish patch at the base of the dark flight feathers, as well as a whitish throat that has smudgy darker streaks. Birds from the Eastern Canaries are paler and less brightly coloured than birds elsewhere in the islands. Madeiran birds are the darkest. Typical calls are a *tet-eh-tet* given in flight and a shorter *tet*; the varied, whistled song is a mix of rattles and trills.

3♂
WEST/CENTRAL

3♀
WEST/CENTRAL

N **1** **Atlantic Canary** L 13 cm
ENDEMIC TO MACARONESIA

This species is the original form of the domestic canary. It is a
very common and widespread resident species on Madeira, Porto
Santo and the Western and Central Canaries, occupying most natural and man-made habitats from sea
level to mountaintop. It is more localised at mid elevations on Gran Canaria and is very scarce and local
on Lanzarote and Fuerteventura. It also occurs in the Azores. It is larger and longer-tailed than European
Serin and has a relatively larger bill and shorter wings. Males **1♂** are more extensively yellow-green from
head to underbelly and are more diffusely streaked above and below than European Serin. Females **1♀**
are duller and rather variable but still show yellowy-green areas on the face and belly, often with distinct
grey areas on the nape and chest. Both sexes show a streaked yellowy-green rump, lacking the pure yellow
tones of European Serin. The engaging and varied trilling and twittering song is a characteristic sound of
the islands; the typical call is a descending *si-si-surr*.

!? **2** **European Serin** L 11 cm

This small finch is a scarce and local breeder in N Tenerife
and on Gran Canaria, where it was possibly introduced, but it
occasionally wanders to other islands in the Canaries. Owing to
the abundance of the very similar Atlantic Canary, however, it
is easily overlooked, unless its distinctive song is heard. It is found mostly in man-made habitat such as
gardens, parks, agricultural areas and golf courses. Smaller than Atlantic Canary, it has a stubbier grey
bill, a larger head and a shorter tail, all contributing to a smaller, more rounded look. This species is also
more restless, bounding around on energetic flights. The male **2♂** has bright yellow around the face and
on the chest, the white underparts are boldly streaked black, and in flight it shows a boldly yellow rump.
The female **2♀** is duller than the male but retains the bold black streaking and the distinctive bright
yellow rump. The typical call is a buzzing trill, but the rapid jangling song of squeaky notes is most unlike
that of Atlantic Canary; it is often given in song flight with slow-motion wingbeats.

3 **European Greenfinch** L 15 cm

This stocky large-billed finch colonised the Canaries in the
20th century and now occurs on all of the islands, although it
apparently does not yet breed on Lanzarote or La Palma; it breeds
in small numbers in a localised area of Madeira. Local or scarce in
wooded areas, including gardens and parks, it appears in larger numbers in winter, at least on the Eastern
Canaries. The male **3♂** is distinctive, largely green, with a greyer face and flanks and bright yellow fringes
to the wing feathers and at the base of the tail. The female and immature **3i** are duller and browner but
still retain some greenish tones, especially on the rump, and show yellowish patches in the wing and tail.
Immatures show more streaking, especially below on a whiter underside. Typical calls include a *jup* and a
rising *joo-it*; the peculiar song consists of a drawn-out wheezy *dweeeeeh*, as well as a more pleasant series
of twitters and trills, often with the wheezy call thrown in.

1

1♂

1♀

2♂

2♀

3♂

3i

1 Common Chaffinch L 14 cm

4 endemic subspecies: Madeira | Central Canaries | La Palma |
El Hierro

The breeding birds of the islands are quite different from those
of the mainland, and the males in particular show subtle differences on each island. These finches are
common and widespread in all wooded habitats on Madeira and the Western and Central Canaries,
including Gran Canaria, but are absent from Porto Santo and occur only as vagrants from the mainland
on Fuerteventura and Lanzarote. All males ♂ have pinkish undersides, grey-blue crowns, bold white
wing bars on blackish wings, and variable back and belly colour as follows: green on the lower back and
rump (Madeira), all-slate-blue back and rump with more white below (La Palma), greenish rump with
less white below (El Hierro), slate blue above with a yellowish-green rump (Tenerife, La Gomera and
Gran Canaria). All females ♀ are duller, grey-brown above and paler below, with a peachy wash to the
throat and an olive tone to the rump, but retain the bold white wing bars. Birds give a range of calls that
vary subtly between islands. These include a soft *pink* call as well as a rippling *cha-cha-cha*; males have a
musical trilling song that rises in pitch to a terminal flourish.

Green on the lower back and rump

1♂

1♂
MADEIRA

1♀
CENTRAL

1♀
MADEIRA

Slate-blue above;
yellowish-green rump

1♂
CENTRAL
CANARIES

Slate-blue above; greenish rump;
less white below

1♂
EL HIERRO

Slate-blue above; slate-blue rump;
more white below

1♂
LA PALMA

Canary Island blue chaffinches The blue chaffinches of the Central Canaries are arguably the most striking endemic birds in the islands. The blue males are quite unlike any other species and fortunately the more striking Tenerife form remains easily seen within its protected habitat. Recent separation of the two forms as distinct species has heightened the importance of on-going conservation work for the critically endangered Gran Canaria Blue Chaffinch.

E **1** ## Tenerife Blue Chaffinch L 17 cm

NT

Endemic to Tenerife

Tenerife Blue Chaffinch, an extraordinary endemic bird found only on Tenerife, was split as a distinct species from the similar form found on Gran Canaria in 2015. It frequents native and replanted Canary Pine forests, as well as those of Monterey Pine, on mountain slopes at elevations of 1,000–2,000 m and feeds primarily on Canary Pine seeds. Tenerife Blue Chaffinch is locally common in the extensive suitable habitat and is most easily seen around picnic spots and water pipes in the Mount Teide National Park. Unmistakable if seen well, it is larger than Common Chaffinch and more front-heavy, with a bulging chest, longer legs and a larger head and bill. The male **1♂** is dark grey-blue above and paler blue-grey below and lacks the prominent white wing bars of Common Chaffinch, instead having two bluish-grey wing bars. The female **1♀** is duller and more like Common Chaffinch, but note the distinctively plain face, large bill and only buffy-white, rather than pure white, wing bars. Tenerife Blue Chaffinch has a distinctive *chap-chee* call, while the simple song is similar to that of Common Chaffinch, consisting of an increasing trill with a flourish at the end.

Tenerife Blue Chaffinch habitat.

Gran Canaria Blue Chaffinch L16cm

Endemic to Gran Canaria

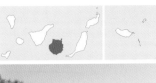

Split from the very similar form on Tenerife and established as a distinct species in 2015, Gran Canaria Blue Chaffinch is now very rare and localised on Gran Canaria, where it favours mature Canary Pine forests with a good understory of a white-flowered shrub known as *Escobón*. It has recently been lost from the isolated forest on Mount Tamadaba and now occurs only in very small numbers in the Pajonales Nature Reserve at around 1,000 m elevation and in nearby areas of Canary Pine forest at Ojeda and Inagua. The remaining suitable forest is rather fragmented and is very vulnerable to fire, with a key area having been lost in 2007. Gran Canaria Blue Chaffinches are smaller than those on Tenerife, and the males 2♂ are greyer and the females 2♀ are paler below. The call is also distinct, the birds producing a weaker *hooit* or *twee* note. Despite a conservation action plan being in place, including trapping feral cats, limiting human access to key habitat in the breeding season, providing corridors between forest patches and, since 2016, releasing birds from a captive breeding programme, the Gran Canaria Blue Chaffinch numbers fewer than 250 birds and remains in critical danger of extinction. The species has the dubious distinction of being the rarest European songbird.

Gran Canaria Blue Chaffinch habitat.

137

1 European Goldfinch L 15 cm

Near-endemic subspecies: Canaries and Madeira
[+ Iberia and NW Africa]

The colourful and distinctive European Goldfinch remains a fairly common and widespread resident on Madeira and Gran Canaria, a local breeder on Fuerteventura and Porto Santo, a scarce declining breeder on Tenerife, La Palma and La Gomera, and only a scarce visitor to El Hierro and Lanzarote. It favours cultivated areas and degraded woodland, where it feeds mostly on thistle seeds. A stocky, big-headed and short-tailed finch, it often forms flocks with other finches in the non-breeding season. The adults are highly distinctive, with a red face bordered white, a black crown and a bright golden yellow band on otherwise black wings. There are bold white spots on the tips of the black wing feathers, the rump is white and the tail is black with white spots. The upperparts are unmarked fawn and contrast with the whiter underparts. The large pointed bill is pale. Young birds are similar but lack bold head markings. The call is a cheery *tik-a-lit*, and the quiet song is a mixed merry trill with the call note mixed in.

2 Common Waxbill L 11 cm

This tiny finch has been introduced from Africa to three of the islands. It is locally numerous on Gran Canaria but very scarce on Tenerife, while a recent introduction to Madeira appears to have established a viable population centred on the S coast. Prefers tall, dense grassy habitat such as reed beds and rushes but will also feed on seed heads of shorter grasses with lush bushy cover nearby, as found in gardens and parks. These tiny grey-brown finches with narrow, pointed tails travel in tight family groups. Close views reveal fine vermiculations to both the darker brown upper-side plumage and the paler buffy underparts. Adults show a narrow red band through the eye, a bright red bill and a pinkish flush to the belly. Juveniles have blacker bills and show less red through the eye. Flocks emit sharp *pit!* notes as they move about; the song consists of a simple three-note *tre-tre-triii*.

3 Trumpeter Finch L 12 cm

Endemic subspecies: Canaries

A small, stocky, large-headed finch of dry areas, Trumpeter Finch is widespread and sometimes common on Lanzarote and Fuerteventura but is scarce and increasingly localised in the S arid zones of Gran Canaria and La Gomera and is close to extirpation on Tenerife. Birds live in dusty plains, dry rocky areas and also locally in agricultural areas near villages, but regularly come to water sources, where they are easiest to see. The male 3♂ has a stocky red bill on a grey head and is largely sandy grey-brown with rich pink areas on the wing, underparts, tail and rump. The female 3♀ is a duller grey-brown and lacks the deep pink areas of the male but retains a stocky pinkish bill and has light pinkish areas on the wing and tail. Both sexes lack streaking above and below. Typical calls are a short nasal *arp* and a simple *chit* or *tee*; the peculiar song consists of a drawn-out nasal *aaaaarrrp* that sounds like a toy trumpet.

1

2

3♂

3♀

Marine mammals

Large whales Five species of large whales are regularly encountered around the islands, including the Sperm Whale, a toothed whale that hunts at depth for large squid, and four similar-looking baleen whales, which sieve the rich waters for fish and crustaceans. The commonest baleen whale is Bryde's Whale, which occurs throughout the year and frequents shallower coastal waters. Other large whales, including Blue Whale, Humpback Whale and North Atlantic Right Whale, are sighted very occasionally in deeper waters offshore from both sets of islands. These records are thought to relate to groups of whales migrating through the islands, although the distribution of these species remains poorly known in the area, and some species may yet prove to be more regular visitors.

VU **1** ## Sperm Whale L 11–18 m

Sperm Whales are present all year round in the seas surrounding Madeira, although are most common in the spring and summer months, from March to September. They are also seen in smaller numbers around the Canaries in spring and summer. These are gregarious whales that often travel in pods of up to 20 animals, spending much time in social interactions, including regular breaching at the surface. They can be slate grey or dark brown above, and the skin is deeply corrugated – like a shrivelled prune. Sperm Whales are easily separated from the other large whales by the absence of a dorsal fin, showing just a small hump instead. They have a much more massive head (roughly one-third of the animal's overall length!) and a broader back, although these features are hard to make out when viewed from a distance. Unlike the baleen whales, Sperm Whales normally raise their large triangular tail flukes vertically above the water prior to diving. They also release a highly distinctive blow that is angled forwards and leftwards to the sea surface. Animals often rest at the surface for long periods between dives, blowing infrequently as they do so.

2 ## Minke Whale L 7–10 m

This smaller baleen whale occurs regularly in small numbers off Madeira from June to August and less regularly around the Canaries in the same months. Although it is generally smaller than the other large whales, size is not always easy to determine at sea. The Minke is another dark grey whale with a long narrow back. However, the tall but small sickle-shaped dorsal fin is located only about two-thirds of the way along the back, so Minkes show a much longer tail stock between the dorsal fin and the tail. Upon surfacing, the rather pointed head often breaks the surface revealing a pale lower jaw, and there is a single central ridge along the snout, which forms a distinct bump in front of the blowhole. The blow is small, low and easily missed. Minkes usually occur singly or more rarely in very small groups and typically appear or roll at the surface five to eight times between dives.

Sperm Whales prefer deep waters, even if fairly close to land.

←——— DIRECTION OF TRAVEL

1

1 DIRECTION OF TRAVEL ⟶

Sperm Whales often raise their tail flukes before a deep dive

2 DIRECTION OF TRAVEL ⟶

DD **1** **Bryde's Whale** L 11–15 m

This is the common large baleen whale around all of the islands and occurs mostly from April to October, although can be seen in any month. It favours shallower waters than Sei Whale, diving in depths of up to 300 m, so is often seen closer inshore and is more likely to be encountered from inter-island ferries and coastal boat trips. Bryde's Whale can be seen singly or in pairs but at favoured spots can also occur in loose groups of up to 20 animals. It is very similar to Sei Whale but is dark smoky grey above rather than blue-grey and shows three parallel ridges between the blowhole and the start of the snout. The dorsal fin is upright and sickle-shaped, as in Sei Whale, but Bryde's Whale is much more active at the surface than Sei Whale and can often be watched engaging in social behaviour. The blow of Bryde's Whale is variable; it can be low and bushy like that of Sei Whale but also tall and column-like, as in Fin Whale.

EN **2** **Sei Whale** L 12–16 m

A large whale that is easily confused with Bryde's Whale, although it is much less common, and sightings are more restricted to the May–September period. Sei Whale also tends to prefer deeper offshore waters. Similar in size and colour to Bryde's Whale, like that species it shows a proportionately rather large, sickle-shaped shark-like dorsal fin about three-quarters of the way along its back. It tends to be blue-grey above and shows a single central ridge between the blowhole and the start of the slender snout. Compared to blow of Fin Whale, Sei Whale's blow looks messier and stays lower to the surface. The blow of this animal typically appears at the same time as the dorsal fin breaks the surface – in Fin Whale the dorsal fin follows the blow. The Sei Whale also tends to sink into dives rather than showing an arched tail stock (the area between the dorsal fin and the tail).

EN **3** **Fin Whale** L 18–26 m

This is the largest whale that is likely to be seen off the islands. It is spotted from time to time off both Madeira and the Canaries but is generally much scarcer than either Sei Whale or Bryde's Whale. This is generally a cool-water species, and the Canaries are very much at the S end of the species' range. Fin Whale shows a very long dark grey back with a small dorsal fin about three-quarters of the way along its length. Its dorsal fin is less erect and more swept back than those of Sei and Bryde's Whales, and it breaks the surface some time after the head is first seen. The area between the dorsal fin and the tail often arches upwards prior to a deep dive. Fin Whales give a very tall, column-like blow upon surfacing that often reaches 8 m above the surface and lasts for several seconds.

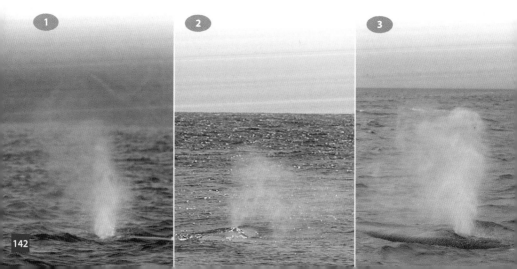

1   DIRECTION OF TRAVEL ⟶

2   DIRECTION OF TRAVEL ⟶

3   DIRECTION OF TRAVEL ⟶

Smaller whales Six species of smaller whale are recorded annually around the islands. The Short-finned Pilot Whale has important populations in these waters and is easily seen from whale-watching trips, particularly in the Canaries. Blainville's Beaked Whale is also regularly seen around the Canaries, although it is rather unobtrusive in habits, while Cuvier's Beaked Whale is more regularly seen in Madeiran waters. Other species of beaked whale have been recorded from time to time, including Gervais's Beaked Whale and Northern Bottlenose Whale in the Canaries and Sowerby's Beaked Whale off Madeira, but sightings of these shy, deep-diving whales are rare and fleeting, and identification is often difficult. Three other small whales, Killer, False Killer and Pygmy Sperm Whale, occur from time to time, and further targeted observation in offshore areas may find these are more regular than current records suggest.

DD ① Short-finned Pilot Whale L 3·5–6·5 m

This is the common small whale around all of the islands. It can be seen in any month but is most numerous in Madeiran waters from November to April, and it would appear that some whales are resident, while others undergo small movements. Detailed study of the pilot whales off the SW coast of Tenerife has identified a population of about 1,000 individuals! Pilot whales are normally seen in family groups resting on the sea surface, often in the morning after a busy night of hunting, and hence seem rather inactive compared to dolphins. Short-finned Pilot Whale looks like a large chunky black dolphin, with a blunt bulbous head, a broad often slightly hooked dorsal fin situated well forward on the back and a long tail stock. It produces a low bushy blow when travelling.

DD ② False Killer Whale L 4–6 m

These small dark whales are seen irregularly off both Madeira and the Canaries, where they sometimes prey upon other species of cetacean, although they typically dive deep for squid. They are active predators and often appear in fast-moving family groups, powering along with their heads and upper bodies above the surface, in a similar manner to Killer Whales, although they will also swim more leisurely between hunts. These are slim-bodied uniformly dark whales with slender tapering heads and a rather tall dorsal fin placed centrally on the back. They typically occur in small family groups, although pods of hundreds have been recorded. False Killer Whales are much slimmer than Killer Whales and lack the distinctive white markings of that species.

DD ③ Killer Whale L 5–9 m

This highly distinctive species, which is actually the world's largest dolphin, occurs only irregularly in the seas around the Canaries and Madeira, but it is hard to overlook because of its striking markings and active behaviour. Killer Whales occur in tight-knit family groups of up to 30 animals. They are active hunters of both fish and other cetaceans and regularly swim at speed at the surface with their heads and upperparts out of the water, revealing a large white patch behind the eye. They also show a pale grey patch on the back behind the dorsal fin. The dorsal fin is characteristically broad-based, triangular and upright; the fin of an adult male can be 2 m tall! Killer Whales often breach, exposing their striking white undersides.

The unmistakable triangular fin of an adult male Killer Whale

1

Females and immatures have smaller fins.

2

3

DD **1** **Pygmy Sperm Whale** L 3–4 m
2 **Dwarf Sperm Whale** L 2–3 m

These are small, shy whales that are occasionally observed in
waters around both sets of islands, but are easily overlooked.
They are very similar, both are roughly dolphin-sized though have a more thickset body and a blunt,
squarish head lacking a beak. They tend to be much more sluggish in behaviour, and are usually seen
resting or moving very slowly at the surface and then sinking down out of sight without diving forward.
They tend to be seen singly or in very small groups. In both species the body is uniformly pale blue-grey
above, and the dorsal fin is very small. The differences between the two species are slight. Pygmy Sperm
Whale **1** has a very small hooked dorsal fin located more than halfway along the back. The rarer Dwarf
Sperm Whale **2** is smaller, has a less blunt head and the dorsal fin, though variable in shape and size, is
broader based and located centrally along the back. Like the much larger Sperm Whale, animals may emit
a reddish-brown substance when disturbed. Pygmy Sperm Whales have also been observed breaching.
They give a very soft, low blow that is angled slightly to the left.

DD **3** **Blainville's Beaked Whale** L 4–6 m

This small whale is resident around the Canaries but is only
rarely seen around Madeira. It is much more unobtrusive in its
habits than Short-finned Pilot Whale, but regular sightings of
individuals and groups of up to 12, particularly off the SW coasts
of La Gomera and Tenerife, indicate a strong population in the area. At sea it looks like a large elongated
dolphin, usually uniformly grey or brown in colour, with a triangular or slightly hooked fin located
about two-thirds of the way along its back. More distinctive is the oddly flattened head and, if seen well,
an oddly raised lower jaw, especially on the male, which from a distance can look like a bump on the
forehead.

4 **Cuvier's Beaked Whale** L 5–7 m

This small whale is seen irregularly off both island groups,
although it is seen more often than Blainville's Beaked Whale
in Madeiran waters. It hunts for squid at depth and has been
recorded diving down to 1,900 m and staying underwater for up
to 40 minutes. It is a little larger and more robust than Blainville's Beaked Whale and is usually paler grey-
brown or brown, with a distinctly paler head in adult animals. The dorsal fin sits two-thirds of the way
down its back and is a little more sickle-shaped than that of Blainville's Beaked Whale. More distinctive
if seen is the shape of the forehead, which slopes gently to the tip of a short distinct beak. Males develop
large tusks for fighting other males and often show pale scars above; they often live separately from groups
of females with calves.

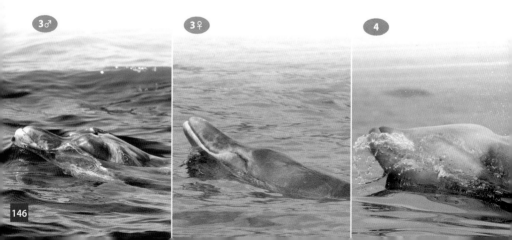

3♂   3♀   4

1

2

← DIRECTION OF TRAVEL

3 ← DIRECTION OF TRAVEL

4 ← DIRECTION OF TRAVEL

Dolphins Seven species of dolphins occur regularly in the seas around the islands, which represent some of the best waters in Europe for a chance to see such a wide range of species. Bottlenose Dolphins are the staple of dolphin-watching cruises, as they are often attracted to boats and are present year-round, but watch for the similar Rough-toothed Dolphin, which is also common in coastal waters around the Canaries. There is also a good chance of encountering large, fast-moving pods of other species, such as Short-beaked Common Dolphin, Striped Dolphin and Atlantic Spotted Dolphin, and warm-water Fraser's and Risso's Dolphins are also possible in the summer months.

① Bottlenose Dolphin L 2–4 m

This is the common resident dolphin of shallower inshore waters around all of the islands, although in Madeira greatest numbers are seen in the warmer months, from March to October. It is innately curious and frequently comes to boats to bow ride or to check out feeding opportunities. Bottlenose Dolphins are very sociable and normally occur in rather dense groups of 5 to 30 animals, although such groups may sometimes combine into larger groups, while odd lone animals, usually male, may loiter in areas frequented by humans. These dolphins are often very active and frequently jump clear of the water when travelling at speed. They are large and robust, with a tall sickle-shaped dorsal fin that is centrally placed on the back. The forehead is curved and leads to a short stubby beak. Uniformly grey above, with paler grey flanks and a lighter belly, they lack bold markings.

② Rough-toothed Dolphin L 2·0–2·5 m

This warm-water dolphin is rare off Madeira but is a common resident of inshore waters in the Canaries. It is a robust animal that appears largely dark grey above and thus from a distance is easily confused with Bottlenose Dolphin. Closer views reveal a distinctly darker grey area on the upper back leading to paler grey flanks and a white underside. There are often whitish or pinkish blotches on the flanks, which sometimes also extend to around the mouth. The head shape is also distinctive, being rather conical, with the flattened curve of the forehead extending smoothly to a long thin beak, which gives them an oddly reptilian look. The centrally placed dorsal fin is broad-based and finely pointed but lacks the distinctive hook shape of the fin of Bottlenose Dolphin. Rough-toothed Dolphins typically occur in groups of 10 to 20 animals, although groups of over 100 have been seen. They are usually less active than other dolphins but when swimming at speed will sometimes hold the head and beak above the water.

③ Risso's Dolphin L 2·5–4·0 m

This large dolphin is a warm-water species that moves north in spring as temperatures rise. It typically occurs in small numbers around the Canaries from February to June and off Madeira from June to October. It feeds mostly at night on squid and spends much of the daytime resting at the surface, although it will also sit upright with its head above the surface and breach when excited or when approached. Risso's Dolphins are gregarious, usually occurring in tight pods of up to 15 animals, and often associate with Short-finned Pilot Whales. They are large robust dolphins with a blunt, rounded head lacking a beak and a large, tall, rather hook-shaped centrally located dorsal fin. Young animals start off dark grey, but they get progressively paler and more scarred as they age, such that older adults can appear to be very pale, although they normally still show a darker dorsal fin and adjacent area of back.

1 Short-beaked Common Dolphin L 1·7–2·5 m

This is a common dolphin around all the islands from December to May but is scarce at other times. Fast-swimming and very active, it usually occurs in large often rather loose groups of up to 500 animals. Groups actively round up fish together, with individuals racing through in different directions, often leaping clear of the water – such gatherings are mesmerising to watch! This is a small streamlined dolphin with a long, slender dark beak and a tall, hook-shaped dorsal fin located halfway down the back. The colouring is distinctive: the blackish grey of the back extends below the dorsal fin in a point, separating a large mustard-yellow patch on the fore-flanks running to the beak from a pale grey patch on the rear flanks. This distinctive flank pattern forms a rough figure of eight and is easily seen when dolphins leap clear of the water. There is also a thin dark stripe running from each flipper to the beak.

2 Striped Dolphin L 1·8–2·5 m

This small active dolphin is seen irregularly off Madeira in February–May and July–October, while it can be seen all year round off the Canaries. A deepwater dolphin, it normally feeds in tight pods of up to 25 animals in pelagic waters out of sight of land. Animals can, however, also mix in with feeding concentrations of Short-beaked Common Dolphins and sometimes feed in close association with Fin Whales. Striped Dolphins are very similar in shape, size and acrobatic behaviour to Short-beaked Common Dolphins. They tend to be shyer and are often less approachable, although will sometimes ride in the wake of boats. The best way of identifying them is from their distinctive flank pattern. They have a pale grey area leading from behind the eye and sweeping up in a thin line through the dark grey upperparts towards the dorsal fin. There is also a thin dark line running from the eye along the lower flanks to the underside of the tail stock, and another shorter dark line runs down from the eye to the flippers.

DD **3** ## Atlantic Spotted Dolphin L 1·9–2·6 m

This small active dolphin can be seen all year round off Madeira, although is most common in March–November, and is present all year around the Canaries, where the largest groups are noted in April. It is largely confined to the tropical and subtropical waters of the Atlantic and is rarely seen elsewhere in Europe. Atlantic Spotted Dolphins typically occur in large dense pods of up to 100 animals that may mix with other similar species. They are similar in size, shape and activity to Short-beaked Common Dolphin and are best identified by the distinctive colouration of adult animals. Calves begin life rather uniformly mid-grey above, with paler grey sides and a white belly. However, as they mature juveniles develop dark spots on their bellies and white spots on their flanks. These spots become denser and spread more widely on adults, which can appear largely blackish with white spots when mature.

4 ## Fraser's Dolphin L 2·0–2·6 m

This small warm-water dolphin is rare around Madeira and uncommon in the Canary Islands, where it occasionally appears in large pods in deep offshore waters. It is sometimes known as Sarawak Dolphin, having been first identified from a skull found on a beach in Sarawak on the island of Borneo. Fraser's Dolphins feed in large, dense active pods and occur throughout the world's tropical and subtropical oceans, although they remain poorly known. Compared to other dolphins they are rather stocky and have an oddly small, triangular and upright dorsal fin. The flippers and tail fluke are also rather small, and there is a short but distinct beak. The colouring is distinctive: blue-grey above and pinkish-white below, with a thick blackish stripe, which thickens and darkens with age, running between the two from the eye to the vent. This stripe is most marked in adult males, giving them a distinctly masked appearance, and it is bordered above by a thin cream-coloured line. There is also a dark stripe running between the jaw base and the flipper.

Seals Only one species of seal occurs around the islands, the very rare and elusive Mediterranean Monk Seal. Numbers of this shy species crashed in the 20th century throughout its Mediterranean range as a result of hunting and disturbance of its nesting beaches, which forced it to resort to nesting in caves. Survivorship of calves is currently very low because of storms and large waves washing out the beaches at the backs of caves. These seals formerly bred on undisturbed open beaches, where survivorship of calves would have been much higher. Fewer than 600 seals remain worldwide; the largest colony nearby, at Cabo Blanco in the W Sahara, underwent a severe population crash in 1997, although the species is now the subject of a targeted conservation plan, and numbers appear to be slowly increasing again. Very occasional recent sightings have been reported from the Eastern Canaries. Numbers on the Desertas Islands of Madeira dropped from some 50 animals in 1978 to just 6–8 animals in 1988 as a result of direct and indirect human disturbance, but complete protection since 1990 has helped numbers there slowly rise, which gives some hope for the future.

CR **1** **Mediterranean Monk Seal** L 2·4 m | W 300–400 kg

This large, critically endangered seal currently occurs only around Madeira, although it formerly inhabited the Canaries, including the islet of Los Lobos (literally, 'the wolves') off Fuerteventura. In Madeira it breeds only in the Desertas Islands, where some 40 animals benefit from the complete protection plan in place since 1990. This small population is showing signs of an increase, and odd seals have occasionally wandered to the S coast of Madeira in recent years. These seals owe their name to their plain colouring, said to resemble monk's robes. Males are black above and whitish below, while females are dark grey above and paler below. Both show broad flat snouts, with very pronounced long nostrils that face upwards, and no obvious external ears. The flippers are rather short and bear small slender claws. Monk Seals feed during the day, diving for fish and molluscs. They breed in caves year-round with a peak in October–November.

Monk seals are very unobtrusive when at sea.

1

Land mammals

As all of the islands have formed without direct connections to the mainland, it is no surprise that the native mammal fauna of the islands is very limited. The original fauna of the Canaries included two species of giant rat, with body lengths of up to 1 m, that were endemic to La Palma and Tenerife respectively, but these appear to have become extinct rapidly after the islands were colonised by humans. The Lava Mouse, which was about twice the size of a House Mouse and had large eyes that suggest it was nocturnal, was also endemic to the Eastern Canaries. It appears to have lasted longer than the giant rats but is thought to have been preyed on by introduced dogs and outcompeted by the introduced House Mouse. The only remaining endemic land mammal is the rarely seen Canarian Shrew, which inhabits the arid lava fields of Lanzarote and Fuerteventura; two other species of shrew have been introduced to Tenerife and Gran Canaria respectively. Lying further offshore than the Canaries, Madeira has no endemic land mammals, and there is no historical evidence to suggest that it ever did. However, a number of non-native mammal species have been introduced to both island groups over the years, including the familiar and destructive Brown and Black Rats, House Mouse and European Rabbit to all the larger islands, as well as Algerian Hedgehog to the Central and Eastern Canaries and Barbary Ground Squirrel to Fuerteventura. Mouflon and Barbary Sheep have been introduced to Tenerife and La Palma respectively for hunting purposes, although both pose a serious threat to endemic plants, and the former is now the subject of a control programme.

❶ ❷ European Rabbit L 38–58 cm including tail of 4–8 cm

The familiar European Rabbit has been introduced to all the main islands of the Canaries and to Madeira, Porto Santo and the Desertas Islands. It first arrived on Porto Santo in 1418 and on the Canaries around the same time or perhaps even earlier. Its original range was in NW Africa and SW Europe, but it has been widely introduced elsewhere for food and now occurs on all continents except Antarctica, though it remains absent from sub-Saharan Africa. These rabbits are exclusively vegetarian, feeding entirely on leaves, buds, bark, roots and seeds and can be destructive grazers of natural habitats. On the islands, rabbits are largely crepuscular and spend much of the heat of the day hidden in burrows, which are placed in both natural and agricultural habitats from the coast to the highest peaks, but particularly in more vegetated areas. Rabbits are widely hunted on the islands; hunters use Canarian warren hounds to locate burrows and then employ a ferret to bring the rabbits out into the open to shoot.

4 **House Mouse** L 12–20 cm including tail of 5–10 cm

This widespread species is found on all the larger islands in the Canaries and on Madeira and Porto Santo. House Mice prefer man-made habitats, so are commonest in urban and agricultural areas, where they often live inside buildings, although they can also occur in most natural habitats. House Mice on Madeira have been shown to be evolving rapidly, and at least six different subspecies are developing through isolation in different parts of the island. Carbon dating shows that these mice have been on Madeira and the Canaries since around AD. 1036, when they may have arrived on Viking longships. Those on Gran Canaria have longer limbs than elsewhere, possibly an adaptation to living in steep volcanic terrain. House Mice vary from pale to dark brown above and can be paler below. They have a pointed snout, small rounded ears, dark eyes and a long, largely hairless tail.

2 (Etruscan) **Pygmy White-toothed Shrew**

L 5–8 cm including tail of 2–3 cm

This widespread shrew has been introduced to the Canaries from Eurasia and currently occurs only on Tenerife but may well spread to other islands. It is widespread on Tenerife, occurring on both sides of the island from the coast up to 2,000 m. This tiny shrew is the lightest mammal in the world, with an average weight of 1.8 g. It is very active and has a very fast metabolism, with a heart rate of 25 beats per second! These shrews prefer moist bushy habitats with plenty of crevices, such as rocks, walls and ruins, as they are incapable of making burrows to live in. They feed mostly on insects up to their own size but will also feed on small lizards. Compared to the other two shrews in the Canaries they are much smaller and lighter-coloured, with pale brown fur above and pale grey fur below. They are largely nocturnal but remain very active at dawn, which is when their high-pitched clicking calls and rapid activity draw attention.

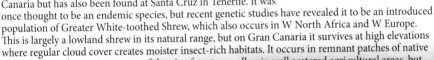

1 Greater White-toothed Shrew

L 9–13 cm including tail of 3–4 cm

This shrew occurs only at high elevations on the N side of Gran
Canaria but has also been found at Santa Cruz in Tenerife. It was
once thought to be an endemic species, but recent genetic studies have revealed it to be an introduced
population of Greater White-toothed Shrew, which also occurs in W North Africa and W Europe.
This is largely a lowland shrew in its natural range, but on Gran Canaria it survives at high elevations
where regular cloud cover creates moister insect-rich habitats. It occurs in remnant patches of native
laurel forest and in moister parts of the pine forest, as well as in well-watered agricultural areas, but
is threatened by rapid urbanisation and by an
increasingly dry climate. The fur can be greyish
or reddish brown above and is yellowish
on the underside. As with all white-
toothed shrews, its teeth are white
at the tips. It is much larger than
Pygmy White-toothed Shrew and
Canarian Shrew, but its range
does not normally overlap
with either species. Individual
pairs will establish and defend
a territory, which is unusual
in mammals. These shrews
are very vocal, producing a
high-pitched twittering sound,
which is the easiest way to
track them down.

3 Canarian Shrew L 6–7 cm including tail of 3 cm

EN

ENDEMIC TO EASTERN CANARIES

This endemic white-toothed shrew is found only on Lanzarote
and Fuerteventura in the Eastern Canaries and on the nearby
islets of Los Lobos and Montaña Clara. It favours arid lava fields
with little or no vegetation, where it hunts for insects and snails in the
crevices and lava tubes, but also occurs in adjacent rocky and sandy
areas and in abandoned agricultural fields. It is smaller than Greater
White-toothed Shrew, and its fur is a more uniform and darker
chocolate brown above. It also shows a more dappled and whiter-
looking belly, as a result of white tips to the hairs. It has
quite large pale ears and unlike many other shrews
does not possess enlarged fore-claws. On Montaña
Clara it is confined to a single sand dune and
often feeds on Atlantic Lizards, which it
immobilises with a bite loaded with
neurotoxin! Canarian Shrew is hard
to see, as it spends much of its day
resting under rocks and unlike
other shrews rarely makes any
twittering calls.

❶ ① Brown Rat L 40–50 cm including tail of 18–25 cm

The cosmopolitan Brown Rat occurs on all the larger islands. Originating from central Asia and China, Brown Rats now inhabit all land masses away from the polar regions. They were introduced to the islands more recently than the Black Rat, appearing on the Canaries in the 18th century. They can occur in any habitat but are probably most numerous in built-up and agricultural areas at lower elevations, where food is easier to find. They are usually nocturnal, but odd individuals may appear in daylight hours. Brown Rats are much larger than Black Rats, and have brown or grey fur above and paler fur below. Compared to Black Rats they have smaller ears and eyes (giving them a 'meaner' look), a more slanted snout and a tail that is shorter than the rest of the body.

❶ ② Black Rat L 12–18 cm including tail of 6–10 cm

Black Rats occur throughout the islands, having been accidentally introduced by humans to Lanzarote as early as the Middle Ages. They originate from SE Asia and India but are now widespread around the world, where they often pose a serious threat to native wildlife and agriculture. On the islands they prefer areas of less disturbed habitat, particularly laurel forest. They eat anything including birds' eggs, invertebrates, vertebrates and vegetative matter. They are a threat to nesting endemic birds and are trapped around nesting areas of Zino's Petrel on Madeira. Black Rats are slightly smaller and more slender-bodied than Brown Rats, with larger ears and eyes (giving them a more friendly look), a more pointed snout and a tail that is longer than the rest of the body. The body fur can be black, but many are brown, paricularly in the laurel forest on Madeira.

❶ **③** **Barbary Ground Squirrel** L 32–44 cm including tail

Introduced as a pet in 1965 from Morocco, this small rodent quickly multiplied to pest proportions on Fuerteventura in the 1980s, although numbers have since declined. Preferring arid rocky areas, it remains the most conspicuous rodent on the island and is easily seen, especially in the central mountains around Betancuria. This is a small greyish-brown or reddish-brown ground squirrel with a bold white stripe down each side, a whitish-grey belly and a bushy grey tail that bears thin black bars along its length. These squirrels are active during the day, living in groups of up to 20 animals, although they often take a siesta in their burrows in the heat of the early afternoon. Some groups at roadside stops are habituated to humans and will beg for peanuts, although they normally feed on native fruits, seeds and insects, as well as on birds' eggs and snails.

❶ **④** **Algerian Hedgehog** L 20–25 cm

This hedgehog is native to North Africa but was introduced to Tenerife, Gran Canaria, Fuerteventura and Lanzarote in the 1890s. It is commonest in lower-lying areas but will also venture high into the mountains. It is easily identified, as it is the only hedgehog on the islands. This is a midsize hedgehog with a long snout, large ears, and soft pale spines that bear darker bands. The face is whitish and, lacking spines on the crown, has a 'friendly' look. The underparts are generally pale. It has relatively long legs, which allow it to run quite fast. It occurs in a range of natural forested and arid habitats but is perhaps most common in parks and gardens. Like most hedgehogs, it is largely nocturnal, although can be active at dusk. Algerian Hedgehogs eat a range of food including insects, small vertebrates and carrion but also take the eggs of ground-nesting birds.

❶ ❶ Mouflon H (to shoulder) 0·9 m to shoulder | L 120 cm |
W 50–55 kg (males), 30 kg (females)

Mouflon is the wild ancestor of domestic sheep and is native to
the Caucasus, N Iraq and N Iran but was introduced to Tenerife
for hunting purposes in the 1970s. Some 70–125 individuals are thought to exist on the island, and there
is a plan in place to slowly eradicate them, as they damage the protected flora in the Teide National Park
and have no natural predators. Most occur at 1,400–3,100 m on summits and along ridges in the centre
of the island in rough lava shrub land (*malpais*), where they feed on grasses and native plants. Mouflon
are very distinctive, with short-haired coats of red-brown with a darker back stripe and a paler patch on
the saddle. Males are larger and have large horns that curve backwards; females are smaller, with much
smaller straight horns that can be lacking altogether. Males rut in the late autumn, and the sexes split into
separate groups during the winter months, when females have their young.

❶ ❷ Barbary Sheep H (to shoulder) 0·8–1·0 m | W 40–140 kg

VU

Barbary Sheep is a rare and declining species of goat that is native
to the rugged mountains and deserts of North Africa. These
animals were introduced to La Palma for shooting purposes and
have spread throughout the N and central parts of the island,
where they are a serious threat to endemic vegetation. They prefer
rough, steep, arid mountainous terrain, where they graze on
bushes, grasses and lichens, and if need be can obtain all the
moisture they require from their food. They are mostly
active in the early morning and late afternoon,
resting during the heat of the day. They are very
shy and can jump vertically over 2 m when
fleeing from danger. Barbary Sheep are
sandy brown above, darkening with
age, and have a slightly paler belly and
a darker line down the back. Males
show shaggy hair on the throat, chest
and mane. The largely smooth horns
are triangular in cross section and
curve outwards, backwards and then
inwards.

Bats

With their powers of flight, bats have been able to colonise the islands over the years, and currently number eight breeding species. Most of the bats require sheltered areas out of the prevailing winds in which to forage at night for flying insects, and many species are therefore restricted mostly to areas with intact forest structure close to roost sites. Populations of many species would have declined as the original forest cover was lost. Seven species of bat breed on the Canary Islands, while just three species occur on Madeira. However, bat distribution is uneven on the Canaries, showing higher diversity on the wetter and more heavily vegetated Western and Central Canaries, while only one species, the widespread Kuhl's Pipistrelle, breeds on Fuerteventura.

The Canary Big-eared Bat is endemic to the Western and Central Canaries, the Madeira Lesser Noctule is an endemic subspecies on Madeira, and the Barbastelle has an endemic subspecies on La Gomera and Tenerife. The Atlantic Islands Pipistrelle occurs on both island groups and is found elsewhere only on the Azores. One further species, the Egyptian Fruit Bat, was accidentally introduced to Tenerife, where it caused problems for native fauna and flora, so was the subject of an eradication programme and is believed to have been extirpated by 2016. Some of the commoner bats may be encountered feeding around outside lights in built-up areas, but many of the bats are rarely seen and remain poorly known. Population sizes of many of the bats are thought to be small and at risk from loss of roosting and feeding habitat and, in particular, overuse of pesticides. For those wanting to see more bats, it is worth joining a professionally organised tour to observe bats emerging from known roost sites.

3 European Free-tailed Bat

L 14 cm including tail of 5 cm | WS 45 cm

This large bat occurs on all the Western and Central Canaries, and there is one old record from Madeira. It is widespread in all habitat zones from the coast to the high mountains on most of the islands where it occurs but is rather localised on Gran Canaria. The flight is fast and direct on long narrow wings, usually at great height, as it hunts over both natural and man-made habitats. It is easily picked up by its regular penetrating *sick, sick* call. This is the largest naturally occurring bat on the islands. It has large, broad forward-pointing ears and a long fleshy tail, of which the final third is unattached by membranes. The long muzzle has distinctive wrinkling around the lips – hence the alternative names of mastiff or bulldog bat. It is a rather dark bat, with black wings, tail membranes and ears and dark grey fur above, although it is paler grey below. This is generally a solitary bat, hiding in both natural and man-made rock crevices during the day, although small groups of females will gather to nurse their young.

Canary Big-eared Bat

EN

L 8 cm including tail of 3·5 cm | WS 25–29 cm

ENDEMIC TO WESTERN AND CENTRAL CANARIES

This rare and endangered midsize bat is endemic to La Palma, El Hierro and Tenerife in the Canaries but may also occur on La Gomera, where much suitable habitat exists. It inhabits coniferous and mixed woodlands between 100 m and 2,300 m elevation and roosts in abandoned buildings as well as in caves and lava tubes. It feeds at night on moths in well-wooded areas. Numbers have declined at the only two known colonies, dropping by 80% at the largest colony, the Cuevas de los Murciélagos on La Palma, in recent years, perhaps as a result of disturbance. The total population is thought to number between 500 and 2,000 individuals, and the species is threatened by the use of pesticides and loss of roosting habitat. Summer colonies consist of up to 30 females, while winter clusters are small, consisting of 1–10 animals. This is a moderately large bat with very broad, long ears, mid-brown fur above and paler fur below.

Grey Long-eared Bat

L 9 cm including tail of 4·5 cm | WS 23–30 cm

This midsize long-eared bat occurs on Madeira and has also been observed on the Desertas Islands. It remains a poorly known and possibly endangered bat on the islands, although it is widespread and common in mainland Europe. It inhabits buildings and caves close to open cultivated land and is thought to avoid dense woodland, although it has been recorded in laurel forest on Madeira. Like other bats, it may have been harmed by overuse of pesticides in the islands. Individuals occasionally fly during the day, but these bats are mostly nocturnal, feeding on moths, flies and beetles, and they hibernate between October and March. This species is similar in size to the Canary Big-eared Bat, but its longer, narrower ears, which have a distinctive fold, are almost as long as the body, the body fur is greyer, and the muzzle is darker.

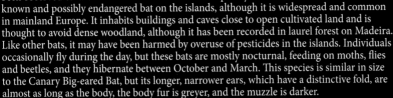

3 Barbastelle L 4·5–6·0 cm | WS 26 cm

3

This rare woodland bat has been recorded only on La Gomera and Tenerife, where recent genetic research has confirmed it to be a subspecies distinct from the mainland populations in S and central Europe and Morocco. Rare throughout its range, this bat favours mature native forest, where it roosts under bark and in natural cavities in damaged or dead trees. Compared to the other midsize bats, it has a distinctive short pug nose, small eyes and short but wide ears that are joined across the forehead by skin. It is a very dark-coloured bat, with black body fur that is usually tipped golden-brown, giving it a slightly frosted appearance. Fast and agile in flight, it specialises in foraging in and around dense woodland.

4 Leisler's Bat / Madeira Lesser Noctule
L 5–7 cm | WS 26–33 cm

Endemic subspecies on Madeira

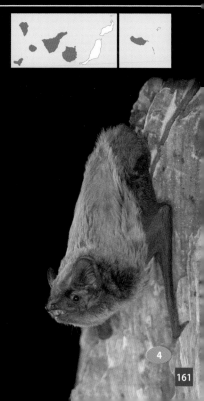

This midsize bat occurs on the Western and Central Canaries and on Madeira; the latter population is regarded as a separate subspecies. It is very much a woodland bat, tied to tall native forest, particularly pine trees in the Canaries, and it often uses tree holes, although it will also visit buildings. The population on Madeira is considered threatened, as the area of suitable habitat is small and habitat quality is slowly declining, and fewer than 1,000 bats are thought to remain. Unlike the similar-size Grey Long-eared Bat and Canary Big-eared Bat, these bats have rather small, rounded ears. They emerge shortly after dusk and fly fast and straight, often at treetop level but also around street lights, and stoop for moths and other flying insects in shallow dives. The body fur is brown and is distinctly paler towards the head and darker towards the rear. The undersides of the arms are also hairy, hence the alternative name Hairy-armed Bat.

4

Pipistrelle bats The three species of pipistrelle bats in the islands are all very similar in appearance and cannot be reliably identified in the field without a bat detector (which picks up echolocation signals) or close views in the hand. Ongoing taxonomic studies further complicate the picture. Only **Atlantic Islands Pipistrelle** occurs on Madeira, which simplifies identification there, although it is rare and endangered on the island. This bat also occurs in the Western Canaries and on Tenerife, where it is often the most commonly seen bat, although ongoing genetic studies may yet reveal this to be a different species to that in Madeira. **Kuhl's Pipistrelle** occurs with Atlantic Islands Pipistrelle on Gran Canaria and Tenerife but is the only pipistrelle on Fuerteventura – and appears to have recently become extirpated on Lanzarote. Kuhl's Pipistrelle is very closely related to Dusky (African) Pipistrelle, and it is currently uncertain to which species the 'Kuhl's' from the Canaries are most closely related, so its name may change in the future. The third bat, **Savi's Pipistrelle**, has recently been discovered to be more closely related to bats of the genus *Hypsugo* than to those of *Pipistrellus*, so it is no longer technically a pipistrelle. It occurs throughout the Western and Central Canaries but is generally more closely tied to non-urban habitats such as rocky gorges and woodland than the others.

E **1** ## Atlantic Islands Pipistrelle

EN

L 3·5–5·0 cm | WS 20–25 cm

ENDEMIC TO MACARONESIA

This small bat is endemic to Macaronesia, occurring on La Palma, El Hierro, La Gomera and Tenerife in the Canaries and on Madeira and Porto Santo, as well as in very small numbers (<300 bats) in the Azores. It is considered endangered, as the population is small throughout its range, suitable habitat is fragmented, and the bat has suffered from overuse of pesticides and predation by feral cats. The species may already be extirpated on Porto Santo, while fewer than 1,000 individuals remain on Madeira, and this population remains highly threatened. Numbers are larger on the Canaries, where it is often the most commonly seen bat on the islands on which it occurs. These bats often roost in caves and rock crevices but will also roost in cracks in buildings. They can occur at over 2,000 m elevation in the Canaries but are more common in the lowlands. They can readily be seen hunting at night, with a jerky erratic flight, around outside lights in towns and over reservoirs, as well as in both agricultural and wooded habitats.

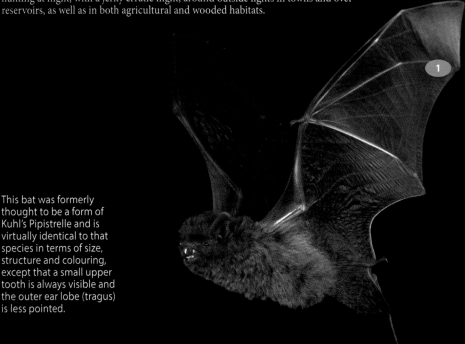

This bat was formerly thought to be a form of Kuhl's Pipistrelle and is virtually identical to that species in terms of size, structure and colouring, except that a small upper tooth is always visible and the outer ear lobe (tragus) is less pointed.

② Savi's Pipistrelle L 4–5 cm | WS 20–25 cm

This small bat occurs on all the main Canary Islands except Lanzarote and Fuerteventura. It does not occur on Madeira. This widespread bat occurs throughout the Mediterranean region, including North Africa and the Middle East, where it is often found in mountainous regions. In the Canaries it is widespread and quite common in more open rocky areas around cliffs and deep ravines as well as in wooded areas. Its preference for less urbanised areas means it is less commonly seen than Atlantic Islands Pipistrelle, although it is the commonest bat on Gran Canaria, where the latter does not occur. Savi's Pipistrelles roost singly or in small numbers in rock crevices and hollow trees. Larger groups of up to 50 females will gather in nursery roosts in late summer. The face, broad rounded ears and wings are black, while the head and upper body are covered in brown fur and the under-body from chin to vent is contrastingly pale. This species has a rounded tail, which is slightly longer than that of Atlantic Islands Pipistrelle, its outer ear lobe (tragus) is broad-based with a tapering rounded tip, and the body fur is often darker.

③ Kuhl's Pipistrelle L 4–5 cm | WS 21–25 cm

This small bat occurs on Fuerteventura, where it is the only breeding bat, so is best seen there. It also occurs on Tenerife, where it overlaps with Atlantic Islands Pipistrelle, and on Gran Canaria, where it is poorly known and appears to be rare. It formerly occurred on Lanzarote but appears to have died out there. This is a widespread species that occurs throughout the Mediterranean region, including North Africa and the Middle East, as well as W Asia. It feeds over a variety of natural and man-made habitats, including woods and deserts, as well as around street lights in urban areas, and has a slow but acrobatic flight. Roosts are often located in buildings, and larger groups of females gather in maternity colonies. Kuhl's Pipistrelle is very similar to Savi's Pipistrelle, but its ears are larger, less rounded and show a pointed outer lobe. The face is not black and the fur on the upperparts ranges from light brown to reddish brown. The underparts are paler, and there is a distinctive pale margin to the dark wings, particularly between the feet and the hands.

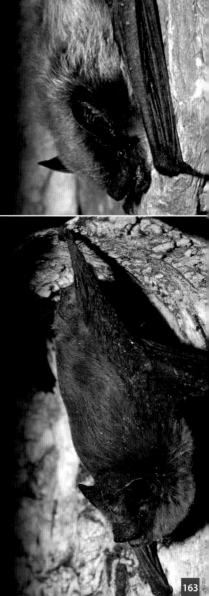

163

Reptiles and Amphibians

Snakes No snakes occur naturally on the islands but the Brahminy Blind Snake and Common Kingsnake have both been introduced accidentally to the Central Canaries. The former is harmless but the latter is a predator of native reptiles.

Lizards One species of lizard, the Madeira Lizard, is endemic to Madeira, while the lizard population of the Canaries represents one of the best examples of island evolution and radiation. Genetic work has revealed that ancestors of both the giant lizards and the smaller lizards originated in North Africa and reached the Eastern Canaries first, having presumably arrived on floating debris, before spreading westwards through the island group, using each new island as a stepping stone, until reaching the youngest and westernmost island, El Hierro.

Giant lizards The original reptile fauna of the Canaries included several very large 'giant' lizards, most of which suffered greatly when humans colonised the islands, presumably as a result of hunting and predation by introduced dogs, cats and rats. The Tenerife Giant Lizard grew to almost 1.5 m in length but sadly appears to have quickly gone extinct, although its smaller cousin, the Tenerife Speckled Lizard, was recently discovered in tiny numbers on the island. The Gran Canaria Giant Lizard, however, survived in good numbers and remains quite common on its home island and has a small introduced population in E Fuerteventura. Even more remarkably, the endemic giant lizards of both El Hierro and La Gomera, which were long thought to be extinct, have both been rediscovered in recent years and are targets of conservation action. Sightings since 2007 of a possible giant lizard on the N coast of La Palma have raised the tantalising possibility that the La Palma endemic species (which grew to a total length of 90 cm) may also survive – although these records may refer instead to large male specimens of the La Palma subspecies of the Western Canaries Lizard. Any really large lizards observed on steep remote slopes on La Palma should be thoroughly checked and photographed whenever possible. The observed lizards were largely dark brown in colour, and some had yellow spots down their sides.

❶ 1 Common Kingsnake L 90 cm

This striking black and white North American snake has been introduced accidentally to Gran Canaria, where it is thriving. By 2014, its population there was estimated at 20,000, with snakes widespread in most habitats. Although non-venomous, it poses a severe threat to all the endemic reptiles on the island.

❶ 2 Brahminy Blind Snake L 17 cm

Originally from Asia, this tiny inconspicuous non-venomous snake has recently been found on Tenerife and Gran Canaria having arrived in the soil of potted plants. Living in the soil, it is rarely seen, but it looks likes a shiny, black unsegmented earthworm.

3 **Madeira Lizard** L 21 cm including tail of 13 cm

ENDEMIC TO MADEIRA

This lizard is very common on all the islands in the Madeiran group and has also been accidentally introduced to the Azores. It occurs commonly in most habitats, including urban areas, from sea level to 1,850 m in the mountains, although it is less common in dense laurel forest and has a preference for rocky places and walls for basking. Adults are variable in colour, ranging from grey to brown, flecked darker and paler above, sometimes with a greenish tinge. Adult males **3♂** can show red or orange below with a bluish throat. Females **3♀** retain a hint of the alternating dark and pale longitudinal stripes of immature lizards and are whitish below, sometimes with darker spots. This is the only naturally occurring lizard on the Madeiran islands, although Boettger's Lizard has been introduced and occurs in and around Funchal.

Atlantic (Haria) **Lizard** L 20 cm including tail of 10 cm

ENDEMIC TO EASTERN CANARIES

This lizard is confined to the islands of Lanzarote and
Fuerteventura and their nearby small islets, although a small
introduced population occurs around Arinaga on the E side of Gran Canaria. It is abundant and easily
seen throughout its native islands and frequents a wide range of habitats, including wooded areas, shrub
land, dry open rocky areas, beaches, urban areas, gardens and agricultural land, up to 800 m elevation. It
is often encountered basking on rocks or bare ground, scuttling away rapidly upon close approach. It is a
small to medium-size lizard with a pointed snout, large coarse scales on the back and a slightly spiny-
looking tail. Adults are dark brown to black with black throats, and males **1♂** show a row of green or blue
spots along the sides. Younger lizards are a paler brown and often show long stripes down the sides and
back.

2 **Boettger's** (Lehr's) **Lizard**
L 20–25 cm incl. tail of up to 15 cm
ENDEMIC TO LA GOMERA AND EL HIERRO
(two separate subspecies)

This is the common lizard on La Gomera and El Hierro, and adjacent islets, and is represented by a different subspecies on each island. It has also been introduced to the Botanical Gardens, Funchal, Madeira and there are odd records from Los Cristianos, Tenerife. It is common in a variety of habitats from open rocky areas, shrub land and open woodland to agricultural and urban habitats, although less common in dense laurel forest and in Canary Pine forest. Boettger's Lizard is very similar to the Western Canaries Lizard, but adults are smaller and the males **2♂** are less brightly coloured, being more uniformly dark grey (including the throat) with a variable amount of blue spotting on the sides. Females **2♀** show the alternating dark and paler longitudinal stripes of immatures, including a broad brown dark-edged stripe down the back, and often show a pale creamy stripe running above and behind the eye and another running lower down the flanks.

2♀
EL HIERRO

2♂
EL HIERRO

Western Canaries Lizard

L up to 50 cm including tail of 25 cm

ENDEMIC TO TENERIFE AND LA PALMA (four separate subspecies)

This is the common lizard on Tenerife and La Palma and their nearby islets, with three different subspecies on Tenerife alone. An introduced population exists at Pajara on Fuerteventura. Reports from Madeira are thought to be in error. It is larger than the closely related Atlantic and Boettger's Lizards and occurs in most habitats except dense forest, from sea level to 3,700 m in the mountains, and is especially fond of walls in agricultural areas. These lizards are fond of ripe bananas and have become rather tame at popular tourist spots, especially on Mount Teide; some are trapped as pests in fruit-growing areas. Adults are dark brown or even black, but breeding males **1♂** show a pale blue throat and two rows of rich blue spots on the sides, as well as variable yellow spotting on the back and flanks, while the smaller females **1♀** show a dark line down the side. Immatures **1i** show alternating dark and pale longitudinal stripes on the back and sides. Animals from the north of Tenerife are larger and more brightly coloured than those from the south, with mature males often showing bars of yellow across the back.

1i LA PALMA

1♀ LA PALMA

1♂ LA PALMA

1 ♀
NORTHERN
TENERIFE

1 ♀
SOUTHERN
TENERIFE

1 ♂
NORTHERN
TENERIFE

1 ♂
SOUTHERN
TENERIFE

169

E **1** ## La Gomera Giant Lizard

CR

L 30–50 cm including tail of up to 30 cm | W up to 0·5 kg

ENDEMIC TO LA GOMERA

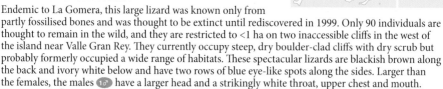

Endemic to La Gomera, this large lizard was known only from partly fossilised bones and was thought to be extinct until rediscovered in 1999. Only 90 individuals are thought to remain in the wild, and they are restricted to <1 ha on two inaccessible cliffs in the west of the island near Valle Gran Rey. They currently occupy steep, dry boulder-clad cliffs with dry scrub but probably formerly occupied a wide range of habitats. These spectacular lizards are blackish brown along the back and ivory white below and have two rows of blue eye-like spots along the sides. Larger than the females, the males **1♂** have a larger head and a strikingly white throat, upper chest and mouth. The females **1♀** are browner on the back and legs. The recovery plan for the species includes removing feral cats from its range, while captive breeding has more than doubled the population.

❶ La Palma Giant Lizard Endemic L 90 cm including tail of up to 40 cm

Endemic to La Palma, this very large lizard was widely thought to be extinct but sightings since 2007 indicate that a remnant population may possibly still exist in the north of the island. Fossil remains reveal a historic range in the more arid littoral zone all around the coast to 800 m altitude on the island, although it avoided denser Laurel and Pine Forest. Recent sightings come from 40-200 m above sea level on the north coast. This species was amongst the very largest and most robust of the giant lizards with thick sturdy legs. As with all giant lizards, the male was larger and larger-headed than the female. The observed lizards were largely dark-brown in colour, whilst some showed yellow spots down the sides. Urgent research is required to ascertain whether the species still survives and what its conservation needs might be.

2 **Hierro Giant Lizard**

L 60 cm including tail of up to 30 cm

ENDEMIC TO EL HIERRO

This large, stocky lizard was thought to be extinct until its rediscovery in 1974. A separate subspecies was lost from the islet of Roque Chico de Salmor in the 1930s. Some 300–400 individuals survive in a few pockets of suitable habitat of about 4 ha in extent at elevations of 350–500 m in the La Fuga de Gorreta cliffs north-east of Frontera. They inhabit areas of steep rocky cliffs with sparse vegetation but were much more widespread formerly, in the absence of predatory cats and rats. Small lizards can run nimbly from these introduced predators, but larger older individuals, particularly ex-captive ones, are easier prey. Hierro Giant Lizards are dark grey (adults) to brown, with a reddish or orange area in the centre of the belly and two rows of pale orange patches running down the sides. Younger females **2i** have a grey back with two rows of orange-green marks and four rows of blackish patches on the sides. A management plan in 1999–2005 returned 387 captive-bred lizards to other parts of the species' original natural habitat on El Hierro, including rocky slopes at El Julan Archaeological Park and in La Dehesa, as well as to the islet of Roque Chico de Salmor, but this lizard remains critically endangered, as the trapping of feral cats around release areas has since stopped.

E **1** **Tenerife Speckled Lizard**

CR

L 50 cm including tail of 30 cm

ENDEMIC TO TENERIFE

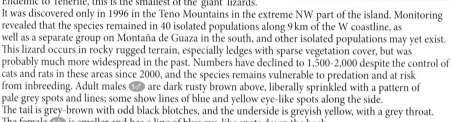

Endemic to Tenerife, this is the smallest of the 'giant' lizards.
It was discovered only in 1996 in the Teno Mountains in the extreme NW part of the island. Monitoring revealed that the species remained in 40 isolated populations along 9 km of the W coastline, as well as a separate group on Montaña de Guaza in the south, and other isolated populations may yet exist. This lizard occurs in rocky rugged terrain, especially ledges with sparse vegetation cover, but was probably much more widespread in the past. Numbers have declined to 1,500-2,000 despite the control of cats and rats in these areas since 2000, and the species remains vulnerable to predation and at risk from inbreeding. Adult males 1♂ are dark rusty brown above, liberally sprinkled with a pattern of pale grey spots and lines; some show lines of blue and yellow eye-like spots along the side. The tail is grey-brown with odd black blotches, and the underside is greyish yellow, with a grey throat. The female 1♀ is smaller and has a line of blue eye-like spots down the back.

Some have a line of blue spots along the back.

Gran Canaria Giant Lizard
L 80–100 cm including tail of up to 60 cm | W up to 0·5 kg
ENDEMIC TO GRAN CANARIA

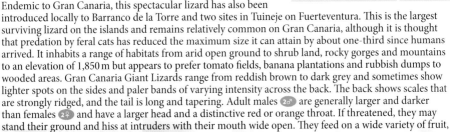

Endemic to Gran Canaria, this spectacular lizard has also been introduced locally to Barranco de la Torre and two sites in Tuineje on Fuerteventura. This is the largest surviving lizard on the islands and remains relatively common on Gran Canaria, although it is thought that predation by feral cats has reduced the maximum size it can attain by about one-third since humans arrived. It inhabits a range of habitats from arid open ground to shrub land, rocky gorges and mountains to an elevation of 1,850 m but appears to prefer tomato fields, banana plantations and rubbish dumps to wooded areas. Gran Canaria Giant Lizards range from reddish brown to dark grey and sometimes show lighter spots on the sides and paler bands of varying intensity across the back. The back shows scales that are strongly ridged, and the tail is long and tapering. Adult males (2♂) are generally larger and darker than females (2♀) and have a larger head and a distinctive red or orange throat. If threatened, they may stand their ground and hiss at intruders with their mouth wide open. They feed on a wide variety of fruit, leaves, flowers and insects.

Skinks Four species of skinks occur in the Canaries, each endemic to different islands. The Eastern Canary Skink is the largest, although it is the least commonly seen species, as it spends most of its time underground or hiding in rock crevices out of the heat of the sun. The three other skinks are more easily seen, particularly when basking on walls in the early morning. Skinks differ from the lizards in having small pointed heads that are barely demarcated from the cylindrical body. The tail and limbs are also relatively shorter, and skinks will resort to a slithering snake-like motion when alarmed. They also have much smoother and shinier scales, giving them a glossy appearance. Differences between the species are mostly small, so location is the best clue to identification, although skinks from S Gran Canaria have distinctive blue or greenish tails.

E **1** **Smooth Skink** L 18 cm including tail of 9 cm

ENDEMIC TO LA GOMERA AND EL HIERRO

Based on genetic data, the skinks on La Gomera and El Hierro have recently been split as a separate species from those on Tenerife. Smooth Skinks are common on both islands from sea level to the summits but are less common in areas of dense laurel forest and pine forest, and are most easily seen basking in rocky areas and on walls. Females are slightly larger than males. Smooth Skinks are very similar to West Canary Skinks but have a slightly more olive-toned or bright coppery-brown back bearing small pale spots, while the sides, belly, legs and tail are blackish.

E **2** **West Canary Skink** L 18 cm including tail of 9 cm

ENDEMIC TO TENERIFE

The West Canary Skink occurs on Tenerife and associated islets, and odd individuals have been introduced to La Palma. This skink is common in most man-made and natural habitats, from sea level to 2,800 m in the mountains, including urban areas and banana plantations, but especially at lower elevations in the north of Tenerife where there is well-developed soil and leaf litter. It can often be seen basking in the sun at the entrance to rock crevices. Like Smooth Skink it is largely grey-brown with a bronzy sheen, bearing rows of small pale spots down the back and with blackish sides. The short legs and tail are darker than the back. Females give birth to one to six fully formed young.

E **3** **Gran Canaria Skink** L 18 cm including tail of 9 cm
ENDEMIC TO GRAN CANARIA

This skink is found only on Gran Canaria and the neighbouring
islet of Gando. It occurs in declining numbers in man-made
and natural habitats from sea level to up to 1,950 m in the mountains, including sandy shorelines and
plantations, although is scarcer in dense forest. Like most skinks it seems to favour rocky areas and stone
walls. The species has declined drastically in recent years from the use of pesticides and predation by alien
predators including the Common Kingsnake (*p. 164*). It looks similar to other skinks in the Canaries,
although it has darker flanks and more frequently shows lines of dark and pale spotting above giving the
appearance of stripes; those from the S part of the island show a vivid blue or greenish tail.

E **4** **Eastern Canary Skink** L to 25 cm
ENDEMIC TO EASTERN CANARIES

This secretive lizard occurs only on Lanzarote, Fuerteventura
and the islet of Los Lobos. It is the largest of the skinks on the
Canaries but is rarely seen, as it lives mostly underground and in rock crevices. It favours moister areas.
On Lanzarote it is largely restricted to the Haria Valley, but it is more widespread on Fuerteventura, where
it occurs in the more vegetated valleys in the centre of the island, around La Oliva in the north and on
Jandia in the south. Historical drought on both islands may have reduced its range. It often lives at the
bases of stone walls and may be found by turning stones over in vegetated areas. Females give birth to
four live young every year. These skinks have proportionately smaller legs and shorter tails and a larger,
fatter body than other skinks. They are variably pale to dark brown or grey above, with extensive pale
spotting, paler below and often show a redder-brown head and snout.

Geckos There are four species of endemic gecko in the Canaries, each found only on its respective island or islands. All are common and appear to have adapted well to human-imposed changes to the islands' habitats, living in buildings and taking advantage of external lights at night as magnets for moths and other invertebrate food. They are all very variable in appearance, as they change their colouration to match their habitat, and are consequently best identified by the island on which they are seen. The larger Moorish Gecko has been introduced to Madeira and Porto Santo, where it is now common in the absence of native gecko species. The smaller Turkish Gecko has been introduced to Tenerife and Gran Canaria, where with care it can be distinguished in urban areas from the native Tenerife and Boettger's Wall Geckos. Another widespread species, Tropical House Gecko, was first sighted in Funchal on Madeira in 2002 and may well become established there. It is much smaller, smoother-skinned and smaller-headed than Moorish Gecko.

 Tenerife (Wall) Gecko L 14 cm including tail of 7 cm

ENDEMIC TO TENERIFE AND LA PALMA

This is the common gecko on Tenerife and La Palma. It occurs in most man-made and natural habitats to 2,300 m elevation, although is rare above 1,800 m and occurs at lower densities in denser woodland. Like all the native geckos it is most common in rocky areas, but it also frequents buildings and will feed on insects drawn to outside lights. It is usually dark grey above and bears dark bands across the back that alternate with paler spots, while the underside is whitish or yellowish, although individuals will lighten to match their background. The head can appear disproportionately large in comparison with the body. The eyes often show golden tones. This is a noisy gecko that makes odd chuckling and chattering sounds at night.

 Boettger's Wall Gecko L 12 cm including tail of 6 cm

ENDEMIC TO GRAN CANARIA, EL HIERRO AND SELVAGENS

Boettger's Wall Gecko has an unusual distribution in that it occurs on Gran Canaria and El Hierro in the Canaries as well as on the Selvagens archipelago north of Lanzarote. It is common on all these islands, frequenting most habitats from the coast to 1,000 m elevation, although is scarce above 800 m and is largely absent from Canary Pine forest. Like most geckos it is most numerous in rocky areas, but it also occurs in buildings. The subspecies on the Selvagens lives in rocky coastal areas and frequents the burrows of petrels, as well as living under rocks. This is another chunky gecko, with a large triangular flattened head. Individuals vary from dark brown to pale grey-brown, depending on substrate, and often show paired darker marks on either side of a pale line down the spine, forming the impression of bars across the back.

3 ## Moorish (Common Wall) **Gecko**

L 16 cm incl· tail of 8 cm

This large plump gecko from the Mediterranean region was introduced to Funchal on Madeira in the 1980s. It has since spread to all parts of that island, and it reached Porto Santo in 2008. There are also reports of this species from urban locations on Tenerife. It occurs in a wide range of natural and urbanised habitats from sea level to 2,300 m elevation, although is generally most common in rocky areas and buildings along the coast and is largely absent from denser woodland. It is largely nocturnal although can also be active on cooler days. Moorish Geckos are generally grey-brown with lighter and darker spots, although they blend with the background and are lighter at night and darker when active in daylight. The skin is covered in spiky tubercles, giving it a very bumpy appearance. Many, particularly younger animals, show a boldly banded tail.

  4 ## Turkish Gecko L 15 cm including tail

This small gecko is native to the Mediterranean region but has been inadvertently introduced to both Tenerife and Gran Canaria, probably by boat. It occurs mostly in houses and in urban settings, often close to ports, hiding within walls in houses and feeding on insects around lights at night. Because of its small size and its largely urban habits, it is not considered a threat to native geckoes. Adults have purple or tan-coloured skin bearing black spots. The Turkish Gecko is best separated from native gecko species by the presence of claws on all of its toes and by its usually more strongly patterned tail bearing alternating rings of pale brown and black.

① Gomera Wall Gecko L 14 cm including tail of 7 cm

ENDEMIC TO LA GOMERA

This gecko is found only on La Gomera, where it is common. It occurs in most natural and man-made habitats from sea level to 850 m on the wetter, N side of the island, although it avoids dense laurel forest, and it is even more numerous in drier rocky areas on the S side of the island, where it occurs to 1,150 m. Gomera Wall Geckos are typically dark grey above with six dark bands crossing the back and many bumpy-looking spines, which appear as white spots. They are mostly active at night but can also be seen in the daytime.

② East Canary Gecko L 16 cm including tail of 8 cm

ENDEMIC TO EASTERN CANARIES

This gecko occurs on Lanzarote and Fuerteventura and their larger associated islets, including Los Lobos. It is not often seen but is actually rather common on these islands in most habitats up to 800 m. It favours dry stony areas and lava flows with a little vegetation, where it hides in crevices and under rocks. It also occurs in buildings and can be seen feeding on moths and other invertebrates around artificial lights at night. The colour of individuals varies with their background, ranging from almost black on dark lava to very pale pink on white-painted walls, while some show a paler stripe down the spine with darker bars across the back. The underside is lighter and is often yellowish towards the vent. These are rather chunky geckos, with a large, rather flattened head and body, stumpy sideways-projecting limbs and large golden-brown eyes with vertical pupils.

Sea turtles Four species of sea turtle are seen regularly in the seas around both sets of islands. The commonest is the Loggerhead Turtle, which is often seen at the surface of inshore waters and should be looked for from inter-island ferries and from cetacean- and seabird-watching vessels. No turtles currently breed on the islands, although they are likely to have done so before humans arrived. Eggs and hatchling Loggerhead Turtles from the Cape Verde islands were released in 2010–13 on Cofete beach on the Jandia peninsula of Fuerteventura as part of a project to bring nesting turtles back to the island. Since nesting females return to the beaches on which they hatched, it is hoped that some of the released turtles that survive the 10–15 years or so to adulthood will return to nest once more on Fuerteventura. Green Turtles are scarcer around the islands but occur regularly in small numbers. The more tropical Hawksbill Turtle is rare off Madeira but occurs regularly in small numbers around the Canaries, while the massive Leatherback Turtle occurs regularly at sea in very small numbers around all the islands. A fifth species, the Kemp's Ridley Turtle, has been recorded very occasionally from both sets of islands.

VU **3** **Leatherback Turtle** L 1·0–1·8 m | W 250–700 kg

This is the largest of the sea turtles and ranges furthest from tropical waters. It occurs regularly in small numbers in the seas around all the islands. Occasional individuals have been seen on beaches on Fuerteventura, which suggests they may once have bred there. Leatherbacks feed on jellyfish and travel huge distances, using ocean currents to reach food-rich areas. They are easily separated from the other sea turtles, as they lack an external shell. Instead they have a very large, tear-shaped body with seven ridges running lengthwise down the back and two very large front flippers. They are usually dark grey or black above, bearing paler marks, with a pale underside. Leatherbacks can appear remarkably barrel-like at the surface until the large blunt head is seen.

Loggerhead Turtle at sea

Green Turtle at sea

EN **1** **Loggerhead Turtle** L 100 cm | W 100 kg

This large sea turtle is by far the commonest species in the area. Many juveniles and some adults are regularly seen around the coasts of all islands throughout the year, particularly in the summer months. Although they have a worldwide distribution in tropical and subtropical oceans, Loggerheads are considered endangered due to loss of nesting sites and the entanglement of large numbers of adults in fishing gear at sea. These turtles are often seen in inshore waters around the islands resting at the surface while between dives to the sea floor, where they forage for bottom-dwelling invertebrates. The shell usually appears reddish-brown, while the skin on the head and sides is brown above and yellowish below.

EN **2** **Green Turtle** L 83–177 cm | W 70–190 kg

This large sea turtle occurs throughout the world's tropical and subtropical oceans but is much scarcer than the Loggerhead Turtle in waters around both sets of islands. Immature Green Turtles are seen most often in the more sheltered waters off the SW coasts of the Central Canaries, and a few found off Tenerife and Gran Canaria have been tagged recently to assess their movements. These animals are from the Atlantic population and occasionally visit the area from breeding sites further south; like all sea turtle populations they are threatened by loss of breeding sites, entanglement with fishing gear and poaching. Green Turtles have a short snout lacking the hooked beak of Hawksbill Turtle. They begin life almost black above and whitish below but turn brown or olive as they mature, by adulthood becoming entirely brown, often with paler spots or rays on the shell and with dark-centred scales on the face.

CR **3** **Hawksbill Turtle** L 70 cm | W 80 kg

This is the smallest of the regularly occurring sea turtles in the area and it is also the rarest. Small numbers are seen around the Canaries, particularly in summer, but this largely tropical species is rare in the cooler waters around Madeira. It is critically endangered worldwide, due to loss of nesting beaches and both deliberate and accidental capture of adults. Hawksbills feed predominantly on sea sponges and jellyfish. Compared to Green and Loggerhead Turtles, Hawksbills have a more elongated and tapering head, which bears a beak-like mouth, and the back of the shell has a serrated edge formed by overlapping scales. The shell typically has an amber-coloured background bearing an irregular pattern of light and dark streaks, with more black and mottled-brown markings on the sides. The head and flippers show dark scales with thin pale margins.

Frogs There are no native amphibians on the islands, but two species from the W Mediterranean have been introduced, and both are locally common in wet places on both sets of islands.

❶ **①** **Perez's Frog** L 4–7 cm

This noisy frog is now widespread throughout all the islands except Fuerteventura and Lanzarote, where it is very localised, and La Gomera from where there are no recent records. It is common and conspicuous in wetter areas at low to mid elevations of all these islands, favouring ponds, irrigation pools, temporary puddles, stream beds, ditches and reservoirs for breeding. Perez's Frogs are chunkier and more conspicuous than Stripeless Tree Frogs. They are rather variable in colour, showing extensive or small patches of rich green above, often with a pale central stripe down the back, all set on a browner background, and with dark spots on the sides of the back and dark blotches on the legs and flanks. These frogs are very vocal day and night, using inflatable cheek sacs to create a range of loud chirruping calls that can sound like clucking chickens, crying babies or even distant sheep!

❶ **②** **Stripeless** (Mediterranean) **Tree Frog** L to 6·5 cm

This striking frog has been introduced to both sets of islands from its native range in the W Mediterranean, including to the Canaries in 1480 by Diego Herrera. It occurs commonly on the wetter Western and Central Canaries, particularly on their N sides, but is very local on the drier Eastern Canaries and some of their satellite islands, such as Alegranza. It is locally common on Madeira, although is generally outnumbered there by Perez's Frog. Stripeless Tree Frog normally occurs at low to mid elevations and breeds in ponds, irrigation pools, reservoirs, ditches, barrancos and even swimming pools, and as a result is often found in agricultural areas, banana plantations and gardens. Mature frogs are typically white below and uniformly bright green above, except for a black line that runs through the eye, broadening behind it and stopping at the shoulder. Contrary to the species' common name, some individuals may also show a stripe down the side. Frogs in drier areas may be brown. The eyes are golden. Each toe ends in a sucker (a feature not found in Perez's Frog) which allows this tree frog to climb up vertical surfaces. It is also much more slender and smooth-skinned than Perez's Frog. Stripeless Tree Frogs are very vocal, using the single large throat sac to create deep quacks as well as loud chuckling sounds.

Dragonflies and Damselflies

The number of dragonflies occurring on the islands is relatively small, thanks to the islands' oceanic isolation and the limited areas of suitable freshwater wetlands. Five dragonflies and one damselfly occur regularly on Madeira and Porto Santo, and 10 dragonflies and two damselflies occur regularly on the Canaries, while a further two migratory dragonfly species have arrived in recent years and could establish permanent populations. All are rather widespread species, except Island Darter, which is endemic to Madeira, Tenerife, Gran Canaria and La Gomera. The smaller Western Canaries and drier Eastern Canaries hold fewer species, with just four regularly occurring species on Lanzarote and seven species, plus one recent arrival, on Fuerteventura. This compares with 11 species on Tenerife, 10 plus one recent arrival on Gran Canaria, eight on La Gomera, six on La Palma and three on El Hierro.

Most species can fly throughout the year in the temperate climate of the islands, but the largest numbers are seen in spring, and a few species, such as Ringed Cascader, do not fly in winter. Many of the African species are highly migratory, and strong S winds can bring influxes of them to the islands, where they can then breed if conditions are suitable. Globe Skimmer has recently reached Gran Canaria in this way, while Long Skimmer has recently reached Fuerteventura; it remains to be seen whether they will establish permanent populations on these islands. There is also a record of a Barbary Featherleg damselfly from Tenerife in March 1971, which is otherwise endemic to North Africa. It is always worth photographing unusual specimens you come across, particularly after S dust-laden storms from North Africa.

NB the vertical lines accompanying each account show the max/min length measured from the front of the head to the tip of the abdomen.

3 Ringed Cascader L 53–58 mm

This boldly marked midsize dragonfly occurs only on Tenerife, La Gomera and Gran Canaria. It is a widespread species in Africa, S Europe, the Middle East and S Asia. However, it prefers fast-flowing sections of permanent streams and rivers, especially rapids, so its habitat is limited on the islands and made more so by the damming of streams at their sources for drinking water and irrigation. It is generally rather local near streams on the islands, but odd individuals will also appear at dams, temporary pools and sheltered beats away from water. Ringed Cascaders fly mostly in the spring and summer months, from March to August. They have long thin bodies and long wings. Adults of both sexes are largely black, with yellow patches down the sides of the abdomen and thin yellow lines down the centre of the abdomen; the female 3♀ shows more distinct black and yellow stripes on the thorax.

3♂   3♀

1. Tropical Bluetail L 28–30mm

A widespread and abundant damselfly, Tropical Bluetail occurs from Africa to Japan and New Guinea and is tolerant of polluted and brackish water including stagnant pools. However, in our area the current known range is restricted to tiny colonies in reservoirs at Las Galletas on Tenerife and near Los Llanos de Ariadne on La Palma. The male 1♂ has a bright blue tip to the abdomen and bright green sides to the thorax and eyes, like Sahara Bluetail (see that species for ID tips). The female 1♀ Tropical Bluetail has only two colour forms on the islands, neither of which is shown by Sahara Bluetail: one has an orangey-brown thorax and a uniformly metallic grey-green abdomen and the other a uniformly blackish abdomen, and neither shows a paler blue or fawn spot near the tip.

2. Sahara Bluetail L 28–30mm

This species is common in its main North African range. It is rather local at or close to freshwater sites on the Canaries, where it has been recorded on all the islands except El Hierro, although it can be seen in quite large groups at favoured sites. The male 2♂ of this species is very similar to Tropical Bluetail, with green sides to the eyes and thorax, and a largely black abdomen bearing a bright blue spot on the last but one segment of the body. The best way to tell males apart is to look at the side edge of the second abdominal segment after the thorax, which has a straight edge in this species but is clearly bulging downwards on Tropical Bluetail. Females 2♀ are highly variable in colouration, but unlike female Tropical Bluetails they always show a paler blue or fawn-coloured spot near the tip of the abdomen.

3. Small Bluetail L 26–32mm

This species occurs only on Madeira and Porto Santo but has a widespread range in Europe, North Africa, Turkey and Russia. It is locally common at suitable sites on both islands, although it tends to have a low weak flight so is easily overlooked. The species quickly colonises temporary pools and flooded areas but also has residual populations in permanent ditches and ponds. Adults have a black abdomen bearing a bold blue spot near the tip, on the last two segments of the body. Immature females 3i are bright orange but become greenish brown as they mature. Small Bluetail is very similar to the two species of bluetails on the Canaries but is thought to be the only damselfly to occur on Madeira currently – although another unknown bluetail species has been caught in the past and may yet still occur.

3i

1♂

1♀

Bluetails

2nd segment
bulging, straight in
Sahara Bluetail 2

2♂

2♀

3♂

3♀

185

1 Vagrant Emperor L 63 mm

This large migratory dragonfly has been recorded on Tenerife and Gran Canaria in the Canaries and on Madeira and Porto Santo, although it must occur on other islands from time to time and can arrive in quite large numbers. It regularly flies long distances over oceans on migration and breeds on the islands when conditions are favourable, in temporary vegetated swamps as well as more open pools. It is smaller and a paler yellowy brown than the similarly patterned Lesser Emperor, and the male 1♂ shows a less complete blue saddle behind the thorax, with the blue largely restricted to the upper surface, and the eyes are brown (not green). Females 1♀ and immatures are darker and duller brown, with a violet-tinged (not blue) saddle.

2 Lesser Emperor L 71 mm

This is another large dragonfly that occurs on the Eastern and Central Canaries, as well as Madeira and Porto Santo, but it has not been recorded from the Western Canaries. This species tends to be less common and more local in occurrence around wetland sites than Blue Emperor, and it can also patrol beats well away from water. It is intermediate in size between Blue Emperor and Vagrant Emperor and shows a straight abdomen. Mature males 2♂ are duller than Blue Emperors and have a dark brown abdomen bearing a bright blue saddle on the segments just behind the thorax fronted by a thin yellow band. This is similar to the pattern of the smaller Vagrant Emperor, but on Lesser Emperor the blue of the saddle wraps right around the body, the eyes are green (not brown), and there are no black markings on the dark brownish thorax. Females 1♀ are similar to males, although the abdomen is duller and the blue saddle is sometimes absent.

3 Blue Emperor L 78 mm

This large, strong-flying species has been recorded on all of the Canary Islands, on Madeira and Porto Santo, and as a migrant to the Selvagens. It requires well-vegetated ponds or reservoirs in which to breed but can be locally common in and around such habitats and is usually the most common of the larger dragonflies. Males 3♂ patrol high over their territories repeatedly to keep other males out and hunt other insect prey, including butterflies. Mature males have a largely sky-blue abdomen with a dark central dorsal stripe and a plain apple-green thorax and head bearing blue eyes. Females 3♀ and immatures are similarly marked to males but are largely green instead of blue. The wings turn yellow-brown with age. A helpful ID tip even when seen against the light is that the abdomen has a downward curve, unlike the straight abdomens of the other large dragonflies.

3♀

1 ♀

1 ♂

2 ♀

2 ♂

3 ♀

3 ♂

① **Epaulet Skimmer** L 39–48 mm

This slim midsize dragonfly occurs on all the Canary Islands except Lanzarote. It is a widespread species and is very common throughout Africa, the Middle East and S Europe. Epaulet Skimmers will use any freshwater habitat for breeding and will also occur well away from water; they are usually outnumbered by the darters. Like the dropwings, Epaulet Skimmers hold their wings forward when resting. The males ①♂ show a pastel-blue abdomen, a greyer-blue thorax and blue eyes, while the females ①♀ are golden brown above, with a pinkish hue on the underside of the thorax and abdomen. Both show a white stripe on the thorax under each wing, which are the 'epaulets' of the name.

①♂ ①♀

② **Long Skimmer** L 60 mm

This widespread species occurs commonly in Africa and the Middle East and is spreading north into S Europe. It has recently colonised Fuerteventura, where it can be seen alongside the more numerous Epaulet Skimmer around pools in barrancos.

Compared to that species, Long Skimmer is obviously larger, with a longer and slimmer abdomen, which bulges markedly near the base. Adults have bright blue eyes, and the mature males ②♂ have a grey-blue thorax and a bluish-black abdomen, while females ②♀ and immatures have a mostly yellowish body bearing a bold black line down the centre that joins with black patches on the sides and across the final two segments.

②♂ ②♀

3 Globe Skimmer L49–52 mm

This large highly migratory species was recorded for the first time in our area on Gran Canaria in January 2013. The species turned up during a period of S winds off the Sahara, and it could occur anywhere on the islands under such conditions. Globe Skimmers turn up annually on oceanic islands such as the Seychelles and will breed given suitable habitat. Adult males **3♂** have a largely reddish-orange abdomen, females **3♀** have an olive abdomen, and both sexes show irregular black markings down the centre. They typically fly high, with broad-angled wings, and show a characteristic wobbling flight.

3♂ 3♀

4 Violet Dropwing L 32–38 mm

This robust darter has recently been recorded at barranco sites on Fuerteventura. It is a widespread species ranging through Africa, the Mediterranean, Arabia and the Near East. It is an adaptable species of semi-arid areas and can breed in ephemeral pools after rains because its larvae develop more quickly than those of other species. Males **4♂** have a beautiful violet thorax, a broad, pinkish-violet abdomen, red eyes and bold red veins on the wings. Females **4♀** have a brownish thorax and a yellow abdomen with dark brown markings. Like the Red-veined Dropwing, this species immediately lowers its wings upon landing.

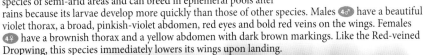

4♂ 4♀

1 Red-veined Dropwing L 32–26 mm

This distinctive dragonfly is a widespread and common species across Africa. It occurs on all of the Western and Central Canaries except for La Palma and is locally common in permanently wet barrancos on the N sides of the islands. The brilliantly coloured males are often seen perched on rocks and vegetation along a stream bed. Males ♂ have a slender, bright red abdomen with black splashes on the sides and a black tip, a purplish-red thorax and bright red veins along the entire length of the wings. Females ♀ and immatures have a yellow-russet abdomen with a pale streak between the wings. All show large crimson eyes and small orange patches at the base of the wings. As with other dropwings, the wings are held forwards and downwards at rest.

2 Red-veined Darter L 40 mm

This thin darter occurs all the Canary Islands except El Hierro, as well as on Madeira and Porto Santo, and it is often the commonest dragonfly. Migrant individuals have even occurred on the dry Desertas and Selvagens Islands. These darters prefer large, weedy waters but will also breed in smaller pools. They are highly migratory and can appear well away from water. Red-veined Darters have much slimmer bodies than Broad Scarlet, with a more tubular abdomen, and appear very similar to Island Darter (see that species for ID tips). Less brightly coloured than Broad Scarlets, males ♂ have a pinkish-red abdomen and a reddish thorax and face. The eyes are red above (brown above in females) and blue below. Females ♀ are yellowish brown, with greener sides to the abdomen. Look for bright red veins in the inner half of the wing on males, and yellow veins on the wings of females. The dark legs show a yellow stripe down the length.

E 3 Island Darter L 45 mm

ENDEMIC TO MADEIRA AND CANARIES

This endemic species occurs on Madeira and Porto Santo, as well as on Tenerife, Gran Canaria and La Gomera, and has also been recorded as a migrant on the Desertas. It is fairly common on Madeira and La Gomera, but is very localised on Tenerife and Gran Canaria. It favours running water but will also use still waters. This darter is closely related to the Common Darter of mainland Europe but differs from it and from Red-veined Darter by having all-black legs. It appears very similar to Red-veined Darter but has a subtly longer, slimmer abdomen lacking black dorsal marks at the tip and longer, slimmer and more pointed-tipped wings. Males ♂ have a slim orange-red abdomen, a yellowish-brown thorax and eyes that are dark reddish brown above and pinkish below, with a short black line crossing in front of them that does not continue down the eye sides. Females ♀ are yellowish brown, like female Red-veined Darter, but lack the yellow veins on the wings and the blue on the lower half of the eyes.

4 Broad Scarlet L 35–40 mm

This robust darter occurs on all the main Canary Islands except Lanzarote and El Hierro. It does not occur on Madeira. It occurs locally at wetland sites, including temporary pools in barrancos and well-watered gardens, but also well away from water, and it is usually outnumbered by Red-veined Darters. Broad Scarlet is a chunky darter with a flat abdomen that broadens in the middle. Males ♂ have a vividly red abdomen and face and a reddish-brown thorax and eyes. Females ♀ are dull yellow-brown and become more olive as they mature but always show a distinctive pale line down the thorax.

Dropwings and darters

1♂ 1♀ 2♂ 2♀ 3♂ 3♀ 4♂ 4♀

191

Butterflies

Resident species A total of 16 butterflies occur regularly on Madeira, with 37 on the Canaries. Many of these can be observed all year round in the equitable climate of the islands, although others occur only as migrants, and several species – the three endemic green-striped whites and Greenish Black-tip – fly mostly December–June, when vegetation is lusher on the drier Eastern Canaries. Other butterflies, such as the graylings, which favour higher elevations in the mountains, fly only in the warmer summer months. Recent work has revealed that many of the butterflies have become sufficiently different from each other on each isolated island to warrant full species status, which has increased their conservation priority status. Madeira Large White sadly appears to have become extinct. This was an endemic subspecies (or possibly species) which favoured north-facing valleys in pristine laurel forest in Madeira. It was formerly widespread and remained common into the 1970s but was last collected in 1986. Despite many searches it has not been seen since and may have succumbed to a virus or parasite brought in when Small Whites were introduced to the island in the early 1970s. The endemic Canary Islands Large White is similarly confined to intact laurel forest and was lost from La Gomera in the 1970s. It still occurs on La Palma and Tenerife but remains vulnerable.

Migrant species The islands see periodic influxes of migrant butterflies; remarkably, these include two species, Monarch and American Painted Lady, from across the Atlantic in North America. Large arrivals of migrants have resulted in breeding populations becoming established in the presence of suitable natural and in particular introduced food plants for the caterpillars. Species such as African Migrant, Monarch, Lang's Short-tailed Blue and Geranium Bronze have colonised the islands this way in recent decades, and others, such as Desert Babul Blue, may also become increasingly widespread. All records of butterflies on the islands will help broaden our knowledge of their status and conservation needs – please submit records via www.ufz.de/lepidiv/.

NB the vertical lines to the right (left, if space dictates) of each account show the max/min length of the forewing, measured as a straight line from where the wing joins the body to the wing tip.

 1 ● **Canary Skipper** WS 24–28mm

ENDEMIC TO WESTERN AND CENTRAL CANARIES

This tiny butterfly is endemic to the Western and Central Canaries and absent from Fuerteventura and Lanzarote. It was formerly considered a subspecies of the widespread Lulworth Skipper but is now regarded as a full species. It is locally common in rather dry, open bushy areas, rocky barrancos and rocky slopes from sea level to 1,800 m in the hills, where the larval food plant (*Brachypodium* grass) grows. Adults fly from March to June (sometimes to late August) at lower elevations, and can be seen into September at higher elevations. They are small golden-brown butterflies that sit with their wings half folded open – a posture unique to this species in the region. There are some yellow-brown spots on the forewing and a darker border along the edges of the wings.

1♂

1♀

2 Queen of Spain Fritillary WS 38–46 mm

This medium-size fritillary occurs on Tenerife, Gran Canaria, La Palma and La Gomera in the Canaries and on Madeira. It is a migrant butterfly that flies from March to October and can be more abundant in some years than others. It flies low over flower-rich sunny areas in both natural and man-made habitats from sea level to high into the mountains, although it tends to avoid densely forested areas. It often basks in bare patches on the ground with the wings held wide open. The forewings are rather pointed, giving this butterfly a rather fast, powerful flight, although it is also somewhat jerky. It is much smaller than Cardinal, and the upperwing pattern is rather similar, with more rounded black spots on an orange-brown background. The underwing, however, is very different, being largely orangey brown with large silvery-white black-rimmed spots on the hindwing.

3 Cardinal WS 64–80 mm

This large fritillary currently occurs on Tenerife, La Palma, El Hierro and La Gomera. Some authorities consider the Canary populations to represent an endemic subspecies. It is scarce but widespread from March to September at the edge of laurel forest at moderate elevations (500–1500 m), where it often glides along paths and lays its eggs on violets and pansies, but is most numerous in pine forests on north-facing slopes. This is the largest of the European fritillaries. The upper side shows a typical complex fritillary pattern of black spots on an orangey-brown background. However, the underside is very striking, being largely plain green on the hindwing and the front corners of the forewing, leaving an isolated panel of orange with black marks in the centre of the forewing.

① **Geranium Bronze** WS 15–27 mm

This tiny butterfly flies year-round and has recently spread to all the Canary Islands, except El Hierro. A caterpillar was found on Madeira in 2002, although the species does not yet appear to have colonised the island. Originally from South Africa, it was introduced to Majorca and was first noted on Lanzarote in 1999 and quickly spread to neighbouring islands, taking advantage of ornamental *Pelargonium* plants, on which its caterpillars feed. It reached Tenerife by 2008 and La Palma by 2015. It is well established in the Eastern Canaries and is becoming increasingly widespread and common in the Central and Western Canaries. It favours coastal areas and hills to 600 m wherever its food plants grow, including within degraded laurel forest. The sexes are alike, brown above with a fine white outer border crossed with dark bars. The grey-brown underside is richly patterned with russet-brown and white bars, and there is a dark spot at the base of two tiny, fine projecting tails on the hindwing.

② **Small White** WS 32–47 mm

This medium-size white butterfly breeds on all the Canary Islands and on Madeira and Porto Santo. Long present on the Canaries, this species only became established on Madeira in the 1970s. Small Whites are now common and widespread in more open habitats on all the islands, including gardens, agricultural areas, roadsides and open scrubby habitats, up to 3,000 m, but are scarcer in more densely forested areas. They look like a smaller version of Large White, with black spots and tips to the forewing and a largely yellow underside, although butterflies from the first generation in spring ②ₛ often show only faint black wing tips.

③ **Large White** WS 63–70 mm

This large white butterfly is a strong migrant from North Africa and could appear on any of the islands, although it has been recorded with certainty only on Lanzarote and Fuerteventura, where it is scarce in the winter months. Large Whites look very similar to Canary Islands Large Whites but are typically found in more open, often man-made habitats such as gardens and agricultural areas. Female Large Whites, on close inspection, have two small black spots (absent in males) on the forewing, which never merge to form a bar as in Canary Islands Large White, and black on the wing tip that is more extensive than on Small White. Large White caterpillars feed on plants of the cabbage family and are considered a major pest of such crops.

> **Ⓔ Madeira Large White** WS 55–65mm. The Madeiran subspecies of Large White, differed in being a little smaller. Apart from size, males looked similar to Large White, though females differed in having less prominent black spots on the upper forewing. Last recorded near Seixal in 1986, its rediscovery would cause a sensation!

Ⓔ ④ **Canary Large White** WS 57–66 mm

VU

ENDEMIC TO LA PALMA, TENERIFE AND LA GOMERA

This endemic counterpart of Large White has only ever occurred on three islands in the Western and Central Canaries, where it requires intact laurel forest. It remains widespread and locally common on La Palma, while it is scarce in the N coastal region of Tenerife and appears to have been extirpated on La Gomera in the 1970s. It favours wet, shaded gullies and cliffs within laurel forest at 200–1,400 m, where the caterpillars feed on an endemic plant (*Crambe*), although it can also feed on introduced species such as Brassicas. It flies mostly from March to October, but odd individuals can be seen on warmer days throughout the winter. This is a large, slow-flying white butterfly with a broad black tip to the upper forewing and two black spots on both sides of the forewing, which are much larger on the male and can merge to form a broad black bar. The underside of the hindwing is powder yellow.

Clouded Yellow WS 52–62 mm

A common bright yellow butterfly that occurs year-round on all the islands, it can be found almost anywhere but particularly favours open grassy areas with flowers and areas under cultivation at low to mid elevations, and in smaller numbers to the tops of the highest peaks. It normally poses with the wings closed, revealing a rich greenish-yellow underwing bearing a distinctive pair of brown-ringed white spots (one large and one small) on the hindwing and a black spot on a richer yellow area on the forewing. The upperwings are rich orangey yellow, bordered black on the outer edge, with a prominent dark spot on the forewing.

African Migrant WS 54–66 mm

This highly migratory species has been recorded on all the Canary Islands since 1995, having first become established there in 1965. It has also been recorded from Madeira and Porto Santo. African Migrants favour exotic flowering shrubs, notably the yellow-flowering *Cassia*, and are often seen around hotel resorts and in parks and gardens at lower levels on the islands. Large arrivals can occur during S winds from Africa, while smaller numbers are now resident all year round. These are rather uniformly coloured butterflies, with broad rounded wings, which fly fast through hotel grounds and rarely stop. Males ♂ are pale yellowish green, females ♀ are yellow, and both show very subtle brown-circled pale dots on the underside. They lack the bright orange on the upperwing and hooked forewing tips of Canary Brimstone.

Canary Brimstone WS 50–70 mm

VU

ENDEMIC TO TENERIFE, LA GOMERA AND LA PALMA

This endemic yellow butterfly is restricted to Tenerife, La Gomera and La Palma and is most numerous on La Gomera. It is local in laurel forest on north-facing slopes at elevations of 600–2,000 m, although it will also occur at times at lower elevations and in other types of forest, including juniper slopes and even cultivated areas close to forest down to 300 m elevation – wherever the larval food plants (*Rhamnus* species) are present. It flies all year round, although it is less active in the winter months. The underwing is pale yellowish green, as in African Migrant, but the forewing has a prominent hooked tip and on the male is largely bright orange on the upper side. There are also prominent pale veins on the underside of the hindwing and a small dark-ringed spot on the underside of either wing.

Madeira Brimstone WS 50–70 mm

EN

ENDEMIC TO MADEIRA

This Madeiran endemic is restricted to dense primary laurel forest at elevations of 500–1,500 m and adjacent flower-rich open areas. The species has declined through habitat loss and has become uncommon and endangered. It looks very similar to Canary Brimstone, with prominently hook-tipped forewings, which are rich orange above in the males, and with pale yellowish-green undersides bearing pale veins.

🅔 ① Gran Canaria Green-striped White WS 36–44 mm

ENDEMIC TO GRAN CANARIA

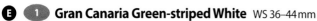

This green-striped white occurs only on Gran Canaria, where it is local at higher elevations in open dry grassland areas with some *Euphorbia* bushes and abundant flowers including Brassicas, which are its food plant. It flies from December to April and appears in two broods. It is very similar in appearance to green-striped whites on Tenerife and Fuerteventura, with triangular wings at rest and broad green stripes on the underside of the hindwing.

🅔 ② Tenerife Green-striped White WS 36–44 mm

ENDEMIC TO TENERIFE

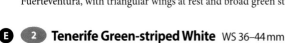

Formerly grouped with the green-striped whites elsewhere in the Canaries, those on Tenerife are subtly smaller but, as a result of recent DNA work, are now regarded as a separate species. They occur almost exclusively from 1,550–3,550 m elevation on the slopes of Mount Teide, where the caterpillars feed on the yellow-flowered endemic plant *Descurainia bourgeana*. Although its range is very restricted, Tenerife Green-striped White is common in these natural and semi-natural habitats, which are protected within the Teide National Park. Butterflies are on the wing from March and fly into the summer at these cooler elevations. It looks very much like the other two green-striped white species, with oddly pointed wings, bold green stripes on the underside of the hindwing and black bars across the tip of the forewing.

🅔 ③ Fuerteventura (Rothschild's) Green-striped White

WS 36–44 mm

ENDEMIC TO FUERTEVENTURA

This green-striped white occurs only on Fuerteventura, where it is locally common at more heavily vegetated sites in the hills of the island, particularly in sheltered gullies and barrancos. The butterfly particularly favours areas of abandoned or marginal cultivated fields where *Sisymbrium erysimoides*, the food plant of the caterpillar, is common. Butterflies are on the wing mostly from December to April, with fewer in May–June, and appear in two broods. Subtly smaller and daintier than Small White, they are very similar to the other green-striped whites, of Tenerife and Gran Canaria, with triangular wings at rest and broad green stripes on the underside of the hindwing.

④ Bath White WS 45–50 mm

This small to medium-size white butterfly breeds commonly on all the Canary Islands but is absent from Madeira. Like Small White, it prefers more open habitats, including gardens, agricultural areas, roadsides and open scrub. It is particularly numerous on the drier Eastern Canaries and on the drier S slopes of the other islands. Like Small White, it can be seen in any month. The most useful feature for separating this species from Small White is the underside of the hindwing, which shows an extensive pattern of green blotches. The upper side is mostly white, but there is an intricate pattern of black blotches near the tip of the forewing and on the lower edge of the hindwing.

⑤ Greenish Black-tip WS 30–34 mm

This small distinctive species occurs only on Fuerteventura and Lanzarote and some of their satellite islands, including Graciosa. This is very much a desert butterfly that thrives in arid conditions, such as those across North Africa. It remains widespread and common in the Eastern Canaries, where it occurs on rocky barren slopes but favours the moister gullies where its larval food plants (*Carrichtera* and *Hirschfeldia*) grow. Greenish Black-tips fly mostly from December to April, with fewer in May–June, as the larval food plants begin to wither away. No other butterfly has the combination of rich yellow upperwings bearing a black bar across the wing tip and a long black spot near the leading edge of the forewing. The underside of the hindwing is greenish grey, while the markings on the upper forewing come through on the underside.

1 African Grass Blue WS 18–26 mm

This tiny blue butterfly occurs on all the main Canary Islands but has not been recorded from Madeira or Porto Santo. It flies all year round and favours sunny irrigated short-grass areas in the lowlands, so is often seen flying over lawns and flower beds in parks and gardens. It flits rapidly low over the ground and rarely stops. African Grass Blues are much smaller than the other widespread blue butterflies. Males ♂ show a dark purplish-blue upper surface with broad dark borders, while females ♀ are mostly dark brown above with a fine white fringe. However, they typically close their wings at rest, revealing buffy underwings bearing numerous small blackish spots with whitish borders and a thin black line towards the rear edge of the hindwing.

2 Desert Babul Blue WS 16–23 mm

In our area, this tiny beautiful blue butterfly is currently known only from Gran Canaria and Fuerteventura. It occurs widely in India, the Middle East and Africa and was first recorded in the Canaries on Gran Canaria in 1982. It frequents the more arid zones in the south of the islands from November to April, where it flies rapidly around trees and occasionally lower over puddles. Its caterpillars feed mainly on thorny acacias. Males ♂ are similar to African Grass Blue, brownish purple above with a bluer area near the wing base, although they lack the prominent dark borders of that species. Females ♀ are a richer brown above than female African Grass Blue and show dark spots on the hindwing. The underside is pale grey with pronounced white and brown dashes and up to five neat black spots on the hindwing.

3 Austaut's Blue WS 29–36 mm

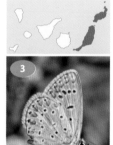

On the islands, this lovely blue butterfly breeds only on Lanzarote and Fuerteventura. Occasional individuals have been recorded from Tenerife, but it has failed to become established there. It flies all year round and favours flower-rich areas in the lowlands and hills, such as areas of cultivation, track edges and gardens. Males ♂ are electric blue above with a fine white border internally edged black, while females ♀ are very similar to Southern Brown Argus, brownish above with a bluish suffusion near the centre. Both sexes show a buffy underwing bearing numerous white-fringed black spots and a row of orange spots near the rear edge.

E 4 Canary Blue WS 28–30 mm
ENDEMIC TO WESTERN AND CENTRAL CANARIES
3 subspecies: La Palma | Gran Canaria | Tenerife and La Gomera

This lovely butterfly is endemic to the Western and Central Canary Islands, absent only from Fuerteventura and Lanzarote. It was apparently lost from El Hierro but was recorded there again in 2014, although may not yet have re-established a permanent population. It remains widespread and locally abundant on the remaining islands in native flower-rich habitats from sea level to up to 3,500 m elevation. It flies mostly between March and October, with odd individuals flying on warmer winter days. It emerges later at higher elevations and is particularly numerous between May and August in the crater of Cañadas del Teide on Tenerife. Oddly, the nearest living relative of this species occurs on islands in the Indian Ocean! These butterflies flit rapidly among the flowers and rarely stop flying during warm sunny conditions. Females ♀ are golden orange above, with some blue near the body, while males ♂ are dark brown above tinged violet-blue, with much dark blue near the body. The underside of the hindwing is variably brown, barred with white and with a bold white zigzag bar and one or two white-centred black spots towards the outer edge.
The underside of the forewing is centrally tawny orange. Specimens from La Palma have broader dark margins to the upperwings and a broader white zigzag bar on the underwing.

1♂ 1♀

2 1

3♂ 3♀

4♂ 4♀

Butterflies

1 Lang's Short-tailed (Common Zebra) Blue

WS 21–30 mm

This small blue butterfly has recently colonised the Canaries, with records from Fuerteventura since 1994 and more recent records from Lanzarote, Gran Canaria, La Gomera, Tenerife and La Palma. It appeared on Madeira in 2001 and on Porto Santo in 2002. It flies all year round in man-made flower-rich habitats such as parks, gardens and nurseries in coastal areas. It is very similar to Long-tailed Blue, as the males are purplish blue above and the females are bluish brown, and both show two fine projecting tails close to a pair of black spots on the rear edge of the hindwing. However, Lang's Short-tailed Blue is smaller, and the dark beige underside is more evenly barred with whitish lines, lacking the single thick white stripe of Long-tailed Blue.

2 Long-tailed Blue WS 32–42 mm

This blue butterfly occurs on all of the islands, where it flies all year round. It is widespread and sometimes common in more open flower-rich habitats, both natural and man-made, from sea level up to 2,000 m, but is most numerous in in weedy agricultural plots at lower elevations that contain its bean and pea food plants. These blues flit rapidly from flower to flower and usually settle with the wings closed, when the most distinctive features on the pale grey-brown underwing are two black dots with orange fringes on the rear edge of the hindwing adjacent to the two fine projecting tails. There is also a distinctive thick white stripe towards the outer edge of the hindwing. Males are violet-blue above, while females are largely brown above with some blue scales.

3 Southern Brown Argus WS 26–35 mm

This small brown member of the blue butterflies group occurs on the Western and Central Canaries but is absent from the Eastern Canaries and Madeira. It can be seen all year round, although is most numerous from March to October. It favours warm, open flower-rich areas in the lowlands and hills, such as gardens and other cultivated areas, forest openings and track edges, although it also occurs in areas of semi-arid natural vegetation, to 2,000 m. The two sexes are alike, being dark brown above with a line of orange spots merging to form a single orange band towards the outer edge of both wings. The underwing pattern is very like the underwing of Austaut's Blue (*page 200*) – so it is fortunate that the ranges of these two species do not overlap.

e 4 Small Copper WS 32–35 mm

Endemic subspecies: Madeira (though not recognised by some)

This small brightly coloured butterfly occurs on all the Canary Islands, and on Madeira and Porto Santo is represented by what may be an endemic form, Madeira Small Copper. On all the islands these butterflies are widespread but rarely numerous, occurring in a wide range of more open man-made and natural habitats, from sea level to at least 2,300 m in the mountains of the Canaries, although they seem to be more restricted to the hills on Madeira. Small Coppers fly all year round, and males often actively defend small flower-rich patches. The sexes are very similar, with rich orange forewings with black margins and spots and black hindwings bearing a wavy orange band near the tip. Females have more rounded wings than males. Butterflies on Madeira show longer dark bars rather than spots on the orange forewing patches, and some show a row of small blue dots in front of the orange band on the hindwing.

4M

1♂ 1♀ 1♀

2♂ 2♀ 2

3 3

4M 4C 4C

E **1** ## Canary Red Admiral WS 61–68 mm

ENDEMIC TO MADEIRA AND CANARIES

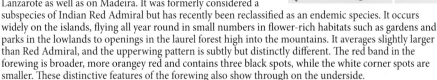

This striking butterfly occurs on all the Canary Islands except Lanzarote as well as on Madeira. It was formerly considered a subspecies of Indian Red Admiral but has recently been reclassified as an endemic species. It occurs widely on the islands, flying all year round in small numbers in flower-rich habitats such as gardens and parks in the lowlands to openings in the laurel forest high into the mountains. It averages slightly larger than Red Admiral, and the upperwing pattern is subtly but distinctly different. The red band in the forewing is broader, more orangey red and contains three black spots, while the white corner spots are smaller. These distinctive features of the forewing also show through on the underside.

2 ## (European) **Red Admiral** WS 55–65 mm

This widespread and familiar European species occurs on all the islands, where numbers are swelled at times by migrants. Red Admirals can be seen in moderate numbers all year round, often around gardens and parks in the lowlands but also at open

sunny spots high into the wooded mountains of the wetter islands. This strong-flying species is largely black above, relieved by white spots near the corners of the forewing and a red band that runs across the forewing and another along the rear edge of the hindwing. The underside of the hindwing is a mottled dark grey, but the distinctive pattern of the upper forewing shows through on the underside.

3 American Painted Lady WS 44–60mm

This American counterpart of Painted Lady currently occurs only on Tenerife and La Palma, although it has been recorded previously on the remaining islands of the Western and Central Canaries and also Madeira. It is unclear whether this species arrived naturally or from an introduction, although it is capable of crossing the Atlantic. It flies all year round in small numbers on Tenerife and La Palma, favouring open flower-rich areas in the lowlands and clearings in the laurel forest. It differs from Painted Lady in being slightly smaller and darker/redder above and on the underside of the forewing, and the largest spot on the forewing corner is usually orange, not white. It also has just two (not four) large blue-centred eyespots on the underside of the hindwing.

4 Painted Lady WS 58–74mm

This widespread migrant butterfly occurs on all the islands. It is most numerous during its winter breeding season and emigrates in the spring, becoming very rare in summer. This species is often numerous in more open sunny habitats, including waste ground, coastal areas, clearings in forests and open hillsides, from sea level to high in the mountains. Many often congregate at favoured feeding spots. Fresh specimens are salmon pink above, but this can fade to orange-brown in the sun. The black forewing tips bear several white spots. The underwing is variegated brown and white, with a row of four black-ringed bluish eyespots on the hindwing.

1 Meadow Brown WS 38–45 mm

This widespread species occurs on the Western and Central Canaries. It is locally common from March to September, although numbers may be swelled in some years by migrants. It prefers, grassy herb-rich areas and occurs from sea level to 1,500 m elevation in the mountains. Meadow Browns often perch with their wings closed, revealing an orangey patch bearing a single dark eyespot on the underside of the forewing and a rather plain grey-brown underside to the hindwing. The upperwing is dark brown but shows extensive orange patches and a large dark eyespot near the corner of the forewing.

2 Speckled Wood WS 46–56 mm

This widespread species occurs in our area only on Madeira and Porto Santo, where it first became established in 1976. It is now common in both open and closed wooded areas, including laurel forest, from sea level to high in the mountains (1,400 m+). On Madeira it appears to have replaced Madeiran Speckled Wood in the lowlands, although the two species can be seen flying together in wooded habitats at mid to high elevations. Compared to Madeiran Speckled Wood, Speckled Wood has yellower spots on the upper surface, three or four (not two) eyespots on the upper side of the hindwing, each surrounded by an orangey-yellow ring, and the outer margin of the forewing is scalloped inwards (concave).

E EN 3 Madeiran Speckled Wood WS 50–60 mm

ENDEMIC TO MADEIRA

This woodland butterfly is endemic to Madeira. It was formerly common and widespread in all wooded habitats from sea level to high into the mountains (1,000 m+) but has retreated to areas of denser laurel and chestnut forest at mid to high elevations in the north and centre of the island since Speckled Wood arrived in 1976. Madeiran Speckled Wood flies year-round, with generally higher numbers in summer, and remains common in suitable habitat, although vulnerable to competition from Speckled Wood. The two species can be seen flying together at habitat boundaries at mid elevations. Compared to Speckled Wood, the Madeiran species has a convex (not concave) outer edge to the forewing, more obvious orange tones to both surfaces of the wing and only two obvious eyespots on the upper side of the hindwing.

E 4 Canary Speckled Wood WS 40–55 mm

ENDEMIC TO WESTERN AND CENTRAL CANARIES

This lovely butterfly is endemic to the Western and Central Canaries, where it occurs on all of the main islands. It flies all year round in wooded or bushy habitats, including gardens, from 200 m to 2,000 m elevation in the mountains, and is widespread and locally common, particularly along paths in laurel forest. The species looks rather similar to Speckled Wood, but fortunately the two do not occur together. Compared to that species, the Canary species has a straight or convex (not concave) outer edge to the forewing and a more prominent white streak and some tiny white dots on the underside of the hindwing.

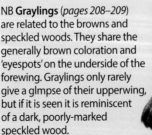

NB **Graylings** (*pages 208–209*) are related to the browns and speckled woods. They share the generally brown coloration and 'eyespots' on the underside of the forewing. Graylings only rarely give a glimpse of their upperwing, but if it is seen it is reminiscent of a dark, poorly-marked speckled wood.

GRAN CANARIA GRAYLING

Endemic graylings The graylings that occur on Madeira and on the Western and Central Canary Islands have originated from ancestral graylings that arrived from the mainland. The group offers a fine example of evolution, with subtle, but large and consistent enough, differences in size and colouration between populations such that they are regarded as six separate species, each restricted to its own island. Those on Madeira are less closely related and are the most brightly coloured, while those on the Canaries are all more subtly marked. All occur on sunny slopes at higher elevations, where they fly in the summer months. Most remain quite common in the right habitat, but those on La Palma and El Hierro are now very localised, and their populations are categorised as vulnerable.

E  ## El Hierro Grayling

VU

WS 55–60 mm
ENDEMIC TO EL HIERRO

This grayling is restricted to two sites on El Hierro. It flies from May to September on very steep grassy cliffs and in adjacent vineyards in barrancos at the base of the cliffs at 300–700 m and extends in smaller numbers up to 1,500 m in the laurel forest. It appears to be absent from Canary Pine forest. The species is threatened by expansion of vineyards in its remaining habitat and also by the intensification of modern agricultural practices in those vineyards, particularly the use of insecticides. Look for this butterfly feeding on ripe fruit. It is very similar to La Palma Grayling but is darker grey on the underside, particularly on the forewing, and of all the graylings shows the strongest contrast between the white border and the black wavy line on the underwing. It is also the largest of the group in the Canaries.

E ## La Palma Grayling

VU

WS 53–56 mm
ENDEMIC TO LA PALMA

This grayling flies from May to September in deep and steep-sided rocky gullies in Canary Pine and laurel forests at 400 m to 1,300 m elevation. It is widespread but very localised on the E and NE side of the island and occurs in an area of less than 20 km^2 that is vulnerable to fire and tourist activities. Probably fewer than 10,000 adult butterflies exist, and the species is considered vulnerable. It looks very similar to Canary Grayling, but it is a little larger and is greyer on the underside, often with a more pronounced white edge to the black wavy line and with a second black wavy line closer to the body on the hindwing.

E ## Gomera Grayling

WS 46-56 mm
ENDEMIC TO LA GOMERA

This grayling is widespread in open country and light woodland at 300 m to 1,200 m elevation. It particularly favours rocky gullies in arid scrubland. Like the other graylings, it flies from May to September, with peak numbers in July–August. It is most similar to Tenerife Grayling, being brownish rather than greyish on the underwing, but has a thicker black wavy line with a more pronounced white edge.

Tenerife Grayling

WS 53–56 mm
ENDEMIC TO TENERIFE

This grayling flies mostly between
1,300 m and 1,700 m elevation in the central mountains, although
it occurs up to 2,300 m in the crater of Las Cañadas del Teide. It is
widespread but local on the island, favouring thinly vegetated rocky
gullies in and above the Canary Pine forest zone. There is only
one brood a year, which flies between April and September. These
graylings often pause to drink in puddles. Large numbers of females
often funnel downhill in the barrancos in the evening and head
back upslope in the morning. Tenerife Graylings are rather plain
dark brown above, with warmer tones towards the corners of the
hindwing and an interrupted white fringe. However, all graylings
typically reveal only the underside, which on this species is rather
brown-toned and shows two distinct dark eyespots on the forewing
and a white-edged black wavy line that cuts across both wings.

  Gran Canaria Grayling

WS 48–55 mm
ENDEMIC TO GRAN CANARIA

This grayling favours thinly vegetated
rocky barrancos in the Canary Pine forest from as low as 400 m to
2,000 m elevation. Some fly as early as April on the warmer S side
of the island, but most fly in July and August. It is locally common
in suitable habitat, and as with Tenerife Grayling, large numbers of
females may congregate and fly downhill in the evening and back
uphill in the morning. It is the smallest grayling in the Canaries and
is most similar to Tenerife Grayling, although it is slightly greyer on
the underside, and the upper forewing can show a pair of pale spots
towards the trailing edge.

  Madeira Grayling

WS 40–52 mm
ENDEMIC TO MADEIRA

This grayling flies in good numbers in well-vegetated
areas in the mountains above 1,000 m, typically from mid-July to
September, although it may emerge as early as June in some years.
It favours more open grassy and heathy areas, as well as forest edge,
and tends to avoid dense laurel forest. Many stop to bask on the
tarmac surface of roads in the mountains, so be extra careful when
you are driving in the hills. It is rather more brightly coloured than
the graylings from the Canaries. Females show a large yellow-
brown patch bearing two eyespots on the forewing, which shows
through on the underwing, while the underside of the hindwing
is variegated dark grey with a broad blackish-edged whitish zigzag
band.

1 **Diadem** (False Plain Tiger) WS 80 mm

This large, widespread butterfly has been recorded recently in our area only on Tenerife, La Gomera and Madeira, but it is a strong-flying migrant, and so it could appear on other islands. It occurs irregularly during onshore winds October–December

and frequents flower-rich coastal areas such as parks and gardens. The sexes are quite different. The male 1♂ is blackish above, bearing a large bold white spot on each of the wings and a smaller white spot near the corner of the forewing. The underside is browner, and the white forewing spots show through, while the hindwing bears a broad white bar. Females 1♀ are very variable and cleverly mimic the poisonous Monarch and Plain Tiger, so are difficult to separate from these species. They are, however, usually smaller than Monarch and Plain Tiger and normally show one black spot on the upper surface of the hindwing that does not show though on the underwing.

2 **Plain Tiger** WS 70–80 mm

This beautiful butterfly occurs on La Palma, La Gomera, Tenerife, Gran Canaria and Fuerteventura in the Canaries. Like Monarch, it flies year-round and can be locally common in flower-rich areas

from sea level to moderate elevations in the hills. It can appear very similar to Monarch and Diadem, but it is intermediate in size between these two species and lacks the prominent black veins on the upperwing of the Monarch. Compared to female Diadems mimicking this species, Plain Tiger tends to show three black spots (not one) on the hindwing, and these always show through to the under surface

3 **Monarch** WS 89–102 mm

This spectacular strong-flying butterfly breeds on all the main Canary Islands except Lanzarote, as well as on Madeira and Porto Santo. Monarch originates from North America, but some individuals regularly cross the Atlantic during W gales in

autumn, from which the local breeding populations have become established. It was first recorded on the Canaries around 1887. Monarchs favour lush flower-rich parks and gardens in the lowlands up to moderate elevations, and they fly all year round. They usually fly alone and are generally quite scarce, although they readily attract attention with their soaring bird-like flight, even down busy urban streets! The largest butterfly on the islands, Monarch shows a striking orange upperwing with many black veins and a white-spotted black border. Some female Diadems mimicking this species can appear similar, some even showing the black veins above, but Diadems usually also show a single black dot on the centre of the hindwing that is lacking in Monarch.

1

1 ♀

2

2

3

3

Rare birds of the region

In addition to the 163 bird species illustrated in this book, a further 325 had been recorded as rare visitors to the Canary Islands (**C**) or Madeira (**M**) up to the end of 2017. The table below lists the 109 species that are rare but are recorded regularly on either island group, as denoted by a tick. The order of species follows Birdlife International.

The species are annotated as follows: ° = ornamental wildfowl; * = definitely/possibly of captive origin; + has bred on the Selvagens in recent years; ‡ bred in the Montado do Pereiro area on Madeira from 2002–10 (the area was damaged by fires in Aug 2010).

Species	C	M
° Mute Swan *Cygnus olor*	✓	
Greylag Goose *Anser anser*	✓	
Ring-necked Duck *Aythya collaris*	✓	
Greater Scaup *Aythya marila*	✓	
Lesser Scaup *Aythya affinis*	✓	
Garganey *Spatula querquedula*	✓	
Gadwall *Mareca strepera*	✓	
American Wigeon *Mareca americana*	✓	
Northern Pintail *Anas acuta*	✓	
Green-winged Teal *Anas carolinensis*	✓	
Black-necked Grebe *Podiceps nigricollis*	✓	
* Greater Flamingo *Phoenicopterus roseus*	✓	
* Lesser Flamingo *Phoeniconaias minor*	✓	
Common Woodpigeon *Columba palumbus*	✓	
European Nightjar *Caprimulgus europaeus*	✓	
Little Swift *Apus affinis*	✓	
Great Spotted Cuckoo *Clamator glandarius*	✓	
Corncrake *Crex crex*	✓	
Spotted Crake *Porzana porzana*	✓	
Little Crake *Zapornia parva*	✓	
Baillon's Crake *Zapornia pusilla*	✓	
Allen's Gallinule *Porphyrio alleni*	✓	
Leach's Storm-petrel *Hydrobates leucorhous*	✓	✓
Sooty Shearwater *Ardenna griseus*	✓	✓
Great Shearwater *Ardenna gravis*	✓	✓
Balearic Shearwater *Puffinus mauretanicus*	✓	
Black Stork *Ciconia nigra*	✓	
White Stork *Ciconia ciconia*	✓	
* Glossy Ibis *Plegadis falcinellus*	✓	
Eurasian Bittern *Botaurus stellaris*	✓	
Squacco Heron *Ardeola ralloides*	✓	
Great White Egret *Ardea alba*	✓	
Great Cormorant *Phalacrocorax carbo*	✓	✓
Eurasian Oystercatcher *Haematopus ostralegus*	✓	
Pied Avocet *Recurvirostra avosetta*	✓	
Eurasian Golden Plover *Pluvialis apricaria*	✓	
American Golden Plover *Pluvialis dominica*	✓	
Eurasian Dotterel *Eudromias morinellus*	✓	
Temminck's Stint *Calidris temminckii*	✓	
White-rumped Sandpiper *Calidris fuscicollis*	✓	
Buff-breasted Sandpiper *Calidris subruficollis*	✓	
Pectoral Sandpiper *Calidris melanotos*	✓	
Jack Snipe *Lymnocryptes minimus*	✓	
Red Phalarope *Phalaropus fulicarius*	✓	
Spotted Sandpiper *Actitis macularius*	✓	
Collared Pratincole *Glareola pratincola*	✓	
Little Gull *Hydrocoloeus minutus*	✓	
Sabine's Gull *Xema sabini*	✓	
Black-legged Kittiwake *Rissa tridactyla*	✓	✓
Slender-billed Gull *Larus genei*	✓	
Mediterranean Gull *Larus melanocephalus*	✓	✓
Audouin's Gull *Larus audouinii*	✓	
Ring-billed Gull *Larus delawarensis*	✓	✓
Common Gull *Larus canus*	✓	
Iceland Gull *Larus glaucoides*	✓	
Great Black-backed Gull *Larus marinus*	✓	✓
+ Sooty Tern *Onychoprion fuscatus*	✓	
Little Tern *Sternula albifrons*	✓	
Common Gull-billed Tern *Gelochelidon nilotica*	✓	
Whiskered Tern *Chlidonias hybrida*	✓	
White-winged Tern *Chlidonias leucopterus*	✓	
Black Tern *Chlidonias niger*	✓	
Arctic Tern *Sterna paradisaea*	✓	✓
Long-tailed Skua *Stercorarius longicaudus*	✓	✓
Arctic Skua *Stercorarius parasiticus*	✓	✓
Pomarine Skua *Stercorarius pomarinus*	✓	✓
Atlantic Puffin *Fratercula arctica*	✓	✓
Eurasian Scops-owl *Otus scops*	✓	✓
Short-eared Owl *Asio flammeus*	✓	✓
* Eurasian Eagle-owl *Bubo bubo*	✓	
European Honey-buzzard *Pernis apivorus*	✓	
Booted Eagle *Hieraaetus pennatus*	✓	
Hen Harrier *Circus cyaneus*	✓	
Long-legged Buzzard *Buteo rufinus*	✓	
European Roller *Coracias garrulus*	✓	✓
Common Kingfisher *Alcedo atthis*	✓	
Eurasian Wryneck *Jynx torquilla*	✓	
Lesser Kestrel *Falco naumanni*	✓	
Eurasian Hobby *Falco subbuteo*	✓	
Peregrine Falcon *Falco peregrinus*	✓	
* Cockatiel *Nymphicus hollandicus*	✓	
* Senegal Parrot *Poicephalus senegalus*	✓	
* Yellow-crowned Amazon *Amazona ochrocephala*	✓	
* Nanday Parakeet *Aratinga nenday*	✓	
* Budgerigar *Melopsittacus undulatus*	✓	
Calandra Lark *Melanocorypha calandra*	✓	
Crested Lark *Galerida cristata*	✓	
Isabelline Warbler *Iduna opaca*	✓	✓
Melodious Warbler *Hippolais polyglotta*	✓	
Sedge Warbler *Acrocephalus schoenobaenus*	✓	
Common Reed-warbler *Acrocephalus scirpaceus*	✓	
Common Grasshopper-warbler *Locustella naevia*	✓	
Red-rumped Swallow *Cecropis daurica*	✓	✓
* Red-whiskered Bulbul *Pycnonotus jocosus*	✓	
Yellow-browed Warbler *Phylloscopus inornatus*	✓	
Iberian Chiffchaff *Phylloscopus ibericus*	✓	
Western Orphean Warbler *Sylvia hortensis*	✓	
* Common Myna *Acridotheres tristis*	✓	
Mistle Thrush *Turdus viscivorus*	✓	
Fieldfare *Turdus pilaris*	✓	
Bluethroat *Cyanecula svecica*	✓	
Common Nightingale *Luscinia megarhynchos*	✓	
Red-breasted Flycatcher *Ficedula parva*	✓	
Desert Wheatear *Oenanthe deserti*	✓	
Black-eared Wheatear *Oenanthe hispanica*	✓	
* Red-cheeked Cordon-bleu *Uraeginthus bengalus*	✓	
* Orange-cheeked Waxbill *Estrilda melpoda*	✓	
‡ Eurasian Siskin *Spinus spinus*	✓	✓
Snow Bunting *Plectrophenax nivalis*		✓

Further reading and websites

Other useful books on the wildlife of Madeira and the Canaries include the following:

Ashmole, P., and M. Ashmole. 2016. *Natural History of Tenerife*. Dunbeath, Scotland: Whittles Publishing Ltd.

Bramwell, D., and Z. Bramwell. 1974. *Wildflowers of the Canary Islands*. Cheltenham: Stanley Thornes Ltd.

Clarke, T. 2006. *Birds of the Atlantic Islands*. Helm Field Guides. London: Christopher Helm.

Clarke, T., and D. Collins. 1996. *A Birdwatchers' Guide to the Canary Islands*. Cley-next-the-sea, Norfolk: Prion Ltd.

Garcia-del-Ray, E. 2011. *Field Guide to the Birds of Macaronesia*. Barcelona: Lynx Edicions.

Hilbers, D., and K. Woutersen. 2014. *Canary Islands – I: Lanzarote and Fuerteventura – Spain*. Arnhem, Netherlands: Crossbill Guides.

Hilbers, D., and K. Woutersen. 2015. *Canary Islands – II: Tenerife and La Gomera – Spain*. Arnhem, Netherlands: Crossbill Guides.

Martin, A., and A. J. Lorenzo. 2001. *Aves del Archipiélago Canario*. La Laguna, Tenerife: Francisco Lemus Editor.

Press, J. R., and M. J. Short. 2016. *Flora of Madeira*. London, England: Pelagic Publishing.

Useful websites include the following:

www.asociacion-zerynthia.org	Spanish NGO overseeing research and conservation of butterflies and their habitats.
www.birdingcanarias.com	Environmentally aware Canaries-based ecotourism company.
www.eurobutterflies.com	Details and photographs of European butterflies, including most species recorded on Madeira and the Canaries.
www.floradecanarias.com	Details and photographs of the vascular plants of the Canaries.
www.floralanzarote.com	Details and photographs of the flora of Lanzarote.
www.iberianwildlife.com	Environmentally aware ecotourism company based in the Iberian peninsula and the Canaries.
www.madeirabirds.com	Details and photographs of the birds, cetaceans, bats, butterflies, dragonflies and bees of Madeira, plus trip reports from an environmentally aware Madeira-based ecotourism company.
www.madeirawindbirds.com	Environmentally aware Madeira-based ecotourism company.
www.neotropico.org	Website and blog posts of the Fundación Neotropico (*see text box below*), including details of sea turtle releases.
www.venturadomar.com	Environmentally aware Madeira-based ecotourism company.

Fundación Neotrópico

The Fundación Neotropico is a not-for-profit organisation based in Santa Cruz, Tenerife, that works at an international level on environmental education, zoological research, fighting against invasive alien species and the rescue of wild fauna. With funding from the Canary Islands government, the Island Council of Tenerife and Santa Cruz de Tenerife Town Hall, it has recently developed education campaigns in the Canaries on the region's threatened marine turtles, its endemic reptiles and its cetaceans, and on invasive alien species in the islands. The organisation's wide range of environmental work includes optimising captive breeding and reinforcement programmes for threatened endemic species in the Canaries, researching and assisting in the conservation of globally threatened sea turtles in the Canaries, including the rescue, rehabilitation and release of injured individuals, and fighting against invasive alien species through rapid response, improved live-capture techniques and quarantine.

FUNDACIÓN NEOTRÓPICO

www.neotropico.org

Photographic and artwork credits

The production of this book would not have been possible without the generous support of the many photographers who kindly supplied their images. In total, over 600 images are featured, representing the work of 92 photographers. Thanks go to the photographers who generously provided access to their entire portfolio of images, and whose work is featured extensively throughout the book. In this respect, particular thanks are due to Andy and Gill Swash (WorldWildlifeImages.com), Hugh Harrop (shetlandwildlife.co.uk), Matt Rowlings (eurobutterflies. com), Luís Dias (www.venturadomar.com), Markus Varesvuo, Paul Verluyten (flickr.com/photos/12001191@N07), Dave Smallshire, Jaime A. de Urioste (Fundación Neotrópico), Tim Taylor (wildimaging.co.uk), Joachim Bertrands (flickr.com/photos/141891542@N04), Raymond de Smet (pbase.com/raydes), Juan Sagardia Pradera, and Mike Watson and Keith Regan. Thanks are also due to Marc Guyt, Roy de Haas and Wil Leurs at the Agami photo agency in the Netherlands (agami.nl) for their invaluable help in sourcing many of the images.

The contribution of every photographer is gratefully acknowledged and each image is itemized in this section, together with the photographer's initials, as coded in the following list: Aah-Yeah [AY]; Ajith U [AU]; Leonardo Ancillotto (flickr.com/photos/leonardoancillotto) [LA]; Miloš Anděra [MA]; Miloš Balla [MBa]; Bill Baston (Agami.nl) [BB]; Matthieu Berroneau (matthieu-berroneau. fr) [MBe]; Joachim Bertrands (flickr.com/photos/141891542@N04) [JBe]; John Bowler [JBo]; Keith Chapman [KC]; Roger & Liz Charlwood (WorldWildlifeImages.com) [RLC]; Yua-Chan Chen [YCC]; Mike Danzenbaker (Agami.nl) [MDan]; Mark Darlaston [MDar]; Roy de Haas (Agami.nl) [RdH]; Raymond de Smet (pbase.com/raydes) [RdS]; Greg & Yvonne Dean (WorldWildlifeImages.com) [GYD]; Luís Dias [LD]; Iosto Doneddu (flickr.com/photos/38480380@N05) [ID]; Theo Douma (Agami.nl) [TD]; Bernard Dupont [BD]; Juan Emilio [JE]; Teresa Farino [TF]; El Coleccionista de Instantes de Fotographía [ECIF]; Hans Germeraad (Agami.nl) [HG]; Lee Gregory (flickr.com/photos/lee_gregory) [LG]; Marc Guyt (Agami.nl) [MG]; Gail Hampshire [GH]; Hugh Harrop (shetlandwildlife.co.uk) [HH]; Stanislav Harvančík [SH]; R. Hutterer [RH]; Dan Irizarry [DI]; Pavel Kirillov [PK]; David Kjaer (davidkjaer.com) [DK]; A. N. Sunesh Kumar [ASK]; Vincent Legrand (Agami.nl) [VL]; Wil Leurs (Agami.nl) [WL]; Karel Mauer (Agami.nl) [KM]; Arnold Meijer (Agami.nl) [AM]; Pete Morris (Agami.nl) [PM]; Tomi Muukkonen (Agami.nl) [TM]; Rolf Nagel (flickr.com/photos/99927961@N06) [RN]; Jens Neef [JN]; Erland Refling Nielsen (flickr.com/photos/23985726@N05) [ERN]; Daniele Occhiato (Agami.nl) [DO]; Rob Olivier (Agami.nl) [RO]; Arie Ouwerkerk (Agami.nl) [AO]; Jari Peltomäki (Agami.nl) [JP]; Tomáš Peš [TP]; Ferran Pestaña [FP]; Lars Petersson (larsfoto.se) [LP]; Walter P. Pfliegler (flickr.com/photos/walter_pfliegler) [WPP]; Juan Sagardia Pradera [JSP]; David V. Raju [DVR]; Noemí Rodriguez [NR]; Matt Rowlings (eurobutterflies.com) [MR]; Pablo Martinez-Darve Sanz (flickr.com/photos/blezsp) [PMDS]; Ran Schols (Agami.nl) [RS]; Tim Sheerman-Chase [TSC]; Dave Smallshire [DS]; Walter Soestbergen (Agami. nl) [WS]; Laurens Steijn (Agami.nl) [LS]; Tim Stenton [TS]; Andy & Gill Swash (WorldWildlifeImages. com) [AGS]; Tim Taylor (wildimaging.co.uk) [TT]; David Tipling (birdphoto.co.uk) [DT]; Jukka Toivanen (flickr.com/photos/155315483@N07) [JT]; Domingo Trujillo González [DTG]; U.S. Fish and Wildlife Service Southeast [USFWC]; Jaime A. de Urioste [JdU]; Dinesh Valke [DV]; Harvey van Diek (Agami. nl) [HvD]; Menno van Duijn (Agami.nl) [MvD]; Nils van Duivendijk (Agami.nl) [NvD]; Chris van Rijswijk (Agami.nl) [CvR]; Lies Van Rompaey [LVR]; Rohan van Twest (flickr.com/photos/90638772@N02) [RvT]; Markus Varesvuo [MVa]; Frank Vassen [FV]; Martijn Verdoes (Agami.nl) [MVe]; Paul Verluyten (flickr. com/photos/12001191@N07) [PV]; Mike Watson & Keith Regan [MW&KR]; Martin Wiemers [MW]; Wim Wilmers (Agami.nl) [WW].

Images reproduced under the Creative Commons Attribution-ShareAlike 2.0 Generic license, the Creative Commons Attribution-Share Alike 3.0 Unported license or the Creative Commons Attribution-ShareAlike 4.0 International license are indicated with "/CC" after the photographer's initials. Images sourced via the photographic agencies Alamy (Alamy.com), FLPA (flpa-images.co.uk), NaturePhoto (naturephoto-cz.com) or Shutterstock (shutterstock.com) are credited in full.

The codes used in the credits below are as follows:

CC = Central Canaries; E = Eastern; EC = Eastern Canaries; EH = El Hierro; GC = Gran Canaria; LG = La Gomera; LP = Las Palmas; M = Madeira; N = Northern; S = Southern; Ten. = Tenerife; W = Western; WC = Western Canaries.

ad. = adult; br. = breeding plumage; fem. = female; fl. = flight; imm. = immature; juv. = juvenile; nonbr. = non-breeding plumage.

Cover Atlantic Canary [LD]. **Frontispiece** Sperm Whale [LD]. **p10** Rock stacks, Madeira [JBo]. **p11** Saltmarsh, Fuerteventura [JBo]; Reservoir, Fuerteventura [JBo]. **p12** Sandy desert, Fuerteventura [JBo]; Rocky desert, Fuerteventura [JBo]. **p13** Subalpine scrub, Tenerife [JBo]; Arid scrubland, Tenerife [JBo]. **p14** Juniper woodland, El Hierro [JBo]; Warmth-loving woodland, La Palma [JBo]. **p15** Laurel Forest, Tenerife [JBo]; Laurel Forest, La Palma [JBo]. **p16** Pine tree, La Palma [JBo]; Pine forest, La Palma [JBo]. **p17** Chanelled river, Madeira [JBo]; Golf course, Tenerife [JBo]; Agricultural terraces, Madeira [JBo]. **p18** Conservation area, Fuerteventura [JBo]. **p19** Re-vegetated slopes, Porto Santo [JBo]. **p20** El Jable Plain, Lanzarote [FV/CC]. **p21** Las Peñitas, Fuerteventura [JBo]; Barranco, Fuerteventura [JBo]. **p22** Scrub on ash slope, Gran Canaria [JBo]; Pine forest, Gran Canaria [JBo]; Pine and birds, Gran Canaria [JBo]. **p23** Pine forest, Tenerife [JBo]; Las Cañadas, Tenerife [JBo]. **p24** Lava plug and forest, La Gomera [JBo]. **p25** Southern slopes, La Gomera [JBo]; Laurel forest path, La Palma [JBo]. **p26** Regenerating forest, El Hierro [JBo]; Juniper, El Hierro [JBo]. **p27** São Vicente, Madeira [JBo]; Desertas Islands [PV]. **p28** Cetacean watching [LD]. **p30** African Blue Tit [JE/CC]. **p31** Lesser Black-backed Gull (ad.) [AGS], (imm.) [KM (Agami)]; Yellow-legged Gull (both) [MG (Agami)]; Black-headed Gull (ad.) [AGS], (imm.) [DO (Agami)]; Sandwich Tern [AO (Agami)]; Roseate Tern [MVa]; Common Tern [HH]. **p32** Black-headed Gull (sum.) [MVa], (win.) [AGS]. **p33** Lesser Black-backed Gull (both) [AGS]; Yellow-legged Gull (ad.) [JBo], (win. and imm.) [DO (Agami)]. **p34** Common Tern [LD]. **p35** Common Tern [HH]; Roseate Tern [MVa]; Sandwich Tern [WL (Agami)]. **p36** *Pterodroma* petrel [LD]. **p37** Zino's Petrel (above) [MVa], (below) [MG (Agami)]; Desertas Petrel (both) [MVa]. **p38** Bulwer's Petrel [LD]. **p39** Bulwer's Petrel [MVa]; White-faced Storm-petrel (above) [LS (Agami)], (below) [MDan (Agami)]. **p40** White-faced Storm-petrel [LD]. **p41** Madeiran Petrel (both) [HH]; European Storm-petrel (both) [MDar]; **p41** Wilson's Storm-petrel (above) [MG (Agami)], (below) [PM (Agami)], (pattering) [HH]. **p42** Cory's Shearwater [HH]. **p43** Cory's Shearwater (both) [HH]; Manx Shearwater (both) [MDan (Agami)]; Macaronesian Shearwater (both) [JSP]. **p44** Northern Gannet [AGS]. **p45** Red-billed Tropicbird [AGS]; Great Skua [HvD (Agami)]; Northern Gannet (ad.) [AGS], (2CY, 3CY) [HH]. **p46** Little Bittern (fl.) [DO (Agami)], (male) [AGS], (fem.) [GYD]. **p47** Black-crowned Night-heron (fl., ad.) [AGS], (juv., imm.) [DO (Agami)]. **p48** Grey Heron (fl.) [DO (Agami)], (ad.) [AGS]; Purple Heron (both) [HH]. **p49** Little Egret (all) [AGS]; Cattle Egret (all) [AGS]. **p50** Sacred Ibis (both) [AGS]; Eurasian Spoonbill (fl.) [DO (Agami)], (ad.) [HH]. **p51** Common Moorhen [AGS]; Common Coot [AGS]. **p52** Northern Shoveler [AGS]; Mallard [AGS]; Marbled Duck [SH]. **p53** Northern Shoveler (both) [AGS]; Mallard (both) [AGS]; Marbled Duck [RdH (Agami)]. **p54** Eurasian Wigeon [AGS]; Common Teal (ad.) [DO (Agami)]. **p55** Eurasian Wigeon (both) [AGS]; Common Teal (male) [HH], (fem.) [DO (Agami)]; Mandarin Duck (both) [AGS]. **p56** Tufted Duck [HH]; Common Pochard [JP (Agami)]; Ruddy Shelduck [Atul Sinai Borker (Shutterstock)]; Tufted Duck [HH]. **p57** Tufted Duck (both) [AGS]; Common Pochard (both) [DO (Agami)]; Ruddy Shelduck [DO (Agami)]. **p59** Grey Plover (br.) [HH], (nonbr.) [Erni (Shutterstock)], (fl.) [DO (Agami)]; Northern Lapwing [Erni (Shutterstock)], (fl.) [DO (Agami)]; Black-winged Stilt [AGS], (male, fem.) [HH]. **p60** Ruddy Turnstone [Erni (Shutterstock)], (nonbr.) [AGS], (br.) [JBo]; Kentish Plover [JP (Agami)], (nonbr.) [FV/CC], (br.) [DO (Agami)]. **p61** Little Ringed Plover (fl.) [RS (Agami)], (ad.) [AGS]; Ringed Plover (fl.) [DO (Agami)], (nonbr.) [AGS], (br.) [HH]. **p62** Sanderling (fl.) [DO (Agami)], (br.) [HH], (nonbr.) [WS (Agami)]. **p62** Little Stint (fl.) [MDan (Agami)], (nonbr.) [AGS]. **p63** Curlew Sandpiper (fl.) [HH], (br.) [Erni (Shutterstock)], (nonbr.) [HH]. **p63** Dunlin (fl., nonbr.) [HH], (br.) [Erni (Shutterstock)]. **p64** Common Redshank [AGS]; Spotted Redshank [DO (Agami)]; Greenshank [MVa]. **p65** Common Redshank [HG (Agami)]; Spotted Redshank (nonbr.) [Erni (Shutterstock)], (br.) [MVa]; (fl.) Greenshank [DO (Agami)]. **p66** Common Sandpiper [MVa]; Green Sandpiper [DO (Agami)]; Wood Sandpiper [AGS]. **p67** Common Sandpiper [DO (Agami)]; Green Sandpiper [DO (Agami)]; Wood Sandpiper [AGS]. **p68** Knot (fl., br) [HH], (nonbr.) [HH], (br.) [JBo]; Ruff (both) [AGS]. **p69** Common Snipe [Erni (Shutterstock)]; Woodcock [DT]. **p70** Bar-tailed Godwit (both) [HH]; Black-tailed Godwit (fl.) [HH], (nonbr.) [AGS]. **p71** Eurasian Curlew (ad.) [MVa], (fl.) [DO (Agami)]; Whimbrel (fl.) [Dave Montreuil (Shutterstock)], (ad.) [CvR (Agami)]. **p72** Black-bellied Sandgrouse [TM (Agami)]. **p73** Cream-coloured Courser [FV/CC]; Stone Curlew (WC) [JBo], (EC) [BB (Agami)]; Black-bellied Sandgrouse (both) [MG (Agami)]. **p75** Common Quail [DO (Agami)]; Barbary Partridge [AO (Agami)]; Red-legged Partridge [AGS]. **p76** Houbara Bustard (fl.) [RdS], (male, fem.) [MW&KR]. **p77** Egyptian Vulture [BB (Agami)], (ad.) [JBe]. **p78** Common Buzzard (fl. C) [JE/CC], (fl. M) [LD], (ad.) [BB (Agami)]; Osprey [RdH (Agami)]; Black Kite [DO (Agami)]. **p79** Osprey [DO (Agami)]; Black Kite [MVa]. **p80** Montagu's Harrier [RO (Agami)]; Marsh Harrier [DO (Agami)]. **p81 male** [JE/CC], (fem.) [JE/CC], (WS (Agami)], [JSP]. **p81** Montagu's Harrier (male) [DO (Agami)], (fem.) Montagu's Harrier [MVa]; Marsh Harrier (male) [MVa], (fem.) DO (Agami)]. **p82** Common Kestrel (fl. EC, fem. EC) [RdS], (fl. WC) [PV], (fem. WC) [JE/CC], (male WC) [JBo]; Barbary Falcon [AGS]; Eleonora's Falcon (both) [AGS]. **p83** Barbary Falcon [FV/CC]; Eleonora's Falcon (dark) [JSP], (pale) [ID]. **p84** Barn Owl [DT], (fl.) [JSP]. **p85** Long-eared Owl (fl.) [JSP], (ad.) [TP]. **p87** Sand Martin (above) [MVa], (below) [RS (Agami)]; House Martin (above) [MVa], (below) [RS (Agami)]; Barn Swallow (above) [JP (Agami)], (below) [MG (Agami)]. **p89** Plain Swift (above) [VL (Agami)], (below) [MG (Agami)]; Common Swift (above) [RS (Agami)], (below) [MvD (Agami)]; Pallid Swift (both) [DO (Agami)]; Alpine Swift (above) [MDan (Agami)], (below) [AGS]. **p91** Laurel Pigeon (both) [JBe]; Bolle's Pigeon (ad.) [JBe], (fl.) [LP]; Trocaz Pigeon (ad.) [PV], (fl.) [LG]. **p93** Eurasian Collared Dove (both) [AGS]; Barbary Dove [RvT]; Rock Dove (both) [HH]. **p94** European Turtle Dove (fl.) [RS (Agami)], (ad.) [AGS]; Laughing Dove (fl.) [RdS, (ad.) [AGS]. **p95** Ring-necked Parakeet [KC], Ring-necked Parakeet (ad.) [JE/CC]; Monk Parakeet (fl.) [AGS], (ad.) [JE/CC]. **p96** Great-spotted Woodpecker (fem.) [MvD (Agami)], (male Ten.) [RLC], (male GC) [JBo]. **p97** European Bee-eater (fl.) [MG (Agami)], (ad.) [GYD]; Common Hoopoe (fl.) [DO (Agami)], (ad.) [FV/CC]. **p98** Great Grey Shrike [JBo];. **p99** Woodchat Shrike [DO (Agami)]; Great Grey Shrike (ad.) [FV/CC], (fl.) [RdS]; Common Cuckoo (fl.) [RS (Agami)], (ad.) [DO (Agami)]. **p100** Red-vented Bulbul [ASK/CC]; Common Starling [HH]. **p101** Golden Oriole (male) [MG (Agami)], (fem.) [MVa].

CREDITS

p103 Common Redstart (both) [AGS]; Black Redstart (both) [DO (Agami)]; Northern Wheatear (both) [DO (Agami)].
p104 Canary Islands Stonechat [JBo]. p105 Whinchat (fem.) [AGS], (male) [DO (Agami)]; Canary Islands Stonechat (fem.)
[RdS], (male) [VL (Agami)]; Common Stonechat (both) [AGS]. p107 Common Blackbird (both) [JBo]; Ring Ouzel (both) [MVa];
Song Thrush [AGS]; Redwing [HH]. p108 European Robin (M) [LD], (GC) [JE/CC], (Ten.) [NvD (Agami)]. p109 Spotted
Flycatcher [AGS]; Pied Flycatcher (fem.) [AGS], (male) [Martin Fowler (Shutterstock)]. p110 African Blue Tit (GC) [JE/CC], (EC,
Ten.) [MW&KR], (EH) [JBo], (LP) [LP]. p112 Red-billed Chough (fl.) [AGS], (ad.) Red-billed Chough [Erni (Shutterstock)].
p113 (fl.) Common Raven [MW&KR], (ad.) BB (Agami)]. p114 Tenerife Kinglet [JBe]; Madeira Firecrest [MDan (Agami)].
p115 Wood Warbler [RS (Agami)]; Western Bonelli's Warbler [DO (Agami)]. p116 Canary Islands Chiffchaff [JBo]. p117
Common Chiffchaff [RS (Agami)]; Canary Islands Chiffchaff [JBo]; Willow Warbler [AM (Agami)]. p119 Garden Warbler [AGS];
Blackcap (both) [TT]; Sardinian Warbler (fem.) [DO (Agami)]; (male.) Sardinian Warbler [JSP]. p120 Spectacled Warbler [JBo];.
p121 Spectacled Warbler (both) [DO (Agami)]; Common Whitethroat (male) [AGS], (fem.) [GYD]; Subalpine Warbler (both)
[HH]. p122 Grey Wagtail [DO (Agami)]; Yellow Wagtail [AGS];. p123 Grey Wagtail (male) [PV], (fem.) [TT]; Yellow Wagtail
(both) [TT]; p123 White Wagtail (both) [HH]. p124 Berthelot's Pipit [MW&KR]; Red-throated Pipit (br.) [RLC], (nonbr.) [DO
(Agami)]. p125 Meadow Pipit [AGS]; Tree Pipit [AGS]. p126 Tawny Pipit [DO (Agami)]; Eurasian Skylark [AGS], (head) [DO
(Agami)]. p127 Short-toed Lark [AGS]; Lesser Short-toed Lark [RdS]. p129 Tree Sparrow [RO (Agami)]; House Sparrow (fem.)
[DO (Agami)], (male) [AGS]; Spanish Sparrow (both) [DO (Agami)]. p130 Rock Sparrow [DO (Agami)]; Corn Bunting [MW&KR].
p131 Common Linnet (M) [PV], (EC) [JBo], (male W, fem. W) [JE/CC]. p132 Atlantic Canary [JBo]. p133 Atlantic Canary
(male) [VL (Agami)], (fem.) [TT]; European Serin (male) [DO (Agami)], (fem.) [MVa]; European Greenfinch (male) [DO
(Agami)], (fem.) [JE/CC]. p134 Common Chaffinch (male M) [TT], (fem. M) [LG], (male. CC) [JE/CC]. p135 Common Chaffinch
(male CC) [JBe], (male EH, male LP) [JBo]. p136 Tenerife Blue Chaffinch (male, fem.) [VL (Agami)], (habitat) [JBo].
p137 Gran Canaria Blue Chaffinch (both) [JBe], (habitat) [JBo]. p138 Trumpeter Finch [JBo]. p139 European Goldfinch
[AGS]; Common Waxbill [DO (Agami)]; Trumpeter Finch (both) [VL (Agami)]. p140 Sperm Whale [LD]; p141 Sperm Whale
(both) [LD]; Minke Whale [LD]. p142 Bryde's Whale [LD]; Sei Whale [LD]; Fin Whale [LD]. p143 Bryde's Whale [LD]; Sei Whale
[LD]; Fin Whale [LD]. p144 Killer Whale [TS]. p145 Short-finned Pilot Whale (both) [LD]; False Killer Whale [LD]; Killer Whale
[LD]. p146 Blainville's Beaked Whale (both) [LD]; Cuvier's Beaked Whale [LD]. p147 Pygmy Sperm Whale [LD]; Dwarf Sperm
Whale [LD]; Blainville's Beaked Whale [LD]; Cuvier's Beaked Whale [LD]. p149 Bottlenose Dolphin [LD]; Rough-toothed
Dolphin [LD]; Risso's Dolphin [LD]. p150 Short-beaked Common Dolphin [TS]; Striped Dolphin [LD]. p151 Atlantic Spotted
Dolphin [LD]; Fraser's Dolphin [TS]. p152 Mediterranean Monk Seal [LD]. p153 European Rabbit [GYD]. p154 House Mouse
[TD (Agami)]; Pygmy White-toothed Shrew [LVR/CC]. p155 Greater White-toothed Shrew [TD (Agami)]; Canarian Shrew
[RH/CC]. p156 Brown Rat [DK]; Black Rat [Miloš Anděra (naturephoto-cz.com)];. p157 Barbary Ground Squirrel [BB (Agami)];
Algerian Hedgehog [Víctor Suárez (Alamy)]. p158 Mouflon [WW (Agami)]; Barbary Sheep [YCC/CC]. p159 European
Free-tailed Bat (both) [LA]. p160 Canary Big-eared Bat [DTG]. p160 Grey Long-eared Bat [DTG]. p161 Barbastelle
[TD (Agami)]; Leisler's Bat [Dietmar Nill (Minden Pictures/FLPA)]. p162 Atlantic Islands Pipistrelle [DTG]. p163 Savi's Pipistrelle
[MA]; Kuhl's Pipistrelle [Michel Rauch (Biosphoto/FLPA)]. p164 Common Kingsnake [JdU]; Brahminy Blind Snake [DVR/CC].
p165 Madeira Lizard (male) [TT], (fem.) [JBo]. p166 Atlantic Lizard (male) [RN], (fem.) [BB (Agami)]. p167 Boettger's Lizard
(fem. EH, male EH) [JBo], (male LG) [WPP]. p168 Western Canaries Lizard (fem., male LP) [JBo]; (male LP) [JdU].
p169 Western Canaries Lizard (fem., N Ten.) [WL (Agami)], (fem., S Ten.) [JdU], (male N Ten., male., S Ten.) [MvD (Agami)].
p170 La Gomera Giant Lizard (all) [JdU]. p171 Hierro Giant Lizard (fem., juv.) [JdU], (male) [JBo]. p172 Tenerife Speckled
Lizard (fem., juv.) [JdU], (male, skin) [NR]. p173 Gran Canaria Giant Lizard (male) [ECIF/CC], (fem., juv) [JBo]. p174 Smooth
Skink [JdU]; West Canary Skink [JdU]. p175 Gran Canaria Skink [JdU]; Eastern Canary Skink [MBe]. p176 Tenerife Gecko [JN];
Boettger's Wall Gecko [JdU]. p177 Moorish Gecko [BD/CC]; Turkish Gecko [GH/CC]. p178 Gomera Wall Gecko [JdU]; East
Canary Gecko [FV/CC]. p179 Leatherback Turtle [Photo Researchers (FLPA)], (beach) [USFWC/CC], (head) [DI].
p180 Loggerhead Turtle [Norbert Wu (Minden Pictures/FLPA)], (head) [LD]; Green Turtle (head) [AGS]. p181 Green Turtle
[MVe (Agami)]; Hawk's-bill Turtle [TSC/CC]. p182 Perez's Frog [PV]; Stripeless Tree Frog [WL (Agami)]. p183 Ringed Cascader
(both) [DS]. p184 Small Bluetail [WS (Agami)]. p185 Tropical Bluetail (male, fem.) [DS]; Sahara Bluetail (male) [JBo],
(fem.) [PMDS]; Small Bluetail (both) [DS]. p186 Blue Emperor [PV]. p187 Vagrant Emperor (fem.) [MBa], (male) [DS]; Lesser
Emperor (fem.) [JT], (male) [DS]; Blue Emperor (both) [DS]. p188 Epaulet Skimmer (male) [DS], (fem.) [JBo]; Long Skimmer
(male) [DS], (fem.) [WL (Agami)]. p189 Globe Skimmer (male) [AGS], (fem.) [DS]; Violet Dropwing (both) [DS].
p191 Red-veined Dropwing (both) [DS]; Red-veined Darter (male) [JE/CC], (fem.) [DS]. p191 Island Darter (male) [DS],
(fem.) [PV]; Broad Scarlet (male) [JE/CC], (fem.) [JBo]. p192 Canary Skipper (under) [WL (Agami)], (male, fem.) [MR].
p193 Queen of Spain Fritillary (both) [PV]; Cardinal (both) [MR]. p194 Geranium Bronze (upper) [JBo], (under) Geranium
Bronze [WL (Agami)]. p195 Small White (upper) [PV], (under) [AGS]; Large White (upper) [AY/CC], (under) [AGS]; Canary
Large White (both) [MR]. p196 Madeira Brimstone [PV]. p197 Clouded Yellow (upper) [PV], (under) [AGS]; African Migrant
(both) [MR]; Canary Brimstone [WL (Agami)]; Madeira Brimstone [PV]. p199 Gran Canaria Green-striped White (both) [MR];
Tenerife Green-striped White (both) [MR]; Fuerteventura Green-striped White (upper) [MR]; Bath White (upper) [JE/CC],
(under) [WL (Agami)]; Greenish Black-tip (both) [MR]. p200 Austaut's Blue [MR]; Canary Blue [MR]. p201 African Grass Blue
(both) [MR]; Desert Babul Blue [MR]; African Grass Blue [WL (Agami)]; Austaut's Blue (both) [MR]; Canary Blue (both) [MR].
p202 Small Copper [JBo]. p203 Lang's Short-tailed Blue (all) [MR]; Long-tailed Blue (male) [JE/CC], (fem.) [MR], (under) [WL
(Agami)]; Southern Brown Argus (upper) [MR], (under) [WL (Agami)]; Small Copper (upper, M, upper EH) [JBo], (under) [WL
(Agami)]. p204 Canary Red Admiral (upper) [JBo], (under) [JE/CC]; Red Admiral (both) [AGS]. p205 American Painted Lady
(both) [WL (Agami)]; Painted Lady (upper) [AGS], (under) [JE/CC]. p207 Meadow Brown (both) [PMDS]; Speckled Wood
(upper) [PV], (under) [MR]; Madeira Speckled Wood (upper) [MR], (under) [TT]; Canary Speckled Wood (upper) [JBo],
(under) [JE/CC]; Gran Canaria Grayling (upper) [MR]. p208 El Hierro Grayling [MW]; La Palma Grayling [MW]; Gomera
Grayling [TF]. p209 Canary Grayling [MW]; Gran Canaria Grayling [MR]; Madeira Grayling [PV]. p210 Diadem [PK/CC].
p211 Diadem (under) [PK/CC], (upper) [AU/CC]; Plain Tiger (under) [DV/CC], (upper) [FP/CC]; Monarch (under) [PV]; (upper)
[TT].

Scientific, Spanish and Portuguese names

The names used for the birds, mammals, reptiles, amphibians, butterflies and dragonflies featured in this book are the generally accepted English names. However, people from many different countries visit Madeira and the Canary Islands, and these names may not therefore be familiar to all. Some visitors will know the species by their universally recognized scientific names and, to help these readers, each species covered in the book is listed in alphabetical order by *scientific name* in the table below, followed by its **English name**, as well as the Spanish and Portuguese name(s) where appropriate, cross-referenced to the page on which the main account for that species appears.

Birds

Accipiter nisus | **Eurasian Sparrowhawk**	Gavilán Común	Gavião da Europa	80
Actitis hypoleucos | **Common Sandpiper**	Andarríos Chico	Maçarico-das-rochas	66
Aix galericulata | **Mandarin Duck**	Pato Mandarín	Pato Mandarim	54
Alauda arvensis | **Eurasian Skylark**	Alondra Común	Laverca	126
Alaudala rufescens | **Lesser Short-toed Lark**	Terrera Marismeña	Calhandrinha-das-marismas	127
Alectoris barbara | **Barbary Partridge**	Perdiz Moruna	Perdiz-moura	74
Alectoris rufa | **Red-legged Partridge**	Perdiz Común	Perdiz	74
Anas crecca | **Common Teal**	Cerceta Común	Marrequinha	54
Anas platyrhynchos | **Mallard**	Ánade Azulón	Pato-real	52
Anthus berthelotii | **Berthelot's Pipit**	Bisbita Caminero	Corre-caminero	124
Anthus campestris | **Tawny Pipit**	Bisbita Campestre	Petinha-dos-campos	126
Anthus cervinus | **Red-throated Pipit**	Bisbita Gorgirrojo	Petinha-de-garganta-ruiva	124
Anthus pratensis | **Meadow Pipit**	Bisbita Común	Petinha-dos-prados	125
Anthus trivialis | **Tree Pipit**	Bisbita Arbóreo	Petinha-das-árvores	125
Apus apus | **Common Swift**	Vencejo Común	Andorinhão-preto	88
Apus pallidus | **Pallid Swift**	Vencejo Pálido	Andorinhão-pálido	88
Apus unicolor | **Plain Swift**	Vencejo Unicolor	Andorinhão-da-serra	88
Ardea cinerea | **Grey Heron**	Garza Real	Garça-real	48
Ardea purpurea | **Purple Heron**	Garza Imperial	Garça-ruiva	48
Arenaria interpres | **Ruddy Turnstone**	Vuelvepiedras	Rola-do-mar	60
Asio otus | **Long-eared Owl**	Búho Chico	Bufo-pequeno	85
Aythya ferina | **Common Pochard**	Porrón Común	Zarro-comum	56
Aythya fuligula | **Tufted Duck**	Porrón Moñudo	Negrinha	56
Bubulcus ibis | **Cattle Egret**	Garcilla Bueyara	Carraceiro	49
Bucanetes githagineus | **Trumpeter Finch**	Camachuelo Trompetero	Trombeteiro	138
Bulweria bulwerii | **Bulwer's Petrel**	Petrel de Bulwer	Alma-negra	38
Burhinus oedicnemus | **Stone Curlew**	Alcaraván	Alcaravão	72
Buteo buteo | **Common Buzzard**	Busardo Ratonero	Águia-d'asa-redonda	78
Calandrella brachydactyla | **Short-toed Lark**	Terrera Común	Calhandrinha	127
Calidris alba | **Sanderling**	Correlimos Tridáctilo	Pilrito-das-praias	62
Calidris alpina | **Dunlin**	Correlimos Común	Pilrito-de-peito-preta	63
Calidris canutus | **(Red) Knot**	Correlimos Gordo	Seixoeira	68
Calidris ferruginea | **Curlew Sandpiper**	Correlimos Zarapitín	Pilrito-de-bico-comprido	63
Calidris minuta | **Little Stint**	Correlimos Menudo	Pilrito-pequeno	62
Calidris pugnax | **Ruff**	Combatiente	Combatente	68
Calonectris borealis | **Cory's Shearwater**	Pardela Cenicienta	Cagarra	42
Carduelis carduelis | **European Goldfinch**	Jilguero	Pintassilgo	138
Catharacta skua | **Great Skua**	Págalo Grande	Alcaide	44
Charadrius alexandrinus | **Kentish Plover**	Chorlitejo Patinegro	Borrelho-de-coleira-interrompida	60
Charadrius dubius | **Little Ringed Plover**	Chorlitejo Chico	Borrelho-pequeno-de-coleira	61
Charadrius hiaticula | **Ringed Plover**	Chorlitejo Grande	Borrelho-grande-de-coleira	61
Chlamydotis undulata | (African) **Houbara Bustard**	Hubara	Hubara	76
Chloris chloris | **European Greenfinch**	Verderón	Verdilhão	132
Circus aeruginosus | **Marsh Harrier**	Aguilucho Laguneroo Occidental	Águia-sapeira	80
Circus pygargus | **Montagu's Harrier**	Aguilucho Cenizo	Águia-caçadeira	80
Columba bollii | **Bolle's Pigeon**	Paloma turqué	Pombo-turqueza	90
Columba junoniae | **Laurel Pigeon**	Paloma Rabiche	Pombo-rabil	90
Columba livia | **Rock Dove**	Paloma Bravia	Pombo-das-rochas	92

LIST OF SPECIES

Phylloscopus canariensis | **Canary Islands Chiffchaff**	Mosquitero Canario	Felosinha das Canárias	116
Phylloscopus collybita | **Common Chiffchaff**	Mosquitero Común	Felosinha	116
Phylloscopus sibilatrix | **Wood Warbler**	Mosquitero Silbador	Felossa-assobiadeira	115
Phylloscopus trochilus | **Willow Warbler**	Mosquitero Musical	Felosa-musical	116
Platalea leucorodia | **Eurasian Spoonbill**	Espátula	Colhereiro	50
Pluvialis squatarola | **Grey Plover**	Chorlito Gris	Tarambola-cinzenta	58
Psittacula krameri | **Ring-necked Parakeet**	Cotorra de Kramer	Periquito-rabijunco	95
Pterocles orientalis | **Black-bellied Sandgrouse**	Ganga Ortega	Cortiçol-de-barriga-preta	72
Pterodroma deserta | **Desertas Petrel**	Petrel Gon-gon	Gon-gon	36
Pterodroma madeira | **Zino's Petrel**	Petrel Freira	Freira	36
Puffinus (lherminieri) baroli | **Macaronesian Shearwater**	Pardela Chica	Pintainho	42
Puffinus puffinus | **Manx Shearwater**	Pardela Piconeta	Fura-bucho do Altántico	42
Pycnonotus cafer | **Red-vented Bulbul**	Bulbul de ventilación roja	Bulbul-vermelho-ventilado	100
Pyrrhocorax pyrrhocorax | **Red-billed Chough**	Chova Piquirroja	Gralha-de-bico-vermelho	112
Regulus madeirensis | **Madeira Firecrest**	Reyezuelo de Madeira	Estrelinha-de-Madeira	114
Regulus (regulus) teneriffae | **Tenerife Kinglet**	Reyezuelo Tinerfeño	Bandeirita	114
Riparia riparia | **Sand Martin**	Avión Zapador	Andorinha-das-barreiras	86
Saxicola dacotiae | **Canary Islands Stonechat**	Tarbilla Canaria	Caldeireta	104
Saxicola rubetra | **Whinchat**	Tarabilla Norteña	Cartaxo-d'arribação	104
Saxicola torquatus | **Common Stonechat**	Tarbilla Común	Cartaxo	104
Scolopax rusticola | **Eurasian Woodcock**	Chocha Perdiz	Galinhola	69
Serinus canaria | **Atlantic Canary**	Canario	Canario-de-terra	132
Serinus serinus | **European Serin**	Verdecillo	Milheirinha	132
Spatula clypeata | **Northern Shoveler**	Pato Cuchara	Pato- colhereiro	52
Spilopelia senegalensis | **Laughing Dove**	Tortola senegalesa	Rola-dos-palmares	94
Sterna dougallii | **Roseate Tern**	Charrán Rosado	Gaivina-rosada	34
Sterna hirundo | **Common Tern**	Charrán Común	Gaivina	34
Streptopelia decaocto | **Eurasian Collared-dove**	Tórtola Turca	Rola-turca	92
Streptopelia roseogrisea | **Barbary Dove**	Tórtola de Cabeza Rosa	Rola-rosada	92
Streptopelia turtur | **European Turtle-dove**	Tórtola Común	Rola-brava	94
Sturnus vulgaris | **Common Starling**	Estornino Pinto	Estorninho-malhado	100
Sylvia atricapilla | **Blackcap**	Curruca Capitotada	Toutinegra-de-barrete	118
Sylvia borin | **Garden Warbler**	Curruca Mosquitera	Felosa-das-figueiras	118
Sylvia cantillans | **Subalpine Warbler**	Curruca Carrasqueña	Toutinegra-de-bigodes	120
Sylvia communis | **Common Whitethroat**	Curruca Zarcera	Papas-amoras-comum	120
Sylvia conspicillata | **Spectacled Warbler**	Curruca Tomillera	Toutinegra-tomilheira	120
Sylvia melanocephala | **Sardinian Warbler**	Curruca Cabecinegra	Toutinegra-dos-valados	118
Tachymarptis melba | **Alpine Swift**	Vencejo Real	Andorinhão-real	88
Tadorna ferruginea | **Ruddy Shelduck**	Tarro Canelo	Pato-casarca	56
Thalasseus sandvicensis | **Sandwich Tern**	Charrán Patinegro	Garajau	34
Threskiornis aethiopicus | **Sacred Ibis**	Ibis sagrado	Ibis-sagrado	50
Tringa erythropus | **Spotted Redshank**	Archibebe Oscuro	Perna-vermelha-bastardo	64
Tringa glarola | **Wood Sandpiper**	Andarríos Bastardo	Maçarico-de-dorso-malhado	66
Tringa nebularia | **Greenshank**	Archibebe Claro	Perna-verde	64
Tringa ochropus | **Green Sandpiper**	Andarríos Grande	Maçarico-bique-bique	66
Tringa totanus | **Common Redshank**	Archibebe Común	Perna-vermelha	64
Turdus iliacus | **Redwing**	Zorzal Alirrojo	Tordo-ruivo	106
Turdus merula | **Common Blackbird**	Mirlo Común	Melro	106
Turdus philomelos | **Song Thrush**	Zorzal Común	Tordo-pinto	106
Turdus torquatus | **Ring Ouzel**	Mirlo de Collar	Melro-de-peito-branco	106
Tyto alba | **Barn Owl**	Lechuza Común	Coruja-das-torres	84
Upupa epops | **Common Hoopoe**	Abubilla	Poupa	97
Vanellus vanellus | **Northern Lapwing**	Avefría Europea	Abibe	58

Mammals

Ammotragus lervia | **Barbary Sheep**	Oveja Barbary		158
Atelerix algirus | **Algerian Hedgehog**	Erizo Moruno		157
Atlantoxerus getulus | **Barbary Ground Squirrel**	Barbary Tierra Ardilla		157
Balaenoptera acutorostrata | **Minke Whale**	Ballena Minke	Baleia Minke	140
Balaenoptera borealis | **Sei Whale**	Rorcual Norteño	Baleia do Norte	142
Balaenoptera edeni | **Bryde's Whale**	Rorcual Tropical	Baleia Tropical	142

LIST OF SPECIES

Balaenoptera physalus | **Fin Whale**	Rorcual Común	Baleia de Barbatana	**142**
Barbastella barbastellus | **Barbastelle**	Murciélago de Bosque		**161**
Crocidura canariensis | **Canarian Shrew**	Musaraña Canaria		**155**
Crocidura russula | **Greater White-toothed Shrew**	Musaraña		**155**
Delphinus delphis | **Short-beaked Common Dolphin**	Delfín Común	Golfinho Comum com Bastão Curot	**150**
Globicephala macrorhynchus | **Short-finned Pilot Whale**	Calderón Tropical	Baleia Piloto de Aletas Curtas	**144**
Grampus griseus | **Risso's Dolphin**	Calderón Gris	Golfinho Cinza	**148**
Hypsugo savii | **Savi's Pipistrelle**	Murciélago Montañero		**163**
Kogia breviceps | **Pygmy Sperm Whale**	Cachalote Pigmaea	Cachoeira pigmeu	**146**
Lagenodelphis hosei | **Fraser's Dolphin**	Delfín de Fraser	Golfinho de Fraser	**151**
Mesoplodon densirostris | **Blainville's Beaked Whale**	Zifio de Blainville	Baleia Bevert de Blainville	**146**
Monachus monachus | **Mediterranean Monk Seal**	Sello Monje Mediteráneo	Selo de Monk Mediteranean	**152**
Mus musculus | **House Mouse**	Ratón	Mouse de Casa	**154**
Nyctalus leisleri | **Leisler's Bat**	Nóctulo Pequeño		**161**
Orca orcinus | **Killer Whale**	Orca	Orca	**144**
Oryctolagus cuniculus | **European Rabbit**	Conejo	Coelho	**153**
Ovis orientalis | **Mouflon**	Muflón		**158**
Physeter macrocephalus | **Sperm Whale**	Cachalote Común	Cachalote	**140**
Pipistrellus kuhlii | **Kuhl's Pipistrelle**	Murciélago de Borde Claro		**163**
Pipistrellus maderensis | **Atlantic Islands Pipistrelle**	Murciélago de Madeira	Bastão de Madeira	**162**
Plecotus austriacus | **Grey Long-eared Bat**		Bastão de Orelo Longa	**160**
Plecotus teneriffae | **Canary Big-eared Bat**	Orejudo Canario		**160**
Pseudorca crassidens | **False Killer Whale**	Falsa Orca	Falso Orca	**144**
Rattus norvegicus | **Brown Rat**	Rata Común	Rato Marrom	**156**
Rattus rattus | **Black Rat**	Rata de Campo	Rato Preto	**156**
Stenella coeruleoalba | **Striped Dolphin**	Delfín Listado	Golfinho Listrado	**150**
Stenella frontalis | **Atlantic Spotted Dolphin**	Delfín Moteado Atlántico	Golfinho Manchado Atlântico	**151**
Steno bredanensis | **Rough-toothed Dolphin**	Delfín Dientes Rugosos	Golfinho de Dentes Ásperos	**148**
Suncus etruscus | **Pygmy White-toothed Shrew**	Musarañita		**154**
Tadarida teniotis | **European Free-tailed Bat**	Murciélago Rabudo		**159**
Tursiops truncatus | **Bottle-nosed Dolphin**	Delfín Mular	Golfinho com Nariz de Garrafa	**148**
Ziphius cavirostris | **Cuvier's Beaked Whale**	Zifio Común	Baleia Bevert de Cuvier	**146**

Reptiles and amphibians

Caretta caretta | **Loggerhead Turtle**	Tortuga Boba	Tartaruga de Gatinho	**180**
Chalcides coeruleopunctatus | **Smooth Skink**	Lisa de La Gomera y El Hierro		**174**
Chalcides sexlineatus | **Gran Canaria Skink**	Lisa Grancanaria		**175**
Chalcides simonyi | **Eastern Canary Skink**	Lisneja		**175**
Chalcides viridanus | **West Canary Skink**	Lisa Dorada		**174**
Chelonia mydas | **Green Turtle**	Tortuga Verde	Tartaruga Verde	**181**
Dermochelys coriacea | **Leatherback Turtle**	Tortuga Laúd	Tartaruga de Couro	**179**
Eretmochelys imbricata | **Hawksbill Turtle**	Tortuga Carey	Tartaruga-de-pente	**181**
Gallotia atlantica | **Atlantic** (Haria) **Lizard**	Lagarto Atlántico		**166**
Gallotia bravoana | **La Gomera Giant Lizard**	Lagarto Gigante de La Gomera		**170**
Gallotia caesaris | **Boettger's** (Lehr's) **Lizard**	Lagarto Tizón de El Hierro y La Gomera		**167**
Gallotia galloti | **Western Canaries Lizard**	Lagarto Tizón		**168**
Gallotia intermedia | **Tenerife Speckled Lizard**	Lagarto Canario Moteado		**172**
Gallotia simonyi | **Hierro Giant Lizard**	Lagarto Gigante de El Hierro		**171**
Gallotia stehlini | **Gran Canaria Giant Lizard**	Lagarto de Gran Canaria		**173**
Hemidactylus turcicus | **Turkish Gecko**	Salamanquesa Rosada		**177**
Hyla meridionalis | **Stripeless Tree Frog**	Ranita Meridional	Sapo de Ávore sem Lixo	**182**
Indotyphlops braminus | **Brahminy Blind Snake**	Brahminy Serpiente Ciega	Brahminy Cobra Cega	**164**
Lampropeltis getula | **Common Kingsnake**			**182**
Pelophylax perezi | **Perez's Frog**	Rana Común	Rã Comum	**182**
Tarentola angustimentalis | **East Canary Gecko**	Perenquén Majorero		**178**
Tarentola boettgeri | **Boettger's Gecko**	Perenquén de Boettger		**176**
Tarentola delalandii | **Tenerife (Wall) Gecko**	Praquén Común		**176**
Tarentola gomerensis | **Gomera Wall Gecko**	Perenquén Gomero		**178**
Tarentola mauritanica | **Moorish Gecko**	Salamanquesa Común	Geco Comum	**177**
Teira dugesii | **Madeira Lizard**		Lagato de parede de Mederião	**165**

Dragonflies

Anax ephippiger | **Vagrant Emperor**	Vagabundo Imperador Libélula	Libélula do Imperador Vagabundo	186
Anax imperator | **Blue Emperor**	Libélula Imperador Azul	Libélula do Imperador Azul	186
Anax parthenope | **Lesser Emperor**	Libélula Menor Imperador	Libélula Menor do Imperador	186
Crocothemis erythraea | **Broad Scarlet**	Libélula de Escarleta		190
Ischnura pumilio | **Small Bluetail**	Pequeña Cola Azul	Pequena Cauda Azul	184
Ischnura saharensis | **Sahara Bluetail**	Cola Azul del Sáhara		184
Ischnura senegalensis | **Tropical Bluetail**	Cola Azul Común		184
Orthetrum chrysostigma | **Epaulet Skimmer**	Libélula Espumadero		188
Orthetrum trinacria | **Long Skimmer**	Libélula largo		188
Pantala flavescens | **Globe Skimmer**	Libélula Globo		189
Sympetrum fonscolombii | **Red-veined Darter**	Libélula de Dardos con Vetas Rojas	Libélula do Veia Vermelha	190
Sympetrum nigrifemur | **Island Darter**	Libélula de la Isla	Libélula da Isla	190
Trithemis annulata | **Violet Dropwing**	Libélula Violeta		189
Trithemis arteriosa | **Red-veined Dropwing**	Libélula Rojo Veteada	Libélula Veia Vermelha	190
Zygonyx torridus | **Ringed Cascader**	Libélula en Cascada Anillada		183

Butterflies

Argynnis pandora | **Cardinal**	Nacara da Pandora		193
Aricia cramera | **Southern Brown Argus**	Morena Común		202
Azanus ubaldus | **Desert Babul Blue**	Aberinto del Desertio		200
Cacyreus marshalli | **Geranium Bronze**	Taladro del Geranio	Borboleta de Gerânio	194
Catopsilla florella | **African Migrant**	Migrador de la Flor de Golfio	Borboleta Africana Migrante	196
Colias croceus | **Clouded Yellow**	Colias Común	Borboleta Amarela Nublada	196
Danaus chrysippus | **Plain Tiger**	Mariposa Tigre	Borboleta Tigre	210
Danaus plexippus | **Monarch**	Mariposa Monarca	Borboleta Monarca	210
Euchloe charlonia | **Greenish Black-tip**	Azufrada Africana		198
Euchloe eversi | **Tenerife Green-striped White**	Blanquiverdosa de Tenerife		198
Euchloe grancanariensis | **Gran Canaria Green-striped White**	Blanquiverdosa de Gran Canaria		198
Euchloe hesperidium | **Fuerteventura Green-striped White**	Blanquiverdosa de Fuerteventura		198
Gonepteryx cleobule | **Canary Brimstone**	Cleopatra canaria		196
Gonepteryx maderensis | **Madeira Brimstone**		Cleopatra da Madeira	196
Hipparchia bacchus | **El Hierro Grayling**	Sátiro de El Hierro		208
Hipparchia gomera | **Gomera Grayling**	Sátiro de La Gomera		208
Hipparchia maderensis | **Madeira Grayling**		Sátiro de Madeira	209
Hipparchia tamadabae | **Gran Canaria Grayling**	Sátiro de Gran Canaria		209
Hipparchia tilosi | **La Palma Grayling**	Sátiro de La Palma		208
Hipparchia wyssii | **Tenerife Grayling**	Sátiro de Tenerife		209
Hypolimnas misippus | **Diadem**	Falsa Mariposa Tigre		210
Issoria lathonia | **Queen of Spain Fritillary**	Espejitos	Espelhos	193
Lampides boeticus | **Long-tailed Blue**	Estriada Canela	Borboleta Azul de Cauda Longa	202
Leptotes pirithous | **Lang's Short-tailed Blue**	Estriada Gris	Borboleta Azul de Cauda Curta	202
Leptotes webbianus | **Canary Blue**	Manto de Canarias		200
Lycaena phlaeas phlaeas | **Small Copper**	Manto Común	Manto de Madeira	202
Maniola jurtina hispulla | **Meadow Brown**	Loba		206
Parage xiphioides | **Canary Speckled Wood**	Ondulada canaria		206
Pararge aegeria aegeria | **Speckled Wood**	Ondulada	Ondulada	206
Pararge xiphia | **Madeiran Speckled Wood**		Ondulada de Madeira	206
Pieris brassicae | **Large White**	Blanca de la Col		194
Pieris cheiranthi | **Canary Large White**	Capuchina Común		194
Pieris rapae | **Small White**	Blanquita de la Col	Pequena Borboleta Branca	194
Polyommatus celina | **Austaut's Blue**	Niña Celina		200
Pontia daplidice | **Bath White**	Blanquiverdosa		198
Thymelicus christi | **Canary Skipper**	Dorada Canaria		198
Vanessa atalanta | **Red Admiral**	Atalanta	Atalanta	204
Vanessa cardui | **Painted Lady**	Cardera	Cardera	205
Vanessa virginiensis | **American Painted Lady**	Cardera Americana	Cardera Americana	205
Vanessa vulcania | **Canary Red Admiral**	Vulcania	Vulcania	204
Zizeeria knysna | **African Grass Blue**	Violetilla		200

Index

This index covers the common (English) names of all the birds, mammals, reptiles, amphibians, butterflies and dragonflies included in this book.

Bold text and **figures** refer to the main species accounts.

Regular text is used for alternative names.

Italicized names and regular figures indicate species that are believed to be extinct.

Italicized numbers indicate other pages on which a photograph appears.